THE AUSTRALIAN
Women's Weekly

THE BUMPER BOOK of KiDS' BiRTHDAY CAKES

a collection of new and favourite recipes

Contents

The Australian Women's Weekly food team started publishing recipes and photographs of birthday cakes for kids way back in the 1950s, and we soon became famous for them. Since that time we've produced many different features in the magazine and in The Weekly's cookbooks, showcasing a vast range of cakes.

I worked in the Test Kitchen in 1980, and times were different then – brainstorming wasn't heard of. The girls in the Test Kitchen just came up with an idea and made it work; we then showed the cake to our boss, Food Editor Ellen Sinclair; if she liked it, we had it photographed in the studio next door – it was as simple as that. There was no food styling, design or layout to work from.

People reminisce about the cakes from their childhood – it has been very entertaining to hear some of the stories about the cakes and of dedicated parents staying up half the night so that the cake could be a complete surprise to their child. In fact, our first birthday cake book, *Children's Birthday Cake Book*, published in 1980, and reprinted many times, as recently as 2011, has now reached three generations – my granddaughters consider this book – along with all of our other kids' cake books – essential reading material, especially around birthday time.

Kids' cakes have become increasingly popular with adults, too; it's not unusual to see a train, a pool or a dolly varden cake made for a 21st birthday party, often with interesting variations on the original cake. Lately, we've heard of several of our kids' cakes being used at weddings, instead of a more traditional wedding cake – now there's a good idea.

While many of the cakes in this book are favourites from previous books, there are a number of new recipes, just so your little ones have even more to choose from. There is a heap of information at the back of the book, along with tips and hints that will help you make the chosen cake. Most of the cakes are relatively easy, some a little fiddly, but all will bring a smile to the face of your child.

Pamela Clark
Editorial and Food Director

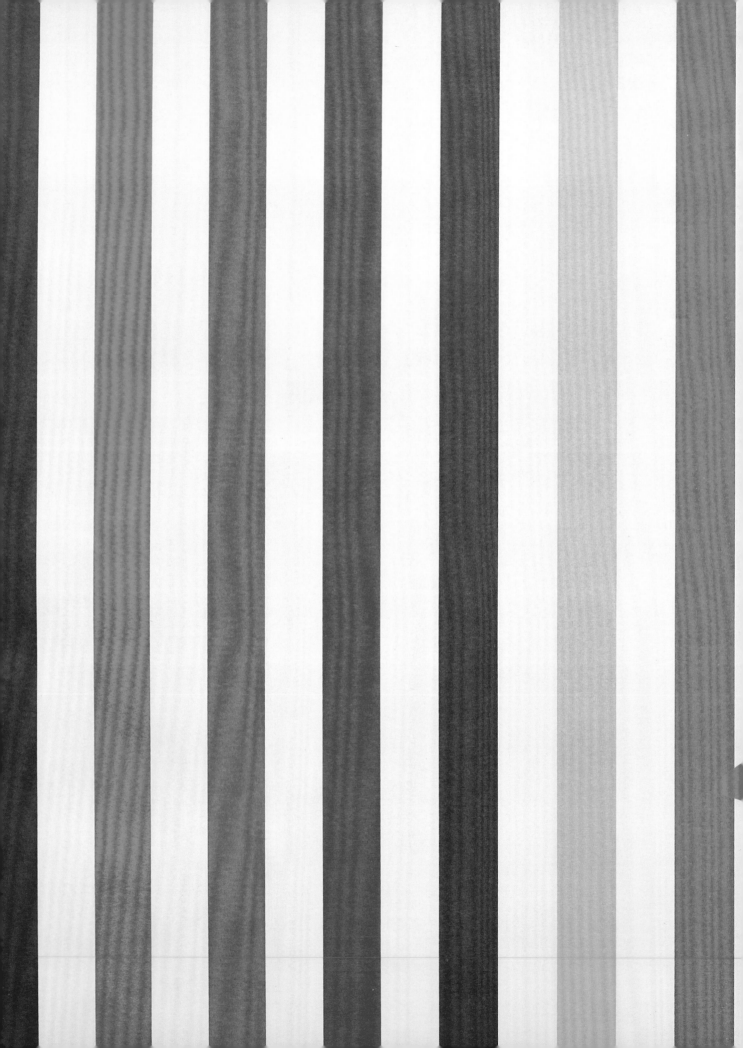

Best-ever
Classics

the magic toadstool

1 Preheat oven to 180°C/350°F. Grease pudding steamers.

2 Make cakes according to directions on packets. Pour enough mixture into pudding steamers until three-quarters full. (Use any leftover mixture to make patty cakes or cupcakes for the party.) Bake smaller pudding about 35 minutes and larger pudding about 55 minutes. Stand cakes in pans 5 minutes before turning out onto wire racks to cool.

3 Level bases of cakes. Secure small cake, cut-side down, on cake board with a little butter cream. Tint half the butter cream yellow; spread all over cake for toadstool stem.

4 Secure large cake, cut-side down, on circle of cardboard with a little butter cream. Position large cake on toadstool stem for toadstool cap. Tint remaining butter cream pink; spread all over cap.

5 Place pink Fruit Sticks side-by-side; trim tops of sticks to make rounded door. Position on toadstool stem for door.

6 Split mint leaves in half horizontally; slice halves into three pieces. Use centre pieces for stems and side pieces as leaves; position around toadstool stem. Position two mini heart lollies at top of each mint stem for flowers.

7 Cut yellow Fruit Stick into thin strips; using a little water, position on two large heart lollies; position on toadstool stem for windows.

8 Position six large heart lollies on cake board at front of toadstool for path; secure with a little butter cream. Decorate toadstool cap with cachous and remaining large heart lollies.

9 Using a little butter cream, attach large marshmallows on top of smaller marshmallows, sprinkle with sifted cocoa; position around toadstool, secure to cake board with a little butter cream. Position fairies around toadstool; secure with a little butter cream.

Split the mint leaves in half through the centre then slice the halves into three pieces.

Position large cake on small cake, then spread pink butter cream over toadstool cap.

TIPS
The large love hearts are the ones with messages on them. Place them word-side down on the cake.

Snow Folk

Use a small sharp, finely serrated knife to trim the cake to a more rounded shape for the snow folk.

1 Preheat oven to 180°C/350°F. Grease three holes of the texas muffin pan; grease three holes of the standard muffin pan.

2 Make cake according to directions on packet. Drop ⅓ cup of the mixture into greased texas pan holes; bake about 25 minutes. Drop 2½ level tablespoons of the mixture into the greased standard pan holes; bake about 20 minutes. Stand cakes in pans 5 minutes before turning, top-side up, onto wire rack to cool.

3 Level cake tops; trim cakes into rounded shapes. Turn larger cakes upside down. Place smaller cakes, top-side up, on top of larger cakes; secure with a little fluffy frosting. Spread cakes all over with frosting. Place marshmallows on top of small cakes for heads. Secure cakes on cake board with a little frosting.

4 Knead ready-made icing on surface dusted with a little sifted icing sugar until icing loses its stickiness. Tint icing orange. Mould into three carrot shapes for noses.

5 Using picture as a guide, make snowgirl. Cut a bow from the red licorice strap and eyes from the black licorice strap. Secure bow, eyes and nose to head with a little frosting. Use pink M&M's for buttons. Position Mallow Bakes around bottom of snowgirl for skirt. Position twigs for arms, and the umbrella on the snowgirl.

6 Using picture as a guide, make snowmen. Cut buttons, bow and scarf from black licorice strap; position on bodies. Cut eyes from black licorice strap. Secure eyes and noses with a little frosting. Position twigs for arms. Make hat bases by cutting two 1.5cm (¾-inch) rounds from the licorice strap; secure to the heads with a little frosting. Make hat tops by cutting two 1cm (½-inch) pieces from the licorice rope; secure to the hat bases with a little frosting.

EQUIPMENT

6-hole (¾-cup/180ml) texas muffin pan
12-hole (⅓-cup/80ml) standard muffin pan
40cm (16-inch) square cake board (page 334)
1.5cm (¾-inch) round cutter

CAKE

½ x 470g (15-ounce) packet butter cake mix
(see 'mixing the cakes' page 345)

1 quantity fluffy frosting
(page 329)

DECORATIONS

3 giant white marshmallows
10g (½ ounce) ready-made white icing (page 329)
pure icing (confectioners') sugar, for dusting
orange food colouring
1 red licorice strap
1 black licorice strap
3 pink mini M&M's
100g (3-ounce) packet Mallow Bakes, halved
6 small cleaned sticks or twigs
1 pink cocktail umbrella
1 black licorice rope

Funny faces

EQUIPMENT

6-hole (¾-cup/180ml)
texas muffin pan

5 texas muffin paper cases

30cm (12-inch) square
cake board (page 334)

CAKE

½ x 470g (15-ounce) packet
butter cake mix
(see 'mixing the cakes' page 345)

½ quantity butter cream
(page 329)

yellow, blue, green, purple and
brown food colouring

PURPLE FUNNY FACE

2 pink Allen's doughnuts

2 small yellow jelly beans

1 Jaffa

1 freckle, halved

1 red sour strap

GREEN FUNNY FACE

2 brown mini M&M's

1 Jaffa

7cm (2¾-inch) piece black
licorice strap

1 candy orange wedge

BROWN FUNNY FACE

7cm (2¾-inch) piece black
licorice strap

1 strawberry and cream
lolly, halved

1 red jelly bean

1 sour worm

BLUE FUNNY FACE

2 blue mini M&M's

2 round peppermints

1 small yellow jelly bean

6cm (2½-inch) piece black
licorice strap

1 yellow Fruit Stick

YELLOW FUNNY FACE

2 blue mini M&M's

2 round peppermints

1 small orange jelly bean

3cm (1¼-inch) piece red
licorice strap

2 candy orange wedges

TIP

You'll have enough cake
mixture left over to make one
more funny face. Make the
whole packet mix and double the
lollies to make 10 faces – there will
be enough mix leftover to make
2 more funny faces, so create
faces of your own.

1 Preheat oven to 180°C/350°F. Line texas muffin pan with paper cases.
2 Make cake according to directions on packet. Drop ⅓ cup of mixture into each paper case; bake about 25 minutes. Stand cakes in pan 5 minutes before turning, top-side up, onto wire rack to cool.
3 Divide butter cream equally into five small bowls; tint yellow, blue, green, purple and brown.

purple funny face Spread purple butter cream over top of one cake. Using picture as a guide, position doughnut lollies for eyes and jelly beans for eyebrows. Position Jaffa for nose and freckle halves for ears. Shape and trim red sour strap to make mouth.

green funny face Spread green butter cream over top of one cake. Using picture as a guide, position M&M's for eyes and Jaffa for nose. Shape and trim a strip of licorice to make mouth and hat brim; top with candy orange wedge to make hat.

brown funny face Spread brown butter cream over top of one cake. Using picture as a guide, trim and position licorice strap. Secure strawberry and cream halves to licorice strap with a little butter cream for eyes. Position jelly bean for nose and sour worm for mouth.

blue funny face Spread blue butter cream over top of one cake. Secure mini M&M's to peppermints with a little butter cream; position for eyes. Using picture as a guide, position jelly bean for nose. Shape a strip of the licorice to make mouth; position on cake. Cut yellow fruit stick into thin strips; position on cake for hair.

yellow funny face Spread yellow butter cream over top of one cake. Secure mini M&M's to peppermints with a little butter cream; position for eyes. Using picture as a guide, position jelly bean for nose. Shape licorice into tongue; position on cake. Position candy orange wedges for ears.

Make the houses by cutting the cake into three or four blocks of varying sizes.

Use a small serrated knife to cut contours into the cake.

Pipe small stepping stones from chocolate.

Tiny town

(page 334)

EQUIPMENT

26cm x 35cm (10½-inch x 14-inch) baking dish

34cm (13½-inch) square cake board (page 334)

2 small paper piping bags (page 338)

small new artist's paint brush

CAKE

3 x 470g (15-ounce) packets butter cake mix

2 quantities butter cream (page 329)

DECORATIONS

⅓ cup (50g) white chocolate Melts

pink, apricot, green, blue and black food colourings

375g (12 ounces) ready-made white icing (page 329)

pure icing (confectioners') sugar, for dusting

⅔ cup (220g) apricot jam, warmed, strained

3 ice-cream wafers

yellow sprinkles

4 green lollipops

13 coloured bullets

1 Preheat oven to 150°C/300°F. Grease and flour baking dish.

2 Make cakes according to directions on packets. Spread mixture into baking dish; bake about 1 hour. Stand cake in dish 10 minutes before turning, top-side up, onto wire rack to cool.

3 Meanwhile, make stepping stones: Melt chocolate (page 339); divide into two small bowls, tint one pink and the other apricot. Spoon pink chocolate into piping bag; pipe small stepping stones onto baking-paper-lined tray. Tap tray on bench to flatten out stepping stones. Repeat with apricot chocolate.

4 Cut a 6cm (2½-inch) slice from the long end of the cake. Cut the slice crossways into three or four blocks of varying sizes for the houses. Refrigerate. Use a small serrated knife to cut some contours into the remaining cake. Secure cake, cut-side up, on cake board with a little butter cream. Colour butter cream pale green; cover cake with butter cream to represent grass.

5 Knead ready-made icing on surface dusted with a little sifted icing sugar until icing loses its stickiness. Reserve one-third of the icing for windows, doors, cars and road. Divide remaining icing into three portions; tint pink, apricot and blue. Wrap each icing, separately, in plastic wrap to prevent drying.

6 To make houses: Brush each house cake with jam. Roll each coloured portion of icing on surface dusted with a little sifted icing sugar until large enough to cover each house. Dust hands with icing sugar, smooth icing over houses; trim around base of each house neatly. Reserve scraps of coloured icing. Roll out a little of the reserved white icing to make windows and doors, mark window panes with the back of a knife; secure windows and doors to houses with a little jam. Trim wafers with a sharp knife to make the roof; join wafers together and to tops of houses with a little butter cream. Position houses on cake.

7 To make road: Tint three-quarters of the remaining reserved icing grey. Roll a narrow strip of icing until long enough to make road. Cut strip of icing about 2.5cm (1-inch) wide; position on cake. Use sprinkles to make road markings; secure each sprinkle to road by brushing a tiny smear of jam onto the road's surface.

8 Mould cars from scraps of coloured icing, secure windows and wheels with a little jam. Position cars on road. Decorate cake with stepping stones, lollipops and bullets.

TIP
The cake can be
completed a day
before the party.

Lucy Ladybird

Ladybird, ladybird, fly away home, there's cake's on the table, there's no time to roam. Kids will love our cherry-red Lucy.

EQUIPMENT

1.25-litre (5-cup)
pudding steamer
12-hole (⅓-cup/80ml)
standard muffin pan
25cm x 30cm
(10-inch x 12-inch)
rectangular cake board
(page 334)

CAKE

1 x 470g (15-ounce) packet
butter cake mix
1 quantity butter cream
(page 329)

black and red food
colourings

DECORATIONS

1 black licorice strap
14 chocolate freckles
2 x 15cm (6-inch) black
chenille sticks
2 yellow Smarties

1 Preheat oven to 180°C/350°F. Grease pudding steamer and one hole of the muffin pan.

2 Make cake according to directions on packet; pour ¼ cup of mixture into muffin hole; bake about 20 minutes. Pour remaining mixture into pudding steamer; bake about 35 minutes. Stand cakes in pans 5 minutes before turning onto wire racks to cool.

3 Using serrated knife, level base of large cake. Cut small segment from side of muffin to make flat. Turn large cake cut-side down; trim dome to make more rounded. Secure large cake on cake board with a little butter cream.

4 Tint ¼ cup of butter cream black; tint remaining butter cream red. Spread red butter cream all over body of ladybird.

5 Position flat side of muffin against body for head; spread all over with black butter cream. Cut an outside strip of licorice from licorice strap; position down centre of ladybird's body. Place freckles on body.

6 Curl one end of each chenille stick; position on cake for antennae. Position Smarties on cake for eyes.

Using a serrated knife, trim the top of the pudding steamer cake so it appears more rounded.

Using a large palette knife, spread the red butter cream all over the ladybird's body.

Position the muffin against the ladybird's body for head, then spread with black butter cream.

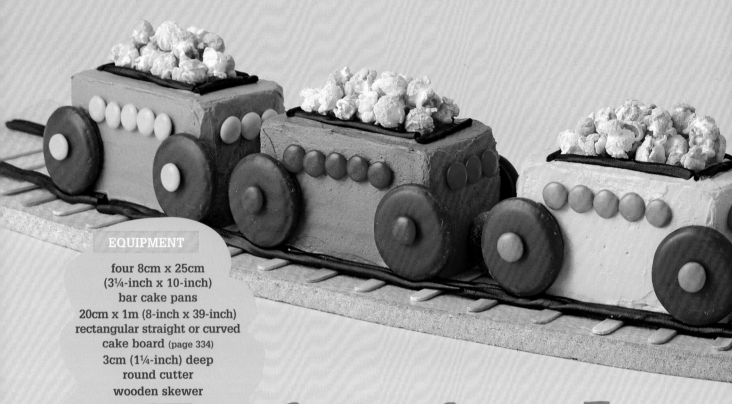

four 8cm x 25cm
(3¼-inch x 10-inch)
bar cake pans
20cm x 1m (8-inch x 39-inch)
rectangular straight or curved
cake board (page 334)
3cm (1¼-inch) deep
round cutter
wooden skewer

CAKE

2 x 470g (15-ounce) packets
butter cake mix
300g (9½-ounce) packet
jam roll
2 quantities butter cream
(page 329)
red, blue, yellow, purple and
green colouring

DECORATIONS

30 ice block sticks
1m (40 inches) black
licorice strap
2 tablespoons chocolate
sprinkles
1 hundreds and
thousands allsort
8 coloured jelly
fruit rings
1 pink ice-cream wafer
1½ cups coloured popcorn
1 yellow chenille stick
(pipe cleaner)
20 Mint Slice biscuits
8 green Smarties
20 pink Smarties
20 orange Smarties
20 red Smarties
20 yellow Smarties

Choo-Choo Train

Requested by many readers of all ages, this is one of our all-time favourite classic cakes.

1 Preheat oven to 180°C/350°F; grease and line bar cake pans. Make cakes according to directions on packets. Divide mixture evenly into pans. Bake cakes about 30 minutes. Stand cakes in pans 5 minutes before turning, top-side up, onto wire racks to cool. Using serrated knife, level cake tops so they are the same height.

2 Place ice-block sticks across cake board. Cut licorice into long thin strips; position for track.

3 Cut each bar cake in half vertically; reserve five halves to make carriages and back of engine. Cut remaining three halves in half horizontally; five of these will form bases of engine and carriages. Cut one quarter off remaining piece to extend engine base; discard remaining cake. Cut 4cm piece from jam roll; using 3cm round cutter, cut a round from the piece of jam roll to make smoke stack, as pictured. Position cake pieces on cake board, as pictured.

4 Divide butter cream into five portions; tint red, blue, yellow, purple and green. Spread engine with red butter cream and carriages with different coloured butter cream.

5 Spread smoke stack with red butter cream, roll in chocolate sprinkles; place on engine. Place hundreds & thousands allsort on engine. Join carriages with fruit rings by making a cut in one ring

TIP
Bar cake pans can be difficult to find these days; if you don't have them, bake the cakes in a large slab or rectangular cake pan or baking dish, then cut out four 8cm x 25cm bar cakes.

and pushing the other ring through it, press into butter cream between carriages. Outline carriage tops and engine with thin strips of licorice. Cut two eyes from licorice strap, position on engine. Cut licorice into 5 x 3cm pieces. Cut thin strip from ice-cream wafer; position at a downwards angle on front of engine. Rest licorice pieces on wafer to form grid.

6 Using toothpick or skewer, make small hole in 5 pieces of popcorn. Thread popcorn onto chenille stick. Position chenille stick in top of smoke stack. Fill each carriage with remaining popcorn.

7 Position Mint Slices for wheels. Position Smarties on engine and carriages. Secure Smarties on wheels with butter cream.

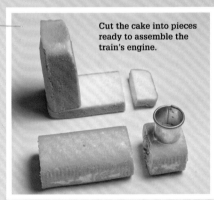

Cut the cake into pieces ready to assemble the train's engine.

The train assembled and ready to ice.

Front view of the engine.

the Penguin Prince

Turn cake cut-side down. Using the paper pattern, cut penguin from cake with a serrated knife.

Mark penguin outlines through the paper pattern onto the cake using a toothpick.

Spread the coloured butter creams onto the cake, using the markings as a guide.

EQUIPMENT

deep 26cm x 36cm
(10½-inch x 14½-inch)
baking dish
35cm x 40cm
(14-inch x 16-inch)
rectangular cake board
(page 334)

CAKE

3 x 470g (15-ounce) packets
butter cake mix

2 quantities
butter cream
(page 329)

black, yellow and
white food colouring

DECORATIONS

2 black Smarties
10cm (4-inch) piece
black licorice strap
1 red bow tie

1 Preheat oven to 180°C/350°F. Grease baking dish; line base and sides with baking paper, extending paper 5cm (2 inches) above sides.
2 Make cakes according to directions on packets. Spread mixture into baking dish; bake about 1 hour. Stand cake in dish 10 minutes before turning, top-side up, onto wire rack to cool.
3 Level cake top. Turn cake cut-side down. Using pattern from pattern sheet, cut out penguin. Secure cake, cut-side down, on cake board with a little butter cream.
4 Using toothpick, and paper pattern as a guide, mark penguin outlines on cake, as pictured.
5 Tint half the butter cream black; tint half the remaining butter cream yellow and the other half white.
6 Spread tummy and eyes with white butter cream, feet and beak with yellow butter cream and remaining top and sides of cake with black butter cream.
7 Position Smarties on cake for eyes. Trim licorice strap into thin strip; position on beak for smile. Position bow tie at penguin's neck.

TIPS
Cake can be made and covered with butter cream a day before the party. Top with popcorn and finish the cake up to three hours before the party. Be sure to remove toothpicks before cutting and serving the cake.

Attach comb to wafers; position comb on top of chicken's head.

Little Chicken

Why did the chicken cross the road? Because he wanted to get away from a horde of hungry little party guests...that's why!

1 Preheat oven to 150°C/300°F. Grease and flour baking dish.

2 Make cakes according to directions on packets. Spread mixture into baking dish; bake about 50 minutes. Stand cake in dish 10 minutes before turning, top-side up, onto wire rack to cool.

3 Level cake top; turn cake cut-side down. Using pattern from pattern sheet, cut out chicken. Secure cake, cut-side down, on cake board with a little butter cream.

4 Tint butter cream yellow; spread all over cake.

5 Using picture as a guide, press popcorn onto body of chicken. Gently push chips into cake for beak. Cut marshmallow in half; position, cut-side up, on cake for eye, top with Skittle. Sprinkle two wafers lightly with a little water (this makes it easier to cut) then cut out feet. Gently push into cake.

6 Knead ready-made icing on surface dusted with a little sifted icing sugar until icing loses its stickiness. Tint red using both red and orange colouring; roll on surface dusted with a little sifted icing sugar into a 3mm (⅛-inch) thickness. Using pattern from pattern sheet, cut out comb. Cut two remaining wafers into same shape as comb but don't trim the base (leave straight). Attach icing comb to wafers with a little butter cream. Gently push base of wafers into cake. Secure comb underneath with toothpicks.

EQUIPMENT

26cm x 35cm (10½-inch x 14-inch) baking dish

35cm (14-inch) square cake board (page 334)

CAKE

2 x 470g (15-ounce) packets butter cake mix

1 quantity butter cream (page 329)

yellow, red and orange food colouring

DECORATIONS

2 cups (20g) popped popcorn

2 small potato chips (crisps)

1 white marshmallow

1 yellow Skittle

4 ice-cream wafers

50g (1½ ounces) ready-made white icing (page 329)

pure icing (confectioners') sugar, for dusting

4 wooden toothpicks

Buzzy Bee

**5 x 12-hole
(1-tablespoon/20ml)
mini muffin pans
12-hole (¹/₃-cup/80ml)
standard muffin pan
2.25-litre (9-cup)
pudding steamer
60 mini muffin paper cases
(28 yellow, 32 dark brown)
35cm (14-inch) square
cake board** (page 334)

CAKE

**2 x 470g (15-ounce) packets
butter cake mix
1½ quantities butter cream**
(page 329)

**yellow and black
food colouring**

TOFFEE

**1 cup (220g) caster
(superfine) sugar
½ cup (125ml) water**

DECORATIONS

**2 blue Smarties
5 red mini M&M's
1 x 30cm (12-inch) black
chenille stick
(pipe cleaner)**

1 Preheat oven to 180°C/350°F. Line mini muffin pans with the paper cases. Grease one hole of the standard muffin pan.

2 Make one cake according to directions on packet. Drop 2 level teaspoons of mixture into each mini paper case; bake about 15 minutes. Drop 2½ level tablespoons of the mixture into the greased hole of the standard muffin pan; bake about 20 minutes. Turn cakes, top-side up, onto wire rack to cool.

3 Reduce oven temperature to 170°C/340°F. Grease pudding steamer. Make remaining cake according to directions on packet. Pour mixture into steamer; bake about 45 minutes. Stand cake in steamer 5 minutes before turning out onto wire rack to cool.

4 Using pattern from pattern sheet, trace two wings onto baking paper. Turn paper over onto an oven tray.

5 To make the toffee: Combine sugar and the water in small saucepan; stir over heat, without boiling, until sugar dissolves. Bring to the boil; boil, uncovered, without stirring, about 10 minutes or until toffee is golden brown. Remove from heat; allow bubbles to subside. Carefully pour toffee onto outline of wing shapes on paper; stand at room temperature until set.

6 Level flat base of pudding cake. Secure cake, cut-side down, on cake board with a little butter cream. Trim top of the pudding cake into a more rounded shape.

7 Trim standard muffin cake into a more rounded shape; trim one side a little flatter and secure this side to the pudding cake with a little butter cream.

8 Tint two-thirds of the butter cream yellow; tint remaining butter cream black. Spread yellow butter cream over body and head of the bee. Spread remaining yellow butter cream over tops of small cakes in the yellow paper cases. Spread black butter cream over tops of small cakes in the brown paper cases. Using picture as a guide, alternate bands of yellow and black cakes to cover the bee's body.

9 Position blue Smarties for eyes and mini M&M's for mouth; secure with a little butter cream, if necessary. Cut chenille stick in half, curl one end of each; insert into cake for antennae. Carefully insert wings into the bee's body just before the party.

Using the pattern sheet, trace two wings onto baking paper, turn paper over onto a flat heatproof surface, like a wooden board or oven tray. After the bubbles have subsided in the toffee, pour the toffee slowly over the wing outlines. Leave toffee to set at room temperature. Position the wings just before the party.

Using a small
serrated knife, trim
the muffin into a
more rounded shape.

TIPS

Make the mini muffins in batches: the cake mixture will be fine to stand at room temperature. Make the toffee wings up to 3 hours before the party. Position the wings just before the party.

If it's too humid to make the toffee wings, shape some craft wire into the wing shapes then cover them with a yellow-tinted cellophane paper.

Fantasy

Robbie Robot

Warning, warning...the kids will be back for more of this cute robot cake. Get your little robotics engineer to help with the decorating.

1 Preheat oven to 170°C/340°F. Grease baking dish and cake pan; line bases and sides with baking paper, extending paper 5cm (2 inches) above sides.

2 Make three cakes according to directions on packets. Spread mixture into baking dish. Make remaining cake according to directions on packet; spread mixture into cake pan. Bake both cakes about 1 hour. Stand cakes in pans 10 minutes before turning, top-side up, onto wire racks to cool.

3 Level cake tops so cakes are the same height; turn cakes cut-side down. Using pattern from pattern sheet, cut out robot's body from large cake, and cut its head, neck and arms from the smaller cake. Position cake pieces, cut-side down, on cake board to form robot shape; secure with a little butter cream.

4 Tint butter cream pale grey; spread all over cake.

5 Using picture as a guide, trim licorice strap to make eyes and to outline body and arms. Trim thin pieces of remaining licorice strap to make mouth and pocket. Cut red jube in half and position for mouth. Position flying saucers for cheeks. Position white sugar-coated almond for nose. Secure white jelly beans to eyes with a little butter cream.

6 Sprinkle robot's neck and feet with choc rocks. Position Hershey kisses as buttons; position silver-coated lollies on robot's shoulders. Cut black jubes in half and, using picture as a guide, position as controls on robot's body. Bend cake decorating wires into desired shape and push ends into top of robot's head to make antennae.

EQUIPMENT

26cm x 35cm (10¼-inch x 14-inch) baking dish

deep 20cm (8-inch) square cake pan

30cm x 40cm (12-inch x 16-inch) rectangular cake board (page 334)

CAKE

4 x 440g (14-ounce) packets butter cake mix
(see 'mixing the cakes' page 345)

2 quantities butter cream
(page 329)

black food colouring

DECORATIONS

60cm (24 inches) licorice strap

1 red jube

2 pink flying saucer lollies

1 white sugar-coated almond

2 white jelly beans

1 cup choc rocks

4 Hershey kisses

12 large silver-coated lollies

4 black jubes

2 x 24-gauge silver cake decorating/florist wires (30cm/12-inches long)

Huff & Puff

This friendly dragon will be loved by both princesses and knights alike. Just change the colour of the butter cream to suit the party.

EQUIPMENT

deep 22cm (9-inch)
round cake pan
12-hole (⅓-cup/80ml)
standard muffin pan
30cm x 45cm (12-inch x 18-inch)
rectangular cake board
(page 334)

CAKE

2 x 470g (15-ounce) packets
butter cake mix
1½ quantities butter cream
(page 329)
pink food colouring

DECORATIONS

1 raspberry licorice strap
1 pink marshmallow
2 red Smarties
2 green Smarties
4 blue Smarties
2 red M&M's
5 blue M&M's
6 green M&M's
3 pink ice-cream wafers
Twinkle Sprinkles or
hundreds and thousands

1 Preheat oven to 180°C/350°F. Grease cake pan; line base and side with baking paper, extending paper 5cm (2 inches) above side. Grease two holes of the muffin pan.

2 Make cakes according to directions on packets; drop 2½ level tablespoons of mixture into greased muffin pan holes. Spread remaining mixture into cake pan. Bake muffins about 20 minutes and large cake about 40 minutes. Stand cakes in pans 5 minutes before turning, top-side up, onto wire rack to cool.

3 Level large cake top; turn, cut-side, down. Using pattern from pattern sheet, cut dragon from cake. Secure dragon on cake board, cut-side down, with a little butter cream.

4 Tint butter cream pink; spread all over cake. Position muffins for eyes; spread all over with butter cream.

5 Cut licorice strap into thin strips; position on cake for outline of dragon. Cut marshmallow in half horizontally; using a little butter cream, secure one red Smartie to each marshmallow half for eyes, position on cake.

6 Cut eyebrows from licorice; position on cake. Position red M&M's on cake for nose; scatter remaining Smarties and M&M's on dragon's face.

7 Cut wafers in half on the diagonal; position five pieces on cake for spikes (discard remaining wafer piece). Sprinkle wafers with sprinkles or hundreds and thousands.

Turn the cake cut-side down, and using the paper pattern, cut the dragon's face from the round cake.

Place the dragon on the cake board, cut-side down, then position the muffins for eyes.

Fairy Trellis

There are fairies at the bottom of the garden, dancing on a summer's breeze with the roses, the butterflies and the bees.

1 Preheat oven to 150°C/300°F. Grease cake pan; line base and side with baking paper, extending paper 5cm (2 inches) above side.

2 Make cake according to directions on packet. Pour enough mixture into pan to fill to three-quarters. (Use any leftover mixture to make cupcakes for the party). Bake cake about 1 hour. Stand cake in pan 5 minutes before turning, top-side up, onto wire rack to cool.

3 Meanwhile, squash and press a large piece of foil into a cylindrical shape, with a base of 8cm (3 inches) and a height of 15cm (6 inches). Stand the foil shape in a glass or cup to make it stable.

4 Stir chocolate in medium heatproof bowl over medium saucepan of simmering water until melted (do not allow water to touch bottom of bowl). Tint about 1 tablespoon of the melted chocolate pink, another tablespoon yellow and another tablespoon green. Place each colour into separate small paper piping bags; pipe different-sized discs of chocolate onto a baking-paper-lined tray. Tap tray on bench to make discs level; stand at room temperature until set.

5 Tint remaining melted chocolate green for trellis; pour into the large piping bag. Using pattern from pattern sheet, pipe chocolate over trellis pattern, starting with rectangle and inside lines first.

6 Stand chocolate a minute or so then, before it sets (it is still pliable, but not runny), drape the chocolate rectangle over the foil cylinder to shape the trellis, stand at room temperature until set. When set, gently peel baking paper from trellis; carefully wind ribbon through trellis.

7 Level top of cake; secure cake, cut-side down, on cake board with a little frosting. Tint fluffy frosting green; spread all over cake.

8 Position trellis on cake before frosting sets. Use tiny dabs of frosting to attach roses to trellis. Position chocolate discs and fairy in garden.

EQUIPMENT

deep 15cm (6-inch) round cake pan
20cm (8-inch) round cake board (page 334) or cake stand
3 small paper piping bags (page 338)
1 large piping bag fitted with a small plain tube

CAKE

1 x 470g (15-ounce) packet butter cake mix
pink, yellow and green food colouring
1 quantity fluffy frosting (page 329)

DECORATIONS

375g (12 ounces) white chocolate Melts
ribbon
ready-made white, yellow and pink sugar roses
fairy ornament

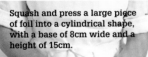
Squash and press a large piece of foil into a cylindrical shape, with a base of 8cm wide and a height of 15cm.

Pipe chocolate over trellis pattern, pipe the rectangle and inside lines first before piping the 'v' shapes.

Drape chocolate over the foil cylinder to shape trellis. Stand at room temperature until set.

Hey diddle diddle

The kids will be over the moon after seeing this cake. It's so easy to make and decorate that you'll also have time for some fun.

EQUIPMENT

deep 22cm (9-inch) round cake pan

33cm (13¼-inch) round cake board (page 334)

CAKE

2 x 470g (15-ounce) packets butter cake mix

1 quantity butter cream (page 329)

yellow food colouring

DECORATIONS

½ cup (110g) white (granulated) sugar

1 black licorice strap

1 Preheat oven to 180°C/350°F. Grease cake pan; line base and side with baking paper, extending paper 5cm (2 inches) above side.

2 Make cakes according to directions on packets; pour mixture into pan. Bake about 1 hour. Stand cake in pan 5 minutes before turning, top-side up, onto wire rack to cool.

3 Level cake top; turn cake cut-side down. Using pattern from pattern sheet, cut moon from cake. Secure cake, cut-side down, on cake board with a little butter cream.

4 Tint butter cream yellow; spread all over cake.

5 Place sugar and yellow colouring in small plastic bag; rub until sugar is evenly coloured. Sprinkle sugar evenly over moon.

6 Cut licorice strap into thin strips; position on cake for eye, mouth and moon outline.

Turn cake cut-side down, position paper pattern. Cut moon from cake with a small serrated knife.

Tint the butter cream yellow, then spread all over the cake.

Place sugar and colouring in a plastic bag; rub together until the sugar is evenly coloured.

Boris the clown

Clowns have been around since ancient Greece, though the red nose has only been around since last century...this clown won't last the day.

1 Preheat oven to 180°C/350°F. Grease cake pans; line bases and sides with baking paper, extending paper 5cm (2 inches) above sides.

2 Make cakes according to directions on packets; divide mixture evenly into pans. Bake cakes about 1 hour. Stand cakes in pans 5 minutes before turning, top-side up, onto wire racks to cool.

3 Place half the butter cream in medium bowl; reserve. Place 2 tablespoons of remaining butter cream in small bowl, tint red. Divide remaining butter cream into two small bowls; tint one green and the other blue.

4 Level cake tops so they are the same height. Turn cakes, cut-side down. Mark a point halfway along top edge of square cake; cut from halfway point to bottom corners to form a large triangle for hat. Cut two even-sided triangles from remaining corners of square cake; discard leftover cake.

5 Secure round cake, cut-side down, on cake board with a little butter cream; position and secure cake triangles on board.

6 Spread plain butter cream over clown's face, spread green butter cream over hat and spread blue butter cream over bow tie.

7 Place noodles in small plastic bag with a few drops of yellow colouring; shake well until noodles are evenly coloured. Spread noodles onto tray to dry; place around face for hair.

8 Cut small pieces of black licorice for each eye and eyebrow; position on clown's face. Outline smile with red licorice strap; spread red butter cream inside smile, repeat for cheeks. Place small strip of black licorice inside smile.

9 Position large gum balls for nose and bow-tie 'knot'; place small gum balls on hat. Outline bow-tie with red licorice straps. Make three-petalled daisy at top of hat with a piece of red licorice strap and a small gum ball.

EQUIPMENT

deep 20cm (8-inch) square cake pan
deep 22cm (9-inch) round cake pan
30cm x 60cm (12-inch x 24-inch) rectangular cake board
(page 334)

CAKE

3 x 470g (15-ounce) packets butter cake mix
2 quantities butter cream
(page 329)
red, green, blue and yellow food colouring

DECORATIONS

100g (3 ounces) fried noodles
1 black licorice strap
1 red licorice strap, cut into thin strips
1 large red gum ball
1 large yellow gum ball
11 small gum balls in assorted colours

Cutting the cake for the hat and bow tie.

Position the cake pieces, cut-side down, on the cake board to form the clown. Secure to board with a little butter cream.

Use food colouring to tint the noodles bright yellow.

Mindy Mermaid

This little mermaid has jumped from the sea and onto the cake plate. If the weather isn't humid, you could use fairy floss for her hair.

EQUIPMENT

three 20cm x 30cm
(8-inch x 12-inch)
rectangular cake pans
70cm (28-inch) square
cake board (page 334)

CAKE

3 x 470g (15-ounce) packets
butter cake mix
3 quantities butter cream
(page 329)

green and flesh
food colouring
vegetable oil, for deep-frying

DECORATIONS

400g (12½ ounces)
mint leaves
3 green Fruit Sticks
2 savoiardi (sponge finger)
biscuits
1 red snake
2 strawberries and creams
blue glossy decorating gel
1 black licorice strap
1 pink Fruit Stick or
Musk Stick
11 Oompas
1 small sea shell
2 scallop shells
250g (8 ounces) bean
thread vermicelli

1 Preheat oven to 180°C/350°F. Grease cake pans; line bases and sides with baking paper, extending paper 5cm (2 inches) above sides.
2 Make cakes according to directions on packets; divide mixture evenly into pans. Bake cakes about 30 minutes. Stand cakes in pans 5 minutes before turning, top-side up, onto wire racks to cool.
3 Level cake tops so they are the same height. Turn cakes, cut-side down. Using pattern from pattern sheet, cut out tail and body of mermaid from two of the cakes. Cut out fin and two semi-circles for head from remaining cake; discard any leftover cake.
4 Secure cakes, cut-side down, on cake board with a little butter cream.
5 Tint two-thirds of the butter cream green; tint remaining butter cream flesh.
6 Spread green butter cream over top and side of tail; spread flesh butter cream over top and side of body and head.
7 Cut mint leaves in half lengthways through centre; cover tail with slightly overlapping mint leaves. Position two green Fruit Sticks to separate tail from body. Position biscuits for arms.
8 Cut mouth from red snake. Position strawberries and creams, upside-down, for eyes; use blue decorating gel to pipe on pupils. Cut two strips of licorice strap for eyelashes; position above eyes.
9 Cut end off pink Fruit Stick; position for belly button. Make necklace with Oompas and small shell; position around neck. Position scallop shells and remaining green Fruit Stick, as pictured, to make bikini top.
10 Deep-fry vermicelli in hot oil until puffed; drain on absorbent paper, cool. Style and shape hair by cutting and separating noodles; position hair around head.

Cut out mermaid body and tail pieces using paper pattern.

Using paper pattern, cut out head and fins.

Position cake pieces, cut-side down, on cake board to form mermaid. Secure to board with a little butter cream.

TIP
If you can't find
Oompas you can use
Cool Fruits or any
round pastel candies.

TIP
The gingerbread house can be assembled 3 days ahead; bake gingerbread a day before it's required and store in an airtight container.

Gingerbread Birdhouse

1 Make gingerbread dough.

2 Preheat oven to 200°C/400°F. Grease oven trays.

3 Roll out gingerbread dough between sheets of baking paper until 1cm (½-inch) thick. Using pattern from pattern sheet, cut out the following shapes ½cm (¼-inch) larger than the pattern: cut 1 x base, 2 x side walls, 2 x front/back walls and 2 x roof panels from dough, re-rolling dough as necessary. Carefully transfer shapes to oven trays. Using heart cutter, cut heart from one of the front/back walls (this will be the front wall).

4 Bake gingerbread about 10 minutes or until firm. Lay pattern on top of warm gingerbread; trim and neaten edges of the gingerbread with a sharp knife to the size of the pattern. Stand gingerbread on trays 5 minutes before transferring to wire racks to cool.

5 Spoon royal icing into piping bag. Pipe a thick line of royal icing along walls and base of gingerbread. Assemble birdhouse on cake board (position a couple of glasses up against the walls to hold them in place). Stand at room temperature until set.

6 Using picture as a guide, secure musk lollies around edge of heart cut-out with royal icing. Trim nerd ropes to outline edges of front and back walls and roof; secure with royal icing. Cover roof panels with sour straps, overlapping slightly; secure to roof with a little butter cream. Make flower using red sour string, fruit wheel and mint leaves, as pictured; secure to front wall with a little royal icing.

gingerbread dough Combine butter, sugar and honey in medium saucepan; stir over low heat until sugar dissolves. Cool 10 minutes. Transfer mixture to a large bowl; stir in rind, eggs and sifted dry ingredients. Turn dough onto a floured surface; knead gently until mixture loses its stickiness; cover, refrigerate 1 hour.

EQUIPMENT

oven trays

6cm (2½-inch) heart cutter

paper piping bag (page 338)

30cm (12-inch) square or round cake board (page 334)

GINGERBREAD

90g (3 ounces) butter

1 cup (200g firmly packed brown sugar

1 cup (250ml) honey

2 teaspoons finely grated lemon rind

3 eggs, beaten lightly

5 cups (750g) plain (all-purpose) flour

1 cup (150g) self-raising flour

1 teaspoon bicarbonate of soda (baking soda)

2 teaspoons ground ginger

1½ teaspoons ground cinnamon

1 teaspoon ground cloves

½ teaspoon ground nutmeg

½ teaspoon ground cardamom

DECORATIONS

2 quantities royal icing (page 329)

½ quantity butter cream (page 329)

100g (3-ounce) packet musk lollies

12 x 26g (¾-ounces) nerd ropes

2 x 160g (5-ounce) packets rainbow sour straps

5cm (2-inch) piece red strawberry sour string

1 yellow fruit wheel

2 mint leaves

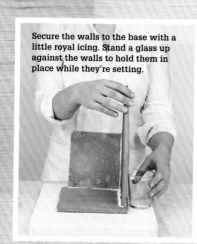

Secure the walls to the base with a little royal icing. Stand a glass up against the walls to hold them in place while they're setting.

Secure the roof panels to the birdhouse with royal icing; hold in place until set.

Rainbow Serpent

Little cakes are perfect for younger children as they each get their very own cake to eat at the party, or take home.

EQUIPMENT

6-hole (¾-cup/180ml)
texas muffin pan
12-hole (¹/₃-cup/80ml)
standard muffin pan
12-hole (1-tablespoon/20ml)
mini muffin pan
35cm x 55cm
(14-inch x 22-inch) rectangular
cake board (page 334)

CAKE

1 x 470g (15-ounce) packet
butter cake mix
1 quantity butter cream
(page 329)
red, orange, yellow, green, blue
and purple food colouring

DECORATIONS

1 triangular purple jube, halved
1 x 30cm (12-inch) black
chenille stick (pipe cleaner)
35g (1-ounce) tube mini M&M's
410g (13-ounce) packet
Smarties

1 Preheat oven to 180°C/350°F. Grease one hole of the texas muffin pan; grease 11 holes of the standard muffin pan; grease two holes of the mini muffin pan.

2 Make cake according to directions on packet. Drop ¹/₃ cup of mixture into greased hole of the texas muffin pan. Drop 2½ level tablespoons of the mixture into the greased holes of the standard muffin pan. Drop 3 level teaspoons of mixture into the greased holes of the mini muffin pan. Bake larger cakes about 20 minutes; bake mini cakes about 15 minutes. Stand cakes in pans 5 minutes before turning, top-side up, onto wire rack to cool.

3 Divide butter cream into six small bowls; tint red, orange, yellow, green, blue and purple.

4 Using picture as a guide, trim the side of the largest cake to make the serpent's head; spread red butter cream all over head. Trim tops of remaining cakes to make them level. Spread with orange, yellow, blue green, purple and red butter cream.

5 Position jube halves for eyes. Cut chenille stick into two 5cm (2-inch) pieces, twist together to make serpent's forked tongue; gently push into front of head. Position cakes on cake board; secure with a little butter cream.

6 Decorate the serpent with M&M's and Smarties.

TIP

You'll have about ½ cup of the cake mixture left over: make more cakes for a longer serpent, if you like. Make the rainbow serpent as long as you like; he could be slithering along the whole length of the party table.

Dolly Varden

Originally a character in a Charles Dickens novel, Dolly has gone on to influence fashion, fish (one is named after her), a cake pan (in the shape of her dress) and all manner of embroideries...what a girl she must have been!

1 Preheat oven to 180°C/350°F. Grease dolly varden pan well.

2 Make cake according to directions on packet; pour mixture into pan. Bake about 1 hour. Stand cake in pan 5 minutes before turning onto wire rack to cool.

3 Spread butter cream all over cake. Gently push doll down into cake to waist level.

4 Halve marshmallows; press marshmallows, cut-side down, alternating pink and white, all over 'skirt' starting from the bottom. Wind ribbon around doll's body to represent bodice, tie at the back in a large bow. Position flower at waist.

EQUIPMENT

dolly varden cake pan
30cm (12-inch) round
cake board (page 334)

CAKE

1 x 470g (15-ounce) packet
butter cake mix
1 quantity butter cream
(page 329)

DECORATIONS

1 doll, legs removed
300g (9½ ounces) pink and
white marshmallows
1m (40 inches) ribbon
artificial flower

Gary Ghost

The fluffy frosting can be applied to the cake the night before, however, it will become crisp and lose its glossy appearance. If you want it shiny, it's best to apply it the morning of the party.

EQUIPMENT

20cm x 30cm (8-inch x 12-inch)
rectangular cake pan
30cm x 40cm (12-inch x 16-inch)
rectangular cake board
(page 334)

CAKE

1 x 470g (15-ounce) packet
butter cake mix
1 quantity fluffy frosting
(page 329)

DECORATIONS

red permanent marker
1 egg shell, halved
2 red Smarties
12 blue Smarties

1 Preheat oven to 180°C/350°F. Grease cake pan; line base and sides with baking paper, extending paper 5cm (2 inches) above sides.

2 Make cake according to directions on packet; spread mixture into pan. Bake about 25 minutes. Stand cake in pan 5 minutes before turning, top-side up, onto wire rack to cool.

3 Level cake top; turn cake cut-side down. Cut two corners off cake, as pictured.

4 Position cake on cake board, cut-side down; position corners for ghost's arms, as pictured. Secure with a little fluffy frosting.

5 Using permanent marker, draw veins in egg shells. Use a little frosting to secure red Smarties in egg shells for eyes.

6 Spread fluffy frosting all over cake. Position egg shells for eyes and blue Smarties for mouth.

Cut the corners off the cake in a rounded shape.

Assemble cake on board, cut-side down. Secure to board with a little butter cream.

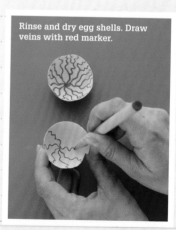

Rinse and dry egg shells. Draw veins with red marker.

Cut out cake using paper pattern.

Cut stars from licorice allsorts.

the Good Witch

There's some hocus pocus going on, and this cake will have the guests under its spell. A purple-covered cake board, or background on the party table, will add to the charm.

1 Preheat oven to 180°C/350°F. Grease cake pan; line base and sides with baking paper, extending paper 5cm (2 inches) above sides.

2 Make cake according to directions on packet; spread mixture into pan. Bake about 25 minutes. Stand cake in pan 5 minutes before turning, top-side up, onto wire rack to cool.

3 Level cake top; turn cake cut-side down. Using pattern from pattern sheet, cut witch from cake. Secure cake, cut-side down, on cake board with a little butter cream.

4 Tint ½ cup butter cream blue; tint remaining butter cream purple. Spread purple butter cream all over cake; spread blue butter cream over face and hands.

5 Cut licorice strap into thin strips; using picture as a guide, position on cake for hat brim, hat tassel, dress and face. Cut stars out of licorice allsorts; position on witch's dress. Position potato straws for hair and Fizzers for eyes.

6 Cut licorice twist in half; position on either side of the witch. Position thin licorice strips for bristles; wind thin licorice around join between bristles and broom handle.

EQUIPMENT

20cm x 30cm (8-inch x 12-inch)
rectangular cake pan

40cm x 50cm (16-inch x 18-inch)
rectangular cake board
(page 334)

CAKE

1 x 470g (15-ounce) packet
butter cake mix

1 quantity butter cream
(page 329)

blue and purple food colouring

DECORATIONS

1 black licorice strap

4 licorice allsorts

2 pink Fizzers

1 packet potato straws

1 black licorice twist

Juggling Jamie

Juggling is so much fun, people have been doing it since ancient Egyptian times. This delightful fellow is constructed from lots of little cakes, so it's simple to make and easy to decorate.

EQUIPMENT

8-hole (½-cup/125ml) mini loaf pan

9-hole (½-cup/125ml) friand pan

2 x 12-hole (1-tablespoon/20ml) mini muffin pans

1cm (½-inch) star cutter

45cm x 55cm (18-inch x 22-inch) rectangular cake board
(page 334)

CAKE

1½ x 470g (15-ounce) packets butter cake mix
(see 'mixing the cakes' page 345)

1 quantity butter cream
(page 329)

blue, purple, green, orange, red and pink food colouring

DECORATIONS

6 green Smarties

6 blue Smarties

3 fruit allsorts

18 red mini M&M's

2 red fruit rings, halved

100g (3-ounce) packet red licorice bootlace

2 blue mini M&M's

2 round peppermints

1 freckle

1 red Smartie

1 green sour strap

10 small pink jelly beans

1 Preheat oven to 170°C/340°F. Grease five holes of the mini loaf pan; grease eight holes of the friand pan; grease 15 holes of the mini muffin pans.

2 Make cakes according to directions on packets. Drop ⅓ cup of the mixture into greased mini loaf pan holes; drop 2½ level tablespoons of mixture into greased friand pan holes. Bake cakes about 25 minutes. Stand cakes in pans 5 minutes before turning, top-side up, onto wire rack to cool.

3 Drop 3 level teaspoons of the mixture into greased mini muffin pan holes; bake about 15 minutes. Stand cakes in pans 5 minutes before turning, top-side up, onto wire rack to cool.

4 Divide butter cream into six small bowls; tint blue, purple, green, orange, red and pale pink.

5 Using picture as a guide, spread butter cream over cake tops. Secure cakes on board with a little butter cream. Use three mini muffin cakes for each foot and two loaf cakes for each leg. Use one loaf cake and two friand cakes for the body. Use two friand cakes for each arm and one mini muffin cake for each hand.

6 Use two friand cakes for the face, two mini muffin cakes for ears and one mini muffin cake for nose. Use four mini muffin cakes for the juggling balls.

7 Position green and blue Smarties on the legs. Slice two fruit allsorts into quarters. Position 13 red mini M&M's and fruit allsorts quarters on body. Use the fruit ring halves to make the frill around clown's neck.

8 Cut a strip of red bootlace for mouth; position on face. Secure blue mini M&M's to peppermints with a little butter cream; position on head for eyes. Trim freckle to make hat; position remaining red mini M&M's at base of hat. Secure red Smartie on top of hat with a little butter cream.

9 Cut green sour strap into strips to make hair; top hands with small pink jelly beans to make fingers. Tie two 20cm (8-inch) pieces of red bootlace into bows; position for shoelaces.

10 Using star cutter, cut four stars from yellow layer of remaining fruit allsort; position on balls.

TIP
There will be about ⅔ cup of the cake mixture left, enough to make 10 more mini muffin balls to share with the guests.

TIPS

Use any leftover cake mixture to make cupcakes. If you like, have the cake prepared for frosting a day ahead: keep the cake in the fridge overnight - a cold cake will make the frosting process easier. Serve the cake as soon as it's browned.

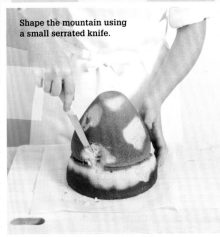

Shape the mountain using a small serrated knife.

Haunted Mountain

If you can't find the snowmen, join a couple of marshmallows together and paint on the faces with a little food colouring.

1 Preheat oven to 150°C/300°F. Grease and flour both pans.

2 Make cakes according to directions on packets. Pour enough mixture into round pan until three-quarters full. Pour enough mixture into dolly varden pan until 4cm (1½ inches) from top of pan. Bake both cakes about 1¼ hours. Stand cakes in pans 5 minutes before turning, top-side down, onto wire rack to cool. Turn oven off (it takes a few hours before the cakes are cold enough to cover with the frosting).

3 Trim tops of both cakes to make flat. Secure round cake, top-side up, on cake board with a little jam. Brush cut surface of cake with warm jam. Position dolly varden cake, cut-side down, on round cake.

4 Using a small serrated knife, shape cakes by hollowing out random areas to give the effect of a rugged mountain, as pictured. Position cake on an oven tray.

5 Position oven shelves to allow for the height of the cake. Preheat oven to 250°C/500°F.

6 Position candle on top of cake, cover cake with frosting, leaving top and wick of candle exposed. Bake cake about 2 minutes or until frosting is browned lightly.

7 Position snow men on cake. Dust cake with sifted icing sugar before serving.

EQUIPMENT

deep 20cm (8-inch) round cake pan
dolly varden cake pan
30cm (12-inch) round cake board (page 334) or plate
oven tray

CAKE

3 x 470g (15-ounce) packets butter cake mix
⅓ cup (110g) apricot jam, warmed, strained
2 quantities fluffy frosting (page 329)

DECORATIONS

short 2.5cm (1-inch) diameter candle
marshmallow snow men
1 tablespoon icing (confectioners') sugar

EQUIPMENT

12-hole (1/3-cup/80ml) standard muffin pan

9-hole (1/2-cup/125ml) friand pan

45cm x 65cm (17-inch x 26-inch) rectangular cake board
(page 334)

CAKE

1½ x 470g (15-ounce) packets butter cake mix
(see 'mixing the cakes' page 345)

1½ quantities butter cream
(page 329)

green, orange and red food colouring

DECORATIONS

15cm x 20cm (6-inch x 8-inch) piece orange cardboard

20cm x 30cm (8-inch x 12-inch) piece yellow cardboard

8 after-dinner mints

200g (6½-ounce) milk chocolate Toblerone

300g (9½-ounce) packet mint leaves

4 red jelly fruit rings

1 orange Smartie

1 brown Smartie

7cm (2¾-inch) piece black licorice strap

2 orange jelly fruit rings

1 x 30cm (12-inch) green chenille stick (pipe cleaner), cut into quarters

1 Preheat oven to 180°C/350°F. Grease nine holes of the muffin pan; grease the friand pan.

2 Make cakes according to directions on packets. Drop 2½ level tablespoons of mixture into greased holes of the muffin pan; bake about 20 minutes. Stand cakes in pan 5 minutes before turning, top-side up, onto wire rack to cool.

3 Reduce oven temperature to 170°C/340°F. Drop 2½ level tablespoons of mixture into greased friand pan holes; bake about 20 minutes. Stand cakes in pan 5 minutes before turning, top-side up, onto wire rack to cool.

Fiery Dragon

In China, dragons traditionally symbolise good luck, which, along with this dragon, is a pretty nice gift to give as a birthday present.

4 Tint two-thirds of the butter cream green. Divide remaining butter cream equally into two small bowls; tint one orange and the other red.

5 Level friand tops. Use three friands to shape dragon's head. Spread green butter cream over tops and sides of each friand.

6 Level muffin tops. Turn eight muffins upside down; spread tops and sides of five muffins with orange butter cream; spread tops and sides of three muffins with red butter cream.

7 Trim the remaining muffin into a triangular shape for the tail; spread top and sides with red butter cream.

8 Using pattern from pattern sheet, cut out dragon's fiery breath from the yellow and orange cardboard. Position on cake board. Using picture as a guide, position cakes on board to make dragon. Position trimmed friands to make head; use the remaining six friands to make a triangular body. Use muffins to make neck and tail. Secure cakes with a little butter cream.

9 Using picture as a guide, cut after-dinner mints into triangles. Use triangular pieces and segments of Toblerone to decorate the dragon's body. Decorate dragon's head and body with mint leaves.

10 Use one red fruit ring to make the eye; top with an orange Smartie. Use brown Smartie for nose. Trim licorice strap to make mouth. Cut remaining red and orange fruit rings in half; use to decorate dragon's neck and tail.

11 Bend one end of each chenille stick to make dragon's legs and feet; position under body.

Use a small sharp, finely serrated knife to trim one end of a friand so the other two sit snugly together for the dragon's head.

Gnome

1 Preheat oven to 170°C/340°F. Grease pans; line bases and sides with baking paper, extending paper 5cm (2 inches) above sides.

2 Make cakes according to directions on packets. Pour two-thirds of the mixture into rectangular pan; pour remaining mixture into round pan. Bake rectangular cake about 45 minutes; bake round cake about 50 minutes. Stand cakes in pans 10 minutes before turning, top-side up, onto wire rack to cool.

3 Level cake tops; turn cakes cut-side down. Using pattern from pattern sheet, cut out gnome's body from rectangular cake. Split round cake in half through centre. Use one half for gnome's head and cut the other half into a triangle for the hat. Using a sharp knife, cut a curved shape into base of triangle so that it fits onto gnome's head. Position cake pieces, cut-side down, on cake board to form gnome; secure with a little butter cream.

4 Reserve half the butter cream. Tint half the remaining butter cream dark green using both the green and blue colourings; tint remaining half black.

5 Spread half of the plain butter cream all over cake; refrigerate for 30 minutes to allow butter cream to set. Spread remaining plain butter cream over gnome's arms and face. Spread black butter cream over boots and green butter cream over gnome's jacket and hat.

6 Using picture as a guide, position Smarties for eyes, gumball for nose, sour string for lips and white marshmallows for beard and eyebrows. Spread butter cream over dried pears; position on cake board, on either side of gnome's head, for ears, secure with a little butter cream. Trim and position licorice strap for belt, and Lattice biscuit for belt buckle.

7 Position mint choc balls around bottom edge of hat for trim. Position orange flying saucers at end of arms for hands and pink flying saucers on face for cheeks.

EQUIPMENT

20cm x 30cm (8-inch x 12-inch)
rectangular cake pan
deep 15cm (6-inch)
round cake pan
30cm x 40cm
(12-inch x 16-inch)
rectangular cake board
(page 334)

CAKE

3 x 440g (14-ounce) packets
butter cake mix
1½ quantities of butter cream
(page 329)

green, blue and black
food colourings

DECORATIONS

2 pink flying saucer lollies
2 orange flying saucer lollies
2 blue Smarties
1 red gum ball
5cm (2-inch) piece red
strawberry sour string
1 x 500g (1 pound) packets
marshmallows
(use white ones only)
2 dried pears
12cm (4¾-inches) black
licorice strap
1 Lattice biscuit
11 mint choc balls

Trim rectangular cake top. Turn cake cut-side down. Place pattern on cake, cut out gnome's body.

Cut round cake in half; use one half for gnome's head. Use other half for hat. Secure to cake board with a little butter cream.

TIPS

Cooked cakes can be frozen for up to one month. Thaw at room temperature for about six hours.

Cake can be iced and decorated one day ahead (except for the bats): keep, covered, in refrigerator if the weather is hot.

Position flying bats about three hours ahead.

Bat Cave

This cave is made up of three different cakes, and while it may look fiddly and complicated to make, it isn't that difficult.

Cut away some of the front of the cake to form cave mouth; pour black glacé icing inside to coat mouth of cave.

1 Preheat oven to 180°C/350°F. Grease square and rectangular cake pans; line bases and sides with baking paper, extending paper 5cm (2 inches) above sides. Grease pudding steamer.

2 Make two of the cakes according to directions on packets; pour into square cake pan. Bake square cake about 1¼ hours. Make remaining packet cakes; pour 4½ cups of mixture into pudding steamer, pour remaining mixture into the rectangular pan. Bake cake in steamer about 50 minutes; bake cake in rectangular pan about 40 minutes. Stand square and rectangular cakes in pans 5 minutes before turning, top-side up, onto wire racks to cool. Turn out cake in pudding steamer onto wire rack to cool.

3 Level cake tops. Using patterns from pattern sheet, cut wall from square cake and cut base from rectangular cake. Carve out mouth of cave from pudding cake.

4 Make black glacé icing. Pour icing into cave; turn cake to evenly coat inside of cave. Stand at room temperature until set.

5 Beat sifted cocoa and brown colouring into butter cream. Secure base, cut-side down, on cake board with a little butter cream. Spread butter cream all over base and wall cakes; stand wall behind base so that the wall is positioned to one end of the base.

6 Slice back of pudding cake (cave) so it will fit flat against the wall. Spread butter cream all over outside of cave; position on top of base, against the wall. Smooth butter cream to cover any joins.

7 Combine coconut with green colouring in a small plastic bag, rub together until coconut is coloured; sprinkle over cake where you are going to place the vines. Position green snakes and leaves to resemble vines.

8 Dab a drop of brown colouring onto absorbent paper, wipe along the length of the bamboo skewers and toothpicks to colour. Push skewers and toothpicks into bat lollies. Using a small paintbrush, paint front of bat lollies with black food colouring; position in and around cave to suggest flying bats.

9 Using picture as a guide, decorate cake with remaining lollies to complete bat cave.

black glacé icing Sift icing sugar into a small heatproof bowl; stir in the water and colouring. Stir over small saucepan of simmering water until icing is spreadable.

EQUIPMENT

deep 22cm (9-inch)
square cake pan
20cm x 30cm (8-inch x 12-inch)
rectangular cake pan
1.75-litre (7-cup) pudding steamer
30cm x 40cm (12-inch x 16-inch)
rectangular cake board
(page 334)
new small artist's paintbrush

CAKE

5 x 340g (11-ounce) packets
chocolate cake mix
(see 'mixing the cakes' page 345)
¼ cup (25g) cocoa powder
brown and green food colouring
3 quantities butter cream
(page 329)

BLACK GLACÉ ICING

1 cup (160g) icing
(confectioners') sugar
1 tablespoon water
black food colouring

DECORATIONS

2 tablespoons shredded coconut
green jelly snakes
mint leaves
3 wooden skewers
2 toothpicks
fruit bat jellies
yellow jelly snake
red jelly snake
red and yellow boiled lollies
50g (1½-ounce) Toblerone
chocolate bar
80g (2½ ounces) milk-
chocolate coated sultanas

Alien

This little extraterrestrial is so likeable that even a horde of hungry alien task force officers may have trouble cutting into it.

EQUIPMENT

deep 12cm (4¾-inch)
round cake pan
deep 20cm (8-inch)
round cake pan
12-hole (1-tablespoon/20ml)
shallow round-based patty pan
30cm x 40cm
(12-inch x 16-inch)
rectangular cake board
(page 334)

CAKE

1½ x 470g (15-ounce) packets
butter cake mix
(see 'mixing the cakes' page 345)
2 quantities butter cream
(page 329)
orange and green
food colouring
1 tablespoon apricot jam,
warmed, strained

DECORATIONS

30g (1 ounce) ready-made
white icing (page 329)
pure icing (confectioners')
sugar, for dusting
1 orange Skittle
5 Tic Tacs
2 swirl pops
13 Froot Loops
2 yellow flying saucers

1 Preheat oven to 160°C/325°F. Grease round pans; line bases and sides with baking paper, extending paper 5cm (2 inches) above sides. Grease one hole of the patty pan.

2 Make cakes according to directions on packets. Drop 1 heaped tablespoon mixture into patty pan hole; bake about 20 minutes. Spread 1⅔ cups mixture into small round pan; bake about 45 minutes. Spread remaining mixture into large round pan; bake about 50 minutes. Stand cakes in pans 5 minutes before turning, top-side up, onto wire racks to cool.

3 Tint butter cream pale orange.

4 Trim 2cm (¾-inch) strip from large cake to make top of alien's body. Trim 1cm (½-inch) strip from small cake to make base of alien's head. Shape top edges of cakes to make rounded. Secure large cake, cut-side up, on cake board with a little butter cream. Secure small cake, cut-side up, on cake board with a little butter cream, joining two flat sides with butter cream. Spread remaining butter cream all over cake.

5 Knead ready-made icing on surface dusted with a little sifted icing sugar until icing loses its stickiness. Roll out three-quarters of the icing on surface dusted with sifted icing sugar, until large enough to cover patty cake. Brush rounded side of patty cake with warmed jam, cover cake wtih icing; trim edge.

6 Tint half the remaining ready-made icing green; roll out on surface dusted with a little sifted icing sugar into a 3mm (⅛-inch) thickness. Cut a 2cm (¾-inch) round from green icing, place on patty cake to make eye; position on alien's head. Place Skittle on eye, secure with a little water. Tint remaining icing orange; roll out on surface dusted with a little sifted icing sugar into a 3mm (⅛-inch) thickness. Shape into mouth, position on cake.

7 Using picture as a guide, decorate cake with Tic Tacs for teeth, swirl pops for antennae, flying saucers for feet and Froot Loops for spots.

TIP
This cake can be completed a day ahead of the party.

the Ghostly Galleon

1 Preheat oven to 180°C/350°F. Grease baking dish; line base and sides with baking paper, extending paper 5cm (2 inches) above sides.

2 Make cakes according to directions on packets; spread mixture into dish. Bake about 1 hour. Stand cake in dish 5 minutes before turning, top-side up, onto wire rack to cool.

3 Level cake top; turn cake cut-side down. Cut cake in half lengthways; cut 7cm (2¾-inch) piece from each half, as pictured.

4 Position cake pieces, cut-side down, on cake board to form galleon, as pictured; secure to board with a little butter cream. Position five skewers in cake, as pictured, to secure cake layers.

5 Trim front of galleon at angles to make bow; discard cake trimmings. Use kitchen scissors to trim skewers to the same height as the cake.

6 Tint butter cream black; spread all over galleon.

7 Decorate galleon with pieces of Curly Wurly, Crazy Bananas and Life Savers. Position milk chocolate block for plank; support plank by placing a piece of skewer or toothpick underneath.

8 Thread large then small cardboard pieces on remaining skewers. Photocopy 6.5cm x 8.5cm (2¾-inch x 3½-inch) Jolly Roger picture from pattern sheet; position at top of centre skewer. Position three masts on galleon.

Cut the cake in half lengthways, then cut a 7cm piece from each of the two halves.

Assemble the cake pieces on the board to form the galleon, then secure with five skewers.

Trim the front of the galleon at angles, then trim skewers to the same height as the cake.

Cut the cake into a clock shape. Keep 'arrow' shape, discard remaining cake, or cut into small shapes and cover with extra butter cream for additional snacks for the party.

Hickory Dickory Dock

(page 334)

EQUIPMENT

20cm x 30cm
(8-inch x 12-inch)
rectangular cake pan
25cm x 35cm (10-inch x
14-inch) rectangular
cake board (page 334)
9cm (3¾-inch) round cutter
small paper piping bag
(page 339)

CAKE

1 x 470g (15-ounce) packet
butter cake mix
1 quantity butter cream
(page 329)
pink food colouring
1 tablespoon cocoa powder
1 tablespoon water

DECORATIONS

400g (12½-ounce) packet
chocolate-covered
licorice bullets
39 pink Smarties
1 black licorice strap
2 chocolate freckles
2 prunes
1 red jelly snake

1 Preheat oven to 180°C/350°F. Grease cake pan; line base and sides with baking paper, extending paper 5cm (2 inches) above sides.

2 Make cake according to directions on packet; spread mixture into pan. Bake about 30 minutes. Stand cake in pan 5 minutes before turning, top-side up, onto wire rack to cool.

3 Level cake top; turn cake cut-side down. Using picture as a guide, cut clock from cake. Secure cake, cut-side down, on cake board with a little butter cream.

4 Using round cutter as a guide, mark a circle on top of the cake to represent face of clock. Place one-quarter of the butter cream in small bowl; tint pink. Stir combined sifted cocoa and the water into remaining butter cream in medium bowl until combined.

5 Spread pink butter cream evenly over face of clock, continue down body of cake to within 4cm (1½ inches) of cake edges, as pictured. Spread chocolate butter cream evenly over rest of cake. Outline cake with chocolate-covered bullets. Outline pink section with Smarties.

6 Spoon remaining chocolate butter cream into piping bag; pipe numbers on clock face. Cut thin strips of licorice and position on cake to make hands of the clock. Using picture as a guide, use thin strips of licorice and freckles to make the pendulums.

7 To make and decorate mice, cut 2 Smarties in half; push into prunes for ears, secure with a little butter cream, if necessary. Cut thin strips of licorice for tails and thin strips of snake for whiskers; secure to prune with a little butter cream. Position mice on cake.

Sally Surprise

This 'cake' is based on the tradition of the piñata - a decorated container filled with treats, released when the piñata is broken.

EQUIPMENT

dolly varden cake pan
(1.5-litre/6-cup capacity)
small hacksaw or
sharp serrated knife
22cm (9-inch) round
cake board (page 334)

CAKE

1 tablespoon vegetable oil
2 x 275g (9-ounce) packets
white chocolate Melts

DECORATIONS

doll (about 30cm/12-inches tall)
30g (1-ounce) pink and white
butterfly sprinkles
1kg (2-pounds) assorted lollies,
approximately
18 ready-made white and
yellow sugar flowers
30cm (12 inches) pink ribbon

1 Cut through doll's waist, using the small saw or knife, and discard bottom half.

2 Using fingers, rub oil evenly over inside surface of cake pan.

3 Melt chocolate in large heatproof bowl over large saucepan of simmering water until smooth (don't let water touch bottom of bowl).

4 Pour half the chocolate into pan; swirl to coat inside of pan evenly. Continue swirling until chocolate begins to set and stops flowing around the pan. Pour remaining melted chocolate (reserving about $1/3$ cup in a small bowl) into pan and continue swirling to coat inside of pan thickly; try to keep chocolate a uniform thickness, particularly at the top edge. Refrigerate about 20 minutes or until chocolate is set.

5 Remelt reserved chocolate, if required. Keeping hair out of the way, dip the doll's upper body into the chocolate to form top part of her dress; sprinkle with butterfly sprinkles. Stand doll on baking paper until beginning to set.

6 Meanwhile, briefly rub a hot cloth around the outside of pan and turn chocolate shell out of pan. Fill shell with assorted lollies; place cake board on top of opening, then invert shell onto cake board. Secure doll on top of chocolate mould with a little melted chocolate; hold in position until the chocolate sets.

7 Use remaining melted chocolate to attach sugar flowers to dress; tie ribbon around doll's waist.

Magic Garden

1 Preheat oven to 180°C/350°F. Line the patty pan with brown standard paper cases; line standard muffin pan with the green and yellow standard paper cases; line mini muffin pans with the mini paper cases.

2 Make cake according to directions on packet. Drop 2½ level tablespoons of the mixture into each paper case in the standard muffin pan. Drop 2 level tablespoons of the mixture into each paper case in the patty pan. Bake cakes about 20 minutes. Stand cakes in pans 5 minutes before turning, top-side up, onto wire rack to cool.

3 Drop 2 level teaspoons of the mixture into the mini paper cases. Bake about 15 minutes. Stand cakes in pans 5 minutes before turning, top-side up, onto wire rack to cool.

4 Design the garden on the board using the cakes before icing them.

5 Divide butter cream into three small bowls. Tint one bowl green and one bowl dark green. Tint half the remaining butter cream brown. Divide remaining plain butter cream equally into three small bowls. Tint yellow, pink and purple.

6 Spread brown butter cream over tops of tree trunk cakes; spread green butter cream over tops of the tree canopy cakes. Spread yellow butter cream over sun cake. Spread pink butter cream over the tops of three mini muffins in pink cases and purple butter cream over the tops of two mini muffins in purple cases; spread the remaining mini muffin cakes with dark green butter cream for garden bed.

7 Reserve three mint leaves; position remaining leaves and the jaffa halves on tree canopy. Use a small sharp knife to cut the remaining mint leaves into thin strips; use to decorate the garden bed.

8 Sprinkle hundreds and thousands over jelly halves. Using picture as a guide, make butterfly by positioning jelly halves, cut-side up, on either side of Musk Stick half; place on tree.

9 Decorate sun with fruit ring halves; position red smarties for eyes and red bootlace for the mouth.

10 Position ladybirds, brown Smarties for rocks, and sour worm in the garden.

11 Position pink and purple Smarties around same coloured cakes to make flower petals. Use yellow rainbow choc-chips to make the flower centres.

12 Use giant marshmallow for rabbit's body and smaller marshmallow for head. Cut remaining marshmallow in half; pinch slightly to shape into rabbit's ears. Position Mallow Bakes for feet and tail. Decorate rabbit's face with Mini Musk for nose, strips of licorice strap for whiskers and blue rainbow choc-chips for eyes; secure to face with a little butter cream.

tip Decorate the garden however you like, using lollies and cute critters. Don't worry about the scale of things, your guests won't mind at all.

Castle for a Princess

Little girls and their dreams of being a princess are fulfilled with this fairy-tale castle...pretty in pink, a princess's favourite colour.

EQUIPMENT

deep 23cm (9¼-inch)
square cake pan

deep 15cm (6-inch)
round cake pan

36cm (14-inch) square
cake board (page 334)

2 bamboo skewers

CAKE

3 x 470g (15-ounce) packets
butter cake mix

3 quantities butter cream
(page 329)

pink food colouring

DECORATIONS

2 x 250g (8-ounce) packets
vanilla creams (biscuits)

5 waffle ice-cream cones

6 ice-cream wafers

130g (4-ounce) packet
candy jewellery

4 heart-shaped lollipops

3 small paper flags

30 sugar cubes

2 pink Mallow Bakes

1 Preheat oven to 130°C/260°F. Grease and flour cake pans.

2 Make cakes according to directions on packets. Pour enough mixture into each pan to fill to three-quarters. (Use any leftover mixture to make cupcakes for the party). Bake cakes about 1¼ hours. Stand cakes in pans 5 minutes before turning, top-side up, onto wire racks to cool.

3 Tint butter cream pink. Level cake tops; secure square cake, cut-side down, on cake board with a little butter cream (allowing space for drawbridge). Using one of the biscuits as a guide, cut rounds out of each corner of the square cake with a small serrated knife.

4 Secure round cake to square cake, cut-side down, with a little butter cream; cover whole cake with butter cream. Stack six biscuits, joining each with butter cream, in each of the cut-out corners of the cake. Using scissors, trim waffle cones to sit flat; position one on each corner and one on the top of the castle to make towers.

5 Remove candy rings from bracelets, position four rings on each lollipop stick, gently push lollipops into corner towers; position flags in top tower. Position sugar cubes using picture as a guide.

6 Using scissors, trim wafers into shapes for windows, door and drawbridge; position on cake. To make chains for drawbridge: cut skewers to about 12cm (4¾ inches) in length. Position a Mallow Bake at one end of each skewer. Slide the candy rings onto the skewers; position another Mallow Bake at end of skewer to hold the candy rings in position; place on cake.

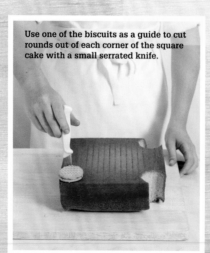

Use one of the biscuits as a guide to cut rounds out of each corner of the square cake with a small serrated knife.

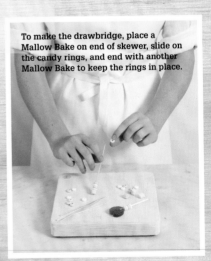

To make the drawbridge, place a Mallow Bake on end of skewer, slide on the candy rings, and end with another Mallow Bake to keep the rings in place.

Gingerbread man

EQUIPMENT

rolling pin
oven tray
23cm x 32cm (9-inch x 13-inch)
swiss roll pan
35cm x 40cm (14-inch x 16-inch)
rectangular cake board (page 334)
pastry brush
small paper piping bag (page 338)

GINGERBREAD

1¼ tablespoons golden syrup
(or treacle)
60g (2 ounces) butter, softened
¼ cup (55g) caster (superfine)
sugar
1 egg yolk
1¼ cups (185g) plain
(all-purpose) flour
½ teaspoon bicarbonate of soda
(baking soda)
1½ teaspoons ground ginger

CAKE

1 x 340g (11-ounce) packet
chocolate cake mix
½ quantity chocolate butter
cream (page 329)

1 quantity royal icing
(page 329)

DECORATIONS

chocolate sprinkles
⅓ cup (110g) apricot jam,
warmed, strained
2 red Smarties
2 green Smarties
2 yellow Smarties
1 black licorice strap
2 white marshmallows
1 brown Smartie, cut in half
1 yellow mini M&M

1 Preheat oven to 180°C/350°F. Grease oven tray. Grease swiss roll pan; line base and sides with baking paper, extending paper 5cm (2 inches) above sides.

2 To make gingerbread man: Pour golden syrup into small heatproof jug; stand jug in small saucepan of simmering water until syrup warms and softens. Beat butter and sugar in small bowl with electric mixer until light and fluffy. Beat in egg yolk. Stir in sifted dry ingredients and warmed syrup. Knead mixture on floured surface until smooth.

3 Using pattern from pattern sheet, roll dough on greased oven tray until it's the size of the gingerbread man pattern. Cut gingerbread man from dough while still on tray. (Make gingerbread biscuits with any leftover mixture.) Bake gingerbread about 20 minutes. Cool on tray.

4 Make the cake according to directions on packet; spread mixture into swiss roll pan. Bake about 20 minutes. Stand cake in pan 5 minutes before turning, top-side up, onto wire rack to cool.

5 Level cake top; turn cut-side down. Position gingerbread man on top of cake; using sharp knife, cut out gingerbread man shape from cake. Position cake and biscuit on cake board. Secure cake to board with a little butter cream; secure gingerbread man to cake with a little butter cream. Spread chocolate butter cream over sides of cake; coat thickly with chocolate sprinkles.

6 Brush gingerbread man lightly, and evenly, with jam to give a glaze. While glaze is still wet, decorate with red, green and yellow Smarties for buttons. Cut marshmallows in half; use bases for eyes. Push brown smartie halves into marshmallows for eyes. Position yellow mini M&M for nose, and thin strips of licorice for mouth and eyebrows.

7 Spoon royal icing into piping bag; pipe around edge of gingerbread to outline. Pipe a dot on each button.

Place the gingerbread man on top of the cake and use a small sharp knife to cut out shape of gingerbread from the cake.

Flying Saucer

If your house is teeming with aliens, you can be sure this UFO cake will be a hit with young space explorers and martians alike.

1 Preheat oven to 170°C/340°F. Grease pan; line base and side with baking paper, extending paper 5cm (2 inches) above side.
2 Make cakes according to directions on packets. Spread mixture into pan; bake about 1 hour 10 minutes. Stand cake in pan 10 minutes before turning, top-side up, onto wire rack to cool.
3 Using sharp serrated knife, sculpt cake to make a flying saucer shape. Secure cake on cake board with a little butter cream.
4 Tint butter cream green with colouring; spread all over cake.
5 Using picture as a guide, position flying saucer lollies as windows. Trim and position licorice bootlace to outline the windows. Position silver lollies between windows and around base; position one silver lolly on top of the flying saucer. Trim and position blue sour strings to outline base of flying saucer. Using picture as a guide, decorate flying saucer with remaining lollies.

EQUIPMENT

deep 25cm (10-inch) round cake pan
36cm (14½-inch) round cake board (page 334)

CAKE

3 x 440g (14-ounce) packets butter cake mix
1 quantity butter cream (page 329)
green food colouring

DECORATIONS

5 flying saucer lollies
50cm (20 inches) licorice bootlace
16 large silver-coated lollies
1 x 56g (2-ounce) packet blue sour strings
20 blue candy snaps

Sculpt the cake so it slopes from the middle out to the edge of the cake.

TIP
You can use
star-patterned wrapping
paper, with a sheet of
baking paper over it, as
a guide when tracing
the stars.

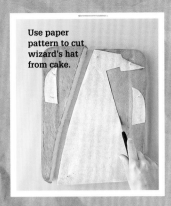
Use paper pattern to cut wizard's hat from cake.

Spread butter cream over cake using palette knife.

Pipe stars; sprinkle half with coloured sprinkles.

Wicked Wizard's hat

With magic and mayhem being all the rage these days, there are sure to be numerous requests for witch and wizard cakes.

EQUIPMENT

deep 26cm x 36cm (10½-inch x 14½-inch) baking dish
45cm x 50cm (17-inch x 18-inch) rectangular cake board
(page 334)
small paper piping bag
(page 338)

CAKE

3 x 470g (15-ounce) packets butter cake mix
2 quantities butter cream
(page 329)
blue and yellow food colouring

DECORATIONS

silver cardboard, for buckle
1 black licorice strap
100g (3 ounces) white chocolate Melts
coloured sprinkles

1 Preheat oven to 180°C/350°F. Grease baking dish; line base and sides with baking paper, extending paper 5cm (2 inches) above sides.
2 Make cakes according to directions on packets; spread mixture into dish. Bake about 1 hour. Stand cake in dish 5 minutes before turning, top-side up, onto wire rack to cool.
3 Level cake top; turn cake cut-side down. Using pattern from pattern sheet, cut hat from cake. Position cake, cut-side down, on cake board to form hat; secure with a little butter cream.
4 Tint butter cream blue; spread all over cake.
5 Trace buckle shape (below); copy onto silver cardboard, then cut out shape. Weave licorice strap through buckle; position on cake.
6 Trace stars (below) onto baking paper. Turn paper over so outlines are underneath. Melt chocolate (page 339); tint yellow, and spoon into piping bag. Pipe over stars; top half the stars with coloured sprinkles, stand at room temperature until set. Carefully lift stars from baking paper; attach to cake with a little butter cream, if necessary.

BUCKLE

STAR

Make one packet of cake mix at a time. Bake two trays of cakes together and, while they're baking, put the cake mixture into the next two trays – this way you'll have an efficient production line. The cakes can be made a day ahead and kept in an airtight container, or frozen for up to three months.

This cake is for a large party (only half the rainbow is shown here). For the best effect, match the paper cases to the colours of the rainbow, that is, to the colours of the frosting and jelly crystals. The sky background (a painted blue board, or blue cardboard) makes it fun, as does the felt 'grass' and the pot of gold at the end of the rainbow.

Rainbow

EQUIPMENT

4 x 12-hole (1-tablespoon/20ml)
mini muffin pans

144 mini muffin paper cases
(35 red, 33 orange, 29 green,
26 blue, 21 purple)

65cm x 1m (26-inch x 39-inch)
rectangular cake board
(page 334)

CAKE

4 x 470g (15-ounce) packets
butter cake mix
(see 'mixing the cakes' page 345)

2 quantities fluffy mock cream
frosting (page 329)

red, orange, green, blue and
purple food colouring

DECORATIONS

5 x 85g (3-ounce) packets
jelly crystals (red, orange,
green, blue and purple)

small gold-coloured
plastic hat or pot

gold-coloured tissue paper

gold-covered chocolate
coins and chocolates

cotton wool

1 Preheat oven to 180°C/350°F. Line mini muffin pans with the paper cases.

2 Make cakes according to directions on packets. Drop 2 level teaspoons of mixture into each paper case; bake about 15 minutes. Stand cakes in pans 5 minutes before turning, top-side up, onto wire racks to cool.

3 Make fluffy mock cream frosting. Divide frosting equally into five small bowls; tint red, orange, green, blue and purple.

4 Pour jelly crystals into separate small bowls. Match the colours of the frosting with the jelly crystals. If the crystals are too pale, make them darker by rubbing some food colouring through the crystals in a sealed small plastic bag.

5 Spread red frosting over cakes in red cases; dip into red jelly crystals. Spread orange frosting over cakes in orange cases; dip into orange jelly crystals. Spread green frosting over cakes in green cases; dip into green jelly crystals. Spread blue frosting over cakes in blue cases; dip into blue jelly crystals. Spread purple frosting over cakes in purple cases; dip into purple jelly crystals.

6 Using picture as a guide, position cakes, starting with the red ones, on cake board. Secure to board with a little frosting.

7 Position gold pot or hat; line with tissue paper then fill with gold-covered coins and chocolates. Pull pieces of cotton wool into cloud shapes and position on board.

Cut two half-circle recesses all the way down two sides of the larger cakes.

Cut one recess all the way down side of the smaller cake.

Royal Castle

1 Preheat oven to 170°C/340°F. Grease pans; line bases and sides with baking paper, extending paper 5cm (2 inches) above sides.

2 Make cakes according to directions on packets. Divide two-thirds of the mixture between 20cm pans; bake about 45 minutes. Spread remaining mixture into smaller pan; bake about 50 minutes. Stand cakes 10 minutes before turning, top-side up, onto wire racks to cool.

3 Level cake tops. Using the round cutter, cut two half-circle recesses all the way down two sides of one 20cm cake (recesses should be towards the front of the cake). Repeat on the second 20cm cake, making sure the recesses line up exactly. (Place the first cake on top of the second cake and use the cutter to make an indent into the top of the second cake to mark the area that should be cut out – this will help keep the recesses in both cakes lined up.)

4 Secure one 20cm cake, cut-side down, to cake board with a little butter cream; secure remaining 20cm cake, cut-side down, on top with a little butter cream.

5 Cut one half-circle recess all the way down the side of the smaller cake. Place cake, cut-side down, on top of the cake stack slightly off centre; secure with a little butter cream.

6 Tint butter cream pale cream, reserve ½ cup; spread remaining butter cream all over the cake.

7 Using picture as a guide, make turrets by stacking 9 larger chocolate biscuits, joining each with butter cream, in each of the recesses on the larger cake. Stack 10 chocolate biscuits, joining each with butter cream, in the recess on the smaller cake. Stack 9 chocolate biscuits, joining each with butter cream, on top of the cake, towards the back. Stack 5 chocolate biscuits, joining each with butter cream, on top of cake, just off centre. Secure smaller chocolate biscuits for windows with a little butter cream.

8 Position jubes around top edges of both cakes, trimming to fit (we used yellow and orange jubes, but use any colour combination you like; you may need to buy more than one packet of jubes for this).

9 Trim one ice-cream wafer into a pointed door shape. Position wafer door, then position second wafer as a 'lowered' drawbridge. Use sherbet straws as drawbridge ropes. Position ice-cream cones on top of each turret, securing with a little butter cream, if necessary. Insert flags into tips of cones.

EQUIPMENT

2 x deep 20cm (8-inch) round cake pans
deep 15cm (6-inch) round cake pan
30cm (12 inch) round cake board (page 334)
4cm (1½-inch) round cutter

CAKE

3 x 440g (14-ounce) packets butter cake mix
1 quantity butter cream (page 329)
cream and black food colouring

DECORATIONS

3 x 150g (4½-ounce) packets chocolate cream sandwich biscuits
mini chocolate cream sandwich biscuits, for windows
1 x 300g (9½-ounce) packet jubes
2 sherbet straws
2 ice-cream wafers
5 ice-cream wafer cones

TIPS
A 2.75-litre (11-cup) metal pudding steamer could be substituted for the dolly varden pan. Use any leftover cake mixture to make extra cupcakes. This cake can be completed two days ahead of the party; the icing flounces will take overnight to dry.

Cut muffin in half and, using skewers, secure to either side of the cake for arms.

Scrunch up some plastic wrap and place it under the ready-made icing to make flounces. When the icing dries, it will look like the ghost is floating.

Flying Ghost

This cute cake would be just right for a halloween party for little ones. Ghostly, but not too scary.

1 Preheat oven to 150°C/300°F. Grease and flour dolly varden and round pans and one hole of the muffin pan.

2 Make cakes according to directions on packets. Pour enough of the mixture into dolly varden pan until 4cm (1½ inches) from top of pan. Pour enough mixture into round pan until three-quarters full. Pour ½ cup (125ml) mixture into muffin pan hole.

3 Bake dolly varden cake about 1¾ hours; round cake about 1¼ hours and muffin about 30 minutes. Turn dolly varden cake out onto wire rack to cool. Turn remaining cakes, top-side up, onto wire racks to cool.

4 Level large base of dolly varden cake to sit flat. Level tops of muffin and round cake to sit flat. Secure round cake, cut-side up, on cake board with a little jam; brush cut surface of cake with a little jam. Position dolly varden cake, cut-side down, on top of round cake. Brush whole cake with warmed jam.

5 To make ghost's arms, cut muffin in half, from top to bottom; attach half a muffin, cut-side down, to each side of cake, secure with skewers, cut so they don't poke out of the cake. Brush arms with more jam.

6 Knead ready-made icing on surface dusted with a little sifted icing sugar until icing loses its stickiness. Roll icing, on surface dusted with a little sifted icing sugar, into a circle large enough to cover cake. Using rolling pin, carefully lift icing over cake, allowing it to drape over head and arms of ghost. Gently pull icing into shape around base of cake, support flounces in icing with scrunched balls of plastic wrap. Remove plastic wrap after icing has become firm.

7 Using scissors, cut licorice into rounds for eyes and oval shape for mouth, secure to icing with a dab of jam. Roll tiny balls of leftover icing for eyes, secure to licorice with jam.

EQUIPMENT

dolly varden cake pan
deep 20cm (8-inch)
round cake pan
6-hole (¾ cup/180ml)
texas muffin pan
30cm (12-inch) round
cake board (page 334)
2 bamboo skewers
rolling pin

CAKE

3 x 470g (15-ounce) packets
butter cake mix
1 cup (320g) apricot jam,
warmed, strained
1.5kg (3 pounds) ready-made
white icing (page 329)
pure icing (confectioners')
sugar, for dusting

DECORATIONS

1 black licorice strap

Join the cakes at the long sides; place pattern on top and cut out using both cakes.

Puss in Boots

This is another one of those charming cakes that look so great, but is really quite easy and simple to make.

EQUIPMENT

two 20cm x 30cm (8-inch x 12-inch) rectangular cake pans
30cm x 40cm (12-inch x 16-inch) rectangular cake board
(page 334)

CAKE

2 x 470g (15-ounce) packets butter cake mix
1 quantity butter cream
(page 329)

green and yellow food colouring

DECORATIONS

1 black licorice strap
2 green Smarties
2 red glacé cherries
1 toothpick

1 Preheat oven to 180°C/350°F. Grease cake pans; line bases and sides with baking paper, extending paper 5cm (2 inches) above sides.
2 Make cakes according to directions on packets; divide mixture evenly into pans. Bake about 30 minutes. Stand cakes in pans 5 minutes before turning, top-side up, onto wire racks to cool.
3 Place cakes side-by-side; trim long sides so the two cakes fit tightly together. Using pattern from pattern sheet, cut puss in boots from cakes; discard excess cake. Position cake pieces, cut-side down, on cake board to form puss in boots; secure with a little butter cream.
4 Tint half the butter cream green; tint remaining butter cream yellow. Spread green butter cream over hat and boots; spread yellow butter cream over remaining cake.
5 Outline cake and define leg with thin strips of licorice, as pictured. Cut nose and paw pads from licorice; position on cake. Use thin strips of licorice for whiskers, eyebrows, mouth and claws. Position green Smarties for eyes, halved glacé cherry for tongue and whole glacé cherry, secured with a toothpick, to tip of hat for pompom.

Cute Monster

This playful- and friendly-looking monster will keep the little ones amused with its bright, cheery colours and smiling face.

EQUIPMENT

26cm x 35cm (10½-inch x 14-inch) baking dish

30cm x 40cm (12-inch x 16-inch) rectangular cake board
(page 334)

CAKE

4 x 440g (14-ounce) packets butter cake mix
(see 'mixing the cakes' page 345)

2 quantities butter cream
(page 329)

blue food colouring

DECORATIONS

2 x 50cm (1½-inch) fruit-flavoured rock candy sticks

1 giant freckle

1 large white chocolate button

1 black mini fruit pastille

20cm (8 inches) licorice bootlace

3 x 25g (¾-ounce) white mini Toblerone chocolate bars

4 white-iced Honey Jumble biscuits

½ cup hundreds and thousands

1 Preheat oven to 170°C/340°F. Grease baking dish; line base and sides with baking paper, extending paper 5cm (2 inches) above sides.

2 Make cakes according to directions on packets. Spread mixture into dish; bake about 1 hour. Stand cake in dish 10 minutes before turning, top-side up, onto wire rack to cool.

3 Level cake top; turn cake cut-side down. Using pattern from pattern sheet, cut out monster; secure cake, cut-side down, to cake board with a little butter cream.

4 Reserve ⅓ cup butter cream; tint remaining butter cream blue. Spread blue butter cream all over cake.

5 Using picture as a guide, push lollipop sticks into monster's head. Position giant freckle in middle of monster's face for the eye; secure chocolate button and mini fruit pastille to eye with a little butter cream. Trim and position licorice bootlace for mouth. Position pieces of mini Toblerone for teeth.

6 Spread the iced biscuits with reserved plain butter cream; dip, iced-side down, into hundreds and thousands. Position iced biscuits on cake board for the monster's arms and legs; secure with a little butter cream.

Castle of Darkness

EQUIPMENT

deep 13cm (5¼-inch)
round cake pan
two deep 20cm (8-inch)
round cake pans
30cm (12-inch) round
cake board (page 334)
2 small paper piping bags
(page 338)

CAKE

3 x 470g (15-ounce) packets
butter cake mix
2 quantities butter cream
(page 329)
blue and yellow
food colouring
2 jam rollettes

DECORATIONS

1 wooden skewer
8cm (3¼-inch) round
black cardboard
6 chocolate mint sticks
150g (4½ ounces) white
chocolate Melts
100g (3 ounces) milk
chocolate Melts
27 sections dark
chocolate Toblerone
artificial spider's web

---

1 Preheat oven to 180°C/350°F. Grease baking dish; line base and sides with baking paper, extending paper 5cm (2 inches) above sides.

2 Make cakes according to directions on packets. Pour mixture into 13cm cake pan until three-quarters full; bake cake about 35 minutes. Divide remaining mixture equally between 20cm pans; bake cakes about 40 minutes. Stand cakes in pans 5 minutes before turning, top-side up, onto wire racks to cool.

3 Level cake tops. Secure one 20cm cake, cut-side up, to cake board with a little butter cream. Tint butter cream blue; spread cake top with ½ cup of the butter cream. Top cake with remaining 20cm cake, cut-side down. Spread cut-side of 13cm cake with ¼ cup of the butter cream; centre, butter-cream down, on 20cm cake stack.

4 Position rollettes on top of stacked cakes; secure with skewer, as pictured. Spread remaining butter cream all over cakes.

5 Make a cut from edge to centre of black cardboard; roll cardboard into a cone shape. Secure with sticky tape on inside of cone; position cone on top of cake.

6 Position mint sticks together on bottom of cake for door.

7 Draw five 3cm x 5.5cm (1¾-inch x 2¼-inch) and seven 2cm x 3cm (¾-inch x 1¼-inch) windows on a sheet of baking paper. Turn paper over so outlines are underneath. Melt white chocolate; tint yellow; spoon into piping bag. Pipe windows onto baking paper; stand until chocolate sets.

8 Melt milk chocolate; spoon into separate piping bag. Pipe spiders onto sheet of baking paper; stand until chocolate sets.

9 Decorate castle with windows, spiders, Toblerone and spider's web.

Place one 20cm cake on cake board then spread the cut side with ½ cup of butter cream.

Stack the jam rollettes on the cake then secure them with a skewer to make a tower.

Make a small cut from the edge to the centre of the black cardboard, then roll it to form a cone.

Pipe different-sized windows onto a sheet of baking paper; stand until the chocolate sets.

Using milk chocolate, pipe spiders
onto a sheet of baking paper; stand
until the chocolate sets.

Adventure

Spaceship Scorpio

Ground control to all junior astronauts! Ice different-sized cupcakes and place them around the ship to represent planets.

EQUIPMENT

two 20cm x 30cm (8-inch x 12-inch) rectangular cake pans
40cm x 50cm (16-inch x 20-inch) rectangular cake board
(page 334)

CAKE

2 x 470g (15-ounce) packets butter cake mix
2 quantities fluffy frosting
(page 329)

DECORATIONS

1 black licorice strap
1 green jelly bean
1 sheet gelatine, optional
1 pink marshmallow
1 white marshmallow
5 licorice allsorts, cut in half
6 Smarties
15g (½-ounce) packet silver cachous
15g (½-ounce) packet gold cachous

1 Preheat oven to 180°C/350°F. Grease cake pans; line bases and sides with baking paper, extending paper 5cm (2 inches) above sides.

2 Make cakes according to directions on packets; divide mixture evenly into pans. Bake about 30 minutes. Stand cakes in pans 5 minutes before turning, top-side up, onto wire racks to cool.

3 Level cake tops so they are the same height; turn cakes, cut-side down, side-by-side. Using pattern from pattern sheet, mark spaceship shape with toothpick or fine skewer. Cut out cake with a sharp knife.

4 Assemble cake pieces on cake board to form spaceship, as pictured; secure to cake board with a little fluffy frosting. Make cockpit from leftover cake; discard any remaining cake. Spread fluffy frosting all over cake.

5 Cut licorice strap into thin strips; using licorice, outline spaceship's edges. Position green jelly bean in cockpit to represent astronaut. Cut sheet gelatine into a shape to represent cockpit window, insert gelatine in front of cockpit to enclose cockpit and astronaut.

6 Position marshmallows on back of ship for lights. Position allsorts for windows and Smarties for spotlights. Position cachous on top of ship as pictured.

Trace pattern onto baking paper; secure on cake with toothpicks.

The cut cake, ready to assemble.

Assemble cake to form a spaceship shape.

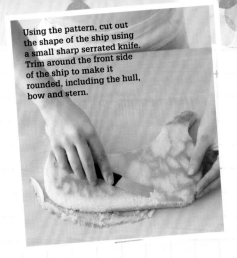

Using the pattern, cut out the shape of the ship using a small sharp serrated knife. Trim around the front side of the ship to make it rounded, including the hull, bow and stern.

Good Ship

The owl and the pussycat went to sea in a beautiful pea-green boat. You can buy the owl and pussycat, rather than make them.

EQUIPMENT

20cm x 30cm (8-inch x 12-inch) rectangular cake pan
5 x 12-hole (1-tablespoon/20ml) mini muffin pans
57 mini paper cases (3 red, 54 green)
40cm x 55cm (16-inch x 22-inch) rectangular cake board (page 334)

CAKE

2 x 470g (15-ounce) packets butter cake mix
1 quantity butter cream (page 329)
green food colouring

DECORATIONS

2 x 140g (4½-ounce) packets green sprinkles (Monster 5s)
3 red jelly fruit rings
180g (5½-ounce) packet Smarties
1 small yellow lollipop
1 grissini bread stick
20cm (8-inch) square unbleached calico
1 cat-shaped soft toy
10cm x 15cm (4-inch x 6-inch) piece brown cardboard
1 mini muffin paper case (brown)
5cm x 5cm (2-inch x 2-inch) piece white cardboard

1 Preheat oven to 180°C/350°F. Grease cake pan; line base and sides with baking paper, extending paper 5cm (2 inches) above sides. Line muffin pans with the paper cases.

2 Make one cake according to directions on packet. Spread mixture into rectangular cake pan; bake about 35 minutes. Stand cake in pan 5 minutes before turning, top-side up, onto wire rack to cool.

3 Make remaining cake according to directions on packet. Drop 2 level teaspoons of mixture into each paper case; bake about 15 minutes. Stand cakes in pans 5 minutes before turning, top-side up, onto wire racks to cool.

4 Level top of large cake. Turn cake cut-side down; using paper pattern from pattern sheet, cut ship from cake. Trim cake to make a curved hull. Secure ship, cut-side down, on cake board with a little butter cream. Discard remaining cake.

5 Reserve 1 tablespoon of the butter cream. Tint remaining butter cream green. Spread two-thirds of the butter cream all over ship; spread remaining butter cream over tops of small cakes in green cases. Sprinkle green hundreds and thousands over cakes. Spread plain butter cream over cakes in red cases.

6 Using picture as a guide, position red cakes in centre of the ship to resemble port holes; top each with a red fruit ring and a red Smartie.

7 Decorate ship with rows of green cakes. Using picture as a guide, position lollipop and Smarties on ship; secure with a little butter cream.

8 Use the bread stick for the mast; position the sail, flags and cat (see tips).

9 Using picture as a guide, make owl. Cut a 7cm (2¾-inch) and 4.5cm (1¾-inch) circle from cardboard. Shape and cut owl's ears from top of smaller circle; tape 'head' to larger circle. Flatten the bown mini paper case; cut a small triangular piece from paper case about 4.5cm (1¾-inch) across, tape to back of owl's head for feathers. Fold paper case so it fits to front of owl for feathers; glue into position. Cut two 2cm (¾-inch) circles from white cardboard for eyes, draw on owl's eyes; glue into position. Use gaffer tape to make and position owl's feet and beak. Position owl on boat.

Fire Engine

EQUIPMENT

14cm x 21cm (5½-inch x 8½-inch) loaf pan

25cm x 30cm (10-inch x 12-inch) rectangular cake board
(page 334)

CAKE

1½ x 470g (15-ounce) packets butter cake mix
(see 'mixing the cakes' page 345)

1 quantity butter cream
(page 329)

red and black food colouring

DECORATIONS

200g (6½ ounces) ready-made white icing (page 329)

pure icing (confectioners') sugar, for dusting

20cm (8-inch) piece black licorice strap,
halved lengthways

black edible writing icing

4 chocolate cream-filled biscuits

8 Smarties

7 mocha sticks

1 Preheat oven to 150°C/300°F. Grease and flour pan.

2 Make cakes according to directions on packets. Pour mixture into pan; bake about 1 hour. Stand cake in pan 5 minutes before turning, top-side up, onto wire rack to cool.

3 Level top of cake; reserve cake scraps. Turn cake, cut-side down, onto surface. Make a shallow cut into cake at one end to a depth of about 5cm (2 inches), for the windscreen; reserve scrap of cake. Secure cake scrap on cake board with a little butter cream to elevate the fire engine slightly off the board (so you can later fit the wheels). Position cake on cake scrap; secure with a little butter cream.

4 Tint butter cream red; spread all over cake.

5 Knead ready-made icing on surface dusted with a little sifted icing sugar until icing loses its stickiness. Roll one-quarter of the icing on surface dusted with sifted icing sugar into a 3mm (⅛-inch) thickness. Using patterns from pattern sheet, cut out windscreen, windows and number plate. Press windscreen and windows onto cake.

6 Tint remaining icing grey using black colouring; roll on surface dusted with a little sifted icing sugar into a 3mm (⅛-inch) thickness. Cut out one 8cm (3¼-inch) square and two 3cm x 7cm (1¼-inch x 2¾-inch) rectangles. Using the side of a small metal spatula or ruler, make indents, 5mm (¼-inch) apart, on rectangles to represent roller doors.

7 Position square on top of fire engine and press roller doors onto sides. Position licorice along sides of fire engine. Shape remaining grey icing into two bumper bars; position on fire engine. Use writing icing to write child's name on number plate. Attach to bumper with a little butter cream. Using a little butter cream, attach biscuits to fire engine for wheels. Use Smarties to make sirens and lights. Trim mocha sticks to make a ladder for the roof.

Make a shallow cut into front of cake, about halfway down cake, to make an indent for the windscreen.

Cut out windscreen, windows and number plate from the rolled ready-made icing.

To make the roller doors, use a small metal spatula (or the blunt edge of a knife) to mark indents in icing.

TIPS
Make sure you use good quality food colouring to make the butter cream a strong red. The fire engine can be completed up to two days before the party.

Make windscreen wipers from scraps of licorice.

HENRI

Rocket Blast

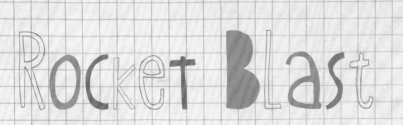

EQUIPMENT

deep 26cm x 36cm
(10½-inch x 14½-inch)
baking dish
35cm x 45cm (14-inch x 18-inch)
rectangular cake board (page 334)
5cm (2-inch) star cutter

CAKE

3 x 470g (15-ounce) packets
butter cake mix
2 quantities butter cream
(page 329)

blue, green and red food colouring
¼ cup (80g) apricot jam,
warmed, sieved

DECORATIONS

2 red licorice straps,
cut into thin strips
1 teaspoon yellow sprinkles
50 blue M&M's
¼ cup (55g) white
(granulated) sugar
3 sparklers

1 Preheat oven to 180°C/350°F. Grease baking dish; line base and sides with baking paper, extending paper 5cm (2 inches) above sides.
2 Make cakes according to directions on packets; spread mixture into dish. Bake about 1 hour. Stand cake in dish 5 minutes before turning, top-side up, onto wire rack to cool.
3 Level cake top; turn cake cut-side down. Using pattern from pattern sheet, cut out rocket ship; reserve leftover cake. Assemble cake on cake board, cut-side down, to form rocket ship; secure with a little butter cream.
4 Tint one-quarter of the butter cream blue. Divide remaining butter cream in half. Tint one half green and the other half red. Using picture as a guide, spread rocket with green and red butter cream.
5 Use strips of red licorice to define and decorate red area. Place star cutter on cake; cover area inside cutter with sprinkles, carefully remove cutter.
6 Mark an 8cm (3¼-inch) circle on cake, press M&M's upright around circle, then fill circle with remaining M&M's.
7 Using cutter, cut stars from reserved cake, spread sides of stars with warm jam.
8 Place sugar and blue food colouring in small plastic bag; rub until sugar is evenly coloured. Lightly sprinkle sides of stars with blue sugar; position around rocket. Spread tops of stars with blue butter cream; sprinkle with blue sugar. Position sparklers in cake; light sparklers just before serving.

Using paper pattern as a guide, cut out cake.

Cake cut into rocket ship shape.

Place star cutter on cake; fill with yellow sprinkles.

Cut stars from reserved cake with star cutter.

Rub colouring into sugar, until sugar is evenly coloured.

Igloo ice-cream cake

The ice-cream should be soft enough to mould; if it starts to melt too much, return it and the igloo to the freezer for 5 minutes or so.

EQUIPMENT

2.25-litre (9-cup) metal
pudding steamer
6-hole (¾ cup/180ml)
texas muffin pan
30cm (12-inch) round
cake board (page 334)
or cake stand
pair each disposable cotton
and latex gloves
plastic ruler

CAKE

1 x 470g (15-ounce) packet
butter cake mix
2 litres (8 cups) vanilla
ice-cream, slightly softened
1 cup (80g) desiccated coconut

DECORATIONS

penguins

1 Preheat oven to 150°C/300°F. Grease and flour pudding steamer and one hole of the muffin pan.

2 Make cake according to directions on packet. Pour ½ cup mixture into muffin pan hole; bake about 35 minutes. Pour remaining mixture into pudding steamer; bake about 1¼ hours. Turn muffin, top-side up, onto wire rack to cool. Stand cake in steamer 5 minutes before turning onto wire rack to cool.

3 Position large cake on baking paper on a flat surface, position muffin against cake for igloo entrance. Using a small sharp serrated knife, shape the large cake into a more rounded shape, shape muffin into a rounded tunnel shape; hollow out a doorway in the muffin. Freeze cake on a metal tray for at least an hour.

4 Protect hands by using cotton and latex gloves together; working quickly mould and shape handfuls of ice-cream over cakes until the ice-cream is about 1cm (½-inch) thick all over. You will need to return the cake to the freezer several times during the shaping of the igloo. When the whole igloo is finished, freeze until firm.

5 Use the side of a plastic ruler or the blunt side of a large heavy knife blade to mark the blocks of ice on the igloo.

6 Position igloo on cake board or stand; sprinkle with coconut, mark the blocks again if necessary. Position penguins just before serving.

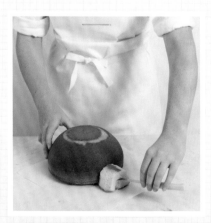

Shape the muffin into a rounded tunnel shape, then hollow out a doorway.

To protect hands from cold, cover in cotton, then latex gloves. Quickly cover igloo all over with ice-cream.

Use a plastic ruler to mark lines all over the igloo to represent 'ice blocks'.

TIPS
This is a great cake to make ahead, it can be completed and frozen, except for the coconut and penguins, at least a week before the party. Use regular ice-cream, not one high or low in fat. Buy small plastic toy penguins or make your own by moulding coloured ready-made white icing.

Pirate Pete

Ho ho ho and a bottle of red cordial will soon have Pete smiling again. We were lucky enough to find an odd-shaped chocolate-coated sultana for the eyebrow, but use some licorice instead.

1 Preheat oven to 180°C/350°F. Grease cake pan; line base and side with baking paper, extending paper 5cm (2 inches) above side.

2 Make cake according to directions on packet; spread into pan. Bake about 45 minutes. Stand cake in pan 5 minutes before turning, top-side up, onto wire rack to cool.

3 Level cake top; turn cake cut-side down. Using pattern from pattern sheet, cut out pirate's face. Secure cake, cut-side down, on cake board with a little butter cream.

4 Tint one-quarter of the butter cream yellow; spread carefully over hat. Spread remaining butter cream over rest of cake for pirate's face.

5 Using pattern from pattern sheet, shape ice-cream wafer for pirate's ear, spread with butter cream; press ear into side of cake. Press chocolate coin (or ring jube) on ear to make earring.

6 Cut a small skull and crossbones out of the cardboard; position on pirate's hat. Trim one side of chocolate biscuit, position on face to represent eye patch; cut thin strip of licorice to make strap of patch. Cut red jelly snake for mouth. Position chocolate bullet, jelly bean and thin strip of licorice for eye. Position thin strip of licorice for moustache, trimmed Clinker for nose and long thin strips of fruit sticks for hair.

EQUIPMENT

deep 22cm (9-inch) round cake pan
30cm (12-inch) round cake board (page 334)

CAKE

1 x 470g (15-ounce) packet butter cake mix
1 quantity butter cream (page 329)
yellow food colouring

DECORATIONS

1 ice-cream wafer
1 gold-covered chocolate coin
black cardboard or paper
1 round chocolate biscuit
1 black licorice strap
1 red jelly snake
1 chocolate-covered licorice bullet
1 green jelly bean
1 Clinker
2 yellow fruit sticks

Solar System

EQUIPMENT

deep 30cm (12-inch)
round cake pan

two 20cm x 30cm (8-inch x
12-inch) rectangular cake pans

2 wooden skewers

3cm (1¼-inch), 4cm (1½-inch),
6cm (2½-inch) and 9cm
(3¾-inch) round cutters

40cm x 1m (16-inch x 39-inch)
rectangular cake board
(page 334)

CAKE

4 x 470g (15-ounce) packets
butter cake mix
(see 'mixing the cakes' page 345)

3 quantities butter cream
(page 329)

orange, red, yellow, blue, green,
and black food colouring

DECORATIONS

3 rainbow sour straps (cut
yellow strips from strap)

1 Preheat oven to 180°C/350°F. Grease cake pans; line bases and sides with baking paper, extending paper 5cm (2 inches) above sides.

2 Make two cakes according to directions on packets; spread into round pan; bake about 50 minutes. Stand cake in pan 5 minutes before turning, top-side up, onto wire rack to cool.

3 Make remaining cakes according to directions on packets. Divide mixture between rectangular pans; bake about 35 minutes. Stand cakes in pans 5 minutes; turn, top-side up, onto wire racks to cool.

4 Level rectangular cake tops; turn cut-side down. Use round cake to make the Sun and rectangular cakes to make the planets. Cut two 3cm (1¼-inch) rounds to make Mercury and Pluto. Cut three 4cm (1½-inch) rounds to make Venus, Mars and Earth. Cut two 6cm (2½-inch) rounds to make Uranus and Neptune. Cut a 9cm (3¾-inch) round from cake to make Jupiter. Using pattern from pattern sheet, cut out Saturn.

5 Place two-thirds of the butter cream in a medium bowl; tint dark orange. Place half the remaining butter cream in a small bowl; tint medium orange. Divide remaining butter cream equally into four small bowls; leave one bowl plain and tint each remaining bowl with one of the suggested colours: red, blue and green.

6 Secure the round cake, top-side up, at the end of the cake board with a little butter cream. Starting from the Sun, and working left to right, position and secure (with a little butter cream) each planet to the cake board as you finish it.

Sun Using picture as a guide, spread about two-thirds of the dark orange butter cream over the top and side of the Sun; roughen with a fork. Dip a bamboo skewer into red colouring, pull through the butter cream to resemble flares.

Mercury Spread top and side of a 3cm cake with dark orange butter cream; roughen with a fork. Dip a bamboo skewer into yellow colouring and pull through the butter cream.

Venus Spread top and side of a 4cm cake with medium orange butter cream blended with a little dark orange butter cream.

Earth Spread top and side of a 4cm cake with blue butter cream; dot with a little green butter cream to resemble land on Earth's surface.

Mars Spread top and side of a 4cm cake with red butter cream blended with a little dark orange butter cream.

Jupiter Spread top and side of a 9cm cake with red butter cream blended with a little dark orange butter cream and plain butter cream to create bands of colour across the planet.

Saturn Tint 1 tablespoon of the plain butter cream yellow. Spread top and side of Saturn and Saturn's rings with medium orange butter cream blended with a little yellow and dark orange butter cream. Top Saturn's rings with yellow strips from sour straps.

Uranus Spread top and side of a 6cm cake with blended blue and green butter cream.

Neptune Spread top and side of a 6cm cake with blue butter cream.

Pluto Tint 1 tablespoon of the plain butter cream with black food colouring to make grey. Spread top and side of a 3cm cake with grey butter cream; blend a little blue butter cream over the top of the grey and swirl through the butter cream.

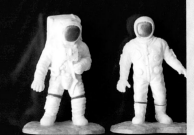

Lolly Goodship

EQUIPMENT

two deep 15cm x 25cm
(6-inch x 10-inch) loaf pans
two 8cm x 26cm
(3¼-inch x 10½-inch)
bar cake pans
35cm x 45cm (14-inch x 18-inch)
rectangular cake board
(page 334)

CAKE

3 x 470g (15-ounce) packets
butter cake mix
2 quantities butter cream
(page 329)
2 ice-cream cones
green, orange, yellow and
blue food colouring

DECORATIONS

6 licorice allsorts
36 five-flavours Life Savers
cotton wool
2 green jelly fruit rings
1 wooden skewer
4 black licorice straps
2 wooden toothpicks

1 Preheat oven to 180°C/350°F. Grease cake pans; line bases and sides with baking paper, extending paper 5cm (2 inches) above sides.

2 Make cakes according to directions on packets; divide two-thirds of the mixture between loaf pans; bake loaf cakes about 40 minutes. Divide remaining mixture equally between bar pans; bake about 25 minutes. Stand cakes in pans 5 minutes before turning, top-side up, onto wire racks to cool.

3 Level cake tops. Trim sides and ends off loaf cakes to form ship hull, as pictured. Secure on cake board with a little butter cream. Round off one end of one bar cake, cut remaining bar cake in half; position on top of ship hull to form second deck. Cut remaining half of bar cake in half lengthways to make upper deck. Trim ice-cream cone tops to make funnels; secure on cake with a little butter cream.

4 Tint one-third of the butter cream green; tint one-third of the remaining butter cream orange, one-third yellow and 1 tablespoon blue. Reserve remaining plain butter cream.

5 Spread reserved plain butter cream over tops of decks and funnels on ship. Spread sides of hull with green butter cream. Spread sides of second deck with orange butter cream. Spread sides of upper deck with yellow butter cream. Spread blue butter cream over second deck to make swimming pool.

6 Cut five allsorts in half (keep one yellow allsort aside); position allsorts and Life Savers around sides of ship as portholes. Press ends of cotton wool onto funnels to make smoke.

7 Cut green jelly fruit rings open and thread onto skewer to make mast. Position on ship.

8 Cut licorice strap into thin strips; position on cake for deck outlines. Position remaining licorice along top of ship.

9 Cut yellow piece out of remaining allsort, cut in half diagonally; insert toothpick into each yellow piece; press into ship for flags.

Trim sides and ends off
loaf cakes to form hull.

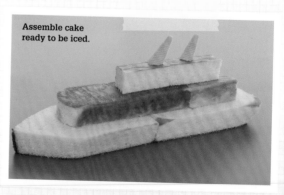

Assemble cake
ready to be iced.

TIPS

You need four 22g (¾-ounce) packets of Life Savers.

Be sure to remove toothpicks, cottonwool and skewer from cake before cutting and serving.

TIP
You will need to buy
a 300g (9-ounce) packet
of chocolate-covered
fruit and nuts for
this cake.

Treasure Island

The perfect cake to end a pirate-themed party. Get the young buccaneers involved in a treasure hunt outside to find the buried gold.

EQUIPMENT

deep 26cm x 36cm (10½-inch x 14½-inch) baking dish

35cm x 45cm (14-inch x 18-inch) rectangular cake board
(page 334)

melon baller or small teaspoon

CAKE

3 x 470g (15-ounce) packets butter cake mix

2 quantities butter cream
(page 329)

blue, yellow and green food colouring

DECORATIONS

2 x 35g (1-ounce) tube mini M&M's

1 tablespoon light brown sugar

1 waffle cone

red and black glossy decorating gel

28 chocolate-covered fruit and nuts

small plastic animals

small plastic trees

1 Preheat oven to 180°C/350°F. Grease baking dish; line base and sides with baking paper, extending paper 5cm (2 inches) above sides.

2 Make cakes according to directions on packets; spread into dish. Bake about 1 hour. Stand cake in dish 5 minutes before turning, top-side up, onto wire rack to cool.

3 Secure cake, top-side up, on cake board with a little butter cream. Using melon baller or small teaspoon, scoop about five deep holes into cake, reserve scoops of cake. Fill holes with half the M&M's; top with reserved scoops of cake.

4 Tint half the butter cream blue; tint one-third of the remaining butter cream yellow. Tint two-thirds of the remaining butter cream green. Reserve remaining plain butter cream.

5 Using picture as a guide, cover top of island with green butter cream. Spread yellow butter cream onto a few edges of the island to resemble the beach; sprinkle yellow butter cream with brown sugar to resemble sand. Swirl blue butter cream with plain butter cream; spread over remaining cake to resemble water.

6 Break tip off waffle cone, push cone into cake for volcano; fill volcano with remaining M&M's through top of waffle cone. Using red decorating gel, pipe around top of cone to make lava.

7 Position chocolate-covered fruit and nuts to form paths. Position animals and trees on island. Using black decorating gel, mark a black cross for the treasure.

Using a melon baller, or small teaspoon, scoop out holes in cake.

Fill the holes with mini M&M's. Push reserved cake into holes to hide treasure.

Cover top of cake with green butter cream.

Trim cake into a rounded shape, slightly pointed at one end.

Shape the ice-cream wafers into the plane's wings and tail.

Jumbo jet

This cake is a good one for budding pilots, flight attendants or for those who just want to travel the world.

EQUIPMENT

14cm x 21cm
(5½-inch x 8½-inch)
loaf pan

6-hole (¾ cup/180ml)
texas muffin pan

30cm (12-inch) square
or round cake board
(page 334)

oven tray

CAKE

1½ x 470g (15-ounce)
packets butter cake mix
(see 'mixing the cakes' page 345)

1 quantity butter cream
(page 329)

blue and grey food
colouring

DECORATIONS

60g (2 ounces) white
chocolate Melts

2 white marshmallows

2cm (¾-inch) piece
black licorice strap

5 ice-cream wafers

candy cake number
decorations

1 Preheat oven to 150°C/300°F. Grease and flour loaf pan and one hole of the muffin pan.

2 Make cakes according to directions on packets. Pour ½ cup mixture into muffin pan hole; bake muffin about 30 minutes. Pour remaining mixture into loaf pan; bake about 50 minutes. Stand cakes in pans 5 minutes before turning, top-side up, onto wire rack to cool.

3 Level top of loaf cake. Using a small serrated knife, trim cake, cut-side up, into a rounded shape, slightly pointed at one end.

4 Reserve ½ cup butter cream, tint remaining butter cream blue. Secure loaf cake to cake board with a little blue butter cream. Spread blue butter cream all over cake.

5 To make propeller: Melt chocolate (page 339); tint grey. Using pattern from pattern sheet, trace propeller shape onto baking paper, then place on tray. Spread chocolate into propeller shape, tap tray on bench; stand at room temperature until chocolate is set. Cut one marshmallow in half; position top half, cut-side down, on propeller for nose cone; secure propeller on plane with a little butter cream.

6 To make cockpit, level top of muffin, turn cut-side down; using a serrated knife, cut into a dome shape. Spread rounded side of muffin with reserved butter cream; secure cockpit on plane with a little butter cream. Position thin strips of licorice for wipers.

7 Using scissors, trim two wafers into large wing shapes. Trim two wafers into smaller wing shapes. Using picture as a guide, position and gently push wings into cake.

8 Trim remaining wafer into shape, rounded at one end, for tail fin. Cut a marshmallow into three slices; position two pieces, cut-side down, onto tail fin. Attach a candy number to the marshmallows with a little butter cream. Gently push tail fin into cake.

play time

fun

celebrate

birthday

TIPS
You need to buy a 80g
(2-ounce) packet of wafers to allow
for breakages. The plane and cockpit
can be made and covered with butter
cream a day ahead. Assemble the
plane - particularly the wings -
as close to serving as possible.

Monster Space Station

1 Preheat oven to 180°C/350°F. Grease cake pan; line base and side with baking paper, extending paper 5cm (2 inches) above side.

2 Make cakes according to directions on packets; pour mixture into pan. Bake about 45 minutes. Stand cakes in pan 5 minutes before turning, top-side up, onto wire rack to cool.

3 Level cake top; turn cake cut-side down. Using 12cm round cutter, cut centre from cake. Using 6cm round cutter, cut centre from round; discard centre. Cut small ring into three pieces, as pictured. Secure the big ring cake, cut-side down, on cake board with a little butter cream.

4 Cut a quarter off one jam roll, position larger piece in hole of cake; discard smaller piece. Cut remaining two jam rolls in half. Position jam rolls at sides and front of space station. Position cut ring pieces, as pictured; secure with a little butter cream.

5 Tint butter cream green; spread all over cake.

6 Using picture as a guide, position Smarties as lights and Life Savers as windows. Position Mini Musks on cake.

7 Cut Musk Sticks and three mint sticks in half; position on cake. Cut the remaining mint sticks into 2cm (¾-inch) pieces, position on cake as lights. Position snowballs and Mint Pattie on cake.

8 Cut licorice into thin strips; use to outline shape of space station.

EQUIPMENT

deep 28cm (11¼-inch)
round cake pan
12cm (4¾-inch) round cutter
6cm (2½-inch) round cutter
45cm x 55cm
(18-inch x 22-inch)
rectangular cake board
(page 334)

CAKE

2 x 470g (15-ounce) packets
butter cake mix
3 x 300g (9½-ounce)
packets jam rolls
2 quantities butter cream
(page 329)

green food colouring

DECORATIONS

32 Smarties
12 Life Savers
30 Mini Musks
3 Musk Sticks
8 chocolate mint sticks
3 snowballs
1 Mint Pattie
1 black licorice strap

Use 12cm cutter to cut centre from cake; use 6cm cutter to cut centre from round.

Cut small ring into three pieces.

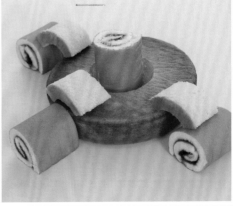

Assemble the cake to form the space station.

Helicopter

Ready for a joy flight or to conduct a rescue, or maybe to report on the traffic conditions.

EQUIPMENT

20cm x 30cm (8-inch x 12-inch) rectangular cake pan

30cm x 40cm (12-inch x 16-inch) rectangular cake board
(page 334)

CAKE

1 x 470g (15-ounce) packet butter cake mix

1 quantity butter cream
(page 329)

apricot and blue food colouring

DECORATIONS

22 chocolate-covered licorice bullets

8 Jaffas

5 ice-cream wafers

1 brown Smartie

3 x 30cm (12-inch) red or orange chenille sticks (pipe cleaners)

shredded coconut

green food colouring

24g (¾-ounce) packet Tic Tacs

1 Preheat oven to 180°C/350°F. Grease cake pan; line base and sides with baking paper, extending paper 5cm (2 inches) above sides.

2 Make cake according to directions on packet; pour into pan. Bake about 30 minutes. Stand cake in pan 5 minutes before turning, top-side up, onto wire rack to cool.

3 Level cake top; turn cake cut-side down. Using pattern from pattern sheet, cut out cake pieces. Position cake pieces on cake board to form helicopter. Discard any leftover cake pieces.

4 Tint ½ cup butter cream apricot; spread over tops and sides of 'skids', position 'skids' on cake board. Secure body of helicopter over 'skids' with a little butter cream. Tint remaining butter cream blue; spread all over body of helicopter.

5 Using picture as a guide, decorate helicopter with bullets and jaffas.

6 Cut one ice-cream wafer into a propeller shape for tail; press into position at rear of helicopter. Secure brown Smartie to propeller with a little butter cream. Make a cross with two chenille sticks, secure in centre with third chenille stick, then fold this in half, twist to form stem, push through centre of helicopter dome. Trim remaining four ice-cream wafers into helicopter blade shape, secure to chenille sticks with a little butter cream.

7 Place coconut and a few drops of green food colouring in ziptop plastic bag; rub with fingertips until coconut is evenly coloured. Sprinkle coconut around helicopter for grass; position Tic Tacs in a circle around cake to represent helicopter pad.

Using pattern, cut shapes from cake.

Assemble the cake ready to ice.

Animals

Cut a 1cm slice from the bottom of each small cake. The large pieces of the cakes are used to make the lion's mane; eight of slices cut from the cakes are used to make the features on the lion's face. The rest of the cake slices are not used.

Larry Lion

This king of the jungle cake will be a hit with young explorers at a jungle-themed safari.

1 Preheat oven to 180°C/350°F. Grease cake pan; line base and side with baking paper, extending paper 5cm (2 inches) above side. Grease friand pans.

2 Make one cake according to directions on packet. Spread mixture into round cake pan; bake about 40 minutes. Stand cake in pan 5 minutes before turning, top-side down, onto wire rack to cool.

3 Make remaining cakes according to directions on packets. Drop 2½ level tablespoons of mixture into each friand hole; bake about 20 minutes. Stand cakes in pans 5 minutes before turning, top-side up, onto wire rack to cool.

4 Secure cake, top-side down, on cake board with a little butter cream.

5 Transfer one-third of the butter cream into a small bowl; tint dark brown. Tint remaining two-thirds of the butter cream caramel. Spread about three-quarters of the caramel butter cream over top and side of round cake.

6 Cut a 1cm (½-inch) slice from the bottom of each small cake; reserve slices. Spread remaining caramel butter cream over bottoms and sides of eight of the reserved slices; top with orange sprinkles. Discard remaining slices. Using picture as a guide, position slices on large cake to make the lion's nose and cheeks.

7 Spread dark brown butter cream over tops of small cakes; position around lion's face. Cut Violet Crumble bars into thin shards, use for the lion's mane.

8 Using scissors, snip tips from top of two marshmallows; place, cut-side up, for eyes. Secure Smarties to top of marshmallows with a little butter cream. Cut licorice into a semi-circle for lion's nose.

9 Cut red sour strap into a semi-circle to make lion's mouth. Using scissors, cut two large triangles from remaining marshmallow for teeth; place at corner of mouth. Position chenille sticks for whiskers.

TIPS
Apart from piping the tacking stitches, the cake can be completed a day ahead of the party. We positioned the owl on a larger cake board decorated with a paper cut-out tree.

Hoot Hoot

This cake is perfect for a first birthday party. It's quite simple to make, so you're not spending lots of time on a creation that probably won't be given its due attention by the birthday child.

EQUIPMENT

deep 20cm (8-inch) square cake pan

30cm (12-inch) square cake board (page 334)

small paper piping bag (page 338)

CAKE

1 x 470g (15-ounce) packet butter cake mix

1 quantity butter cream (page 329)

yellow and blue food colouring

250g (8 ounces) ready-made white icing (page 329)

pure icing (confectioners') sugar, for dusting

DECORATIONS

4 white chocolate bullets

1 Preheat oven to 150°C/300°F. Grease cake pan; line base and sides with baking paper, extending paper 5cm (2 inches) above sides.

2 Make cake according to directions on packet. Spread mixture into pan; bake about 35 minutes. Stand cake in pan 5 minutes before turning, top-side up, onto wire rack to cool.

3 Knead ready-made icing on surface dusted with a little sifted icing sugar until icing loses its stickiness. Roll out about one-third of the icing between sheets of baking paper into a 3mm (⅛-inch) thickness; cut out two 2.5cm (1-inch) circles for eyes. Tint some of the icing scraps yellow, roll out between baking paper; using pattern from pattern sheet, cut out beak. Tint remaining icing pale blue, roll between sheets of baking paper; using pattern, cut out eyes.

4 Tint scraps and remaining icing a darker shade of blue, roll between sheets of baking paper; cut out 1cm (½-inch) circles for pupils of eyes. Using pattern from pattern sheet, cut out wings from remaining icing.

5 Meanwhile, tint butter cream yellow.

6 Level top of cake; turn, cut-side down. Using pattern, cut out owl shape. Secure cake on cake board with a little butter cream.

7 Reserve 2 tablespoons of butter cream, spread remaining butter cream all over cake.

8 Using picture as a guide, position cut-out pieces of icing for eyes, beak and wings to cake (dab the backs of each piece with a tiny bit of water to help secure them together).

9 Fill piping bag with reserved butter cream, snip end from bag, pipe tacking stitches on wings, as pictured. Position bullets to form feet.

Charlotte the Sheep

While this looks cute enough for a baby's first birthday, it's best not to use the popcorn - instead, pipe some of the frosting over the sheep to make its woolly coat.

1 Preheat oven to 170°C/340°F. Grease pan; line base and sides with baking paper, extending paper 5cm (2 inches) above sides.
2 Make cakes according to directions on packets. Spread mixture into pan; bake about 2 hours. Stand cake in pan 10 minutes before turning, top-side up, onto wire rack to cool.
3 Level cake top; using a sharp serrated knife, split cake in half horizontally. Using pattern from pattern sheet, cut out the head and body from cakes. Using picture as a guide, secure the body, cut-side down, on the cake board with a little fluffy frosting. Secure head on top of body with a little fluffy frosting.
4 Heat oil in large saucepan. Add popping corn; stir to coat kernels in oil. Cook, covered, shaking pan occasionally, about 5 minutes or until popping stops. Transfer popcorn to large heatproof bowl, cool.
5 Meanwhile, spread fluffy frosting all over head and body of sheep.
6 Using picture as a guide, position popcorn all over cake, leaving the face uncovered. Cut marshmallow in half; position marshmallow halves as ears. Secure two almonds on ears with a little fluffy frosting. Position remaining almond for nose. Position licorice rounds for eyes. Position licorice tubes at base of body for legs, pushing into frosting to secure. Cut remaining licorice rounds in half and position for feet, securing to cake board with a little fluffy frosting. Using scissors, cut licorice strap into a thin strip, position on sheep's face for mouth.

EQUIPMENT

deep 30cm (12-inch)
round cake pan
40cm (14-inch) round
cake board (page 334)

CAKE

6 x 440g (14-ounce) packet
butter cake mix
(see 'mixing the cakes' page 345)

1 quantity fluffy frosting
(page 329)

1 tablespoon vegetable oil
½ cup (120g) popping corn

DECORATIONS

1 white marshmallow
3 pink sugar-coated almonds
4 salted licorice rounds
4 licorice tubes
10cm (4-inch) piece licorice
strap

TIP
You can use ready-made
air-popped popcorn
instead of making your
own; you will need
about 8 cups.

Position mint leaves, overlapping slightly, over three-quarters of the peacock's body.

Position the lollipops for tail, pushing lollipop sticks into peacock's body to secure; trim sticks to fit, as necessary.

Using a sharp knife, cut the mint leaves in half lengthways.

Princely Peacock

You'll be prouder than a peacock when you present this cake at the party. The design is mainly in the placement of the lollies.

1 Preheat oven to 170°C/340°F. Grease baking dish; line base and sides with baking paper, extending paper 5cm (2 inches) above sides.

2 Make cakes according to directions on packets. Pour mixture into baking dish; bake about 1 hour. Stand cake in dish 10 minutes before turning, top-side up, onto wire rack to cool.

3 Level cake top; turn cake cut-side down. Using pattern from pattern sheet, cut out peacock's body; secure to cake board with a little butter cream.

4 Tint butter cream turquoise using all the colourings; spread all over the cake.

5 Cut mint leaves in half lengthways; using picture as a guide, and starting at the bottom end of the cake, position the mint leaves, overlapping slightly, over three-quarters of peacock's body. Reserve some of the mint leaf halves for the tail.

6 Trim the sticks from one yellow, red and green lollipop quite short and position in the peacock's head to secure. Position Jols lolly for eye. Using picture as a guide, position remaining lollipops for tail, pushing lollipop sticks into peacock's body to secure (trim sticks to fit, as necessary). Position freckles and reserved mint leaves on tail, secure with a little butter cream.

EQUIPMENT

26cm x 35cm (10½-inch x 14-inch) baking dish

30cm x 40cm (12-inch x 16-inch) rectangular cake board
(page 334)

CAKE

4 x 440g (14-ounce) packets butter cake mix
(see 'mixing the cakes' page 345)

1½ quantities butter cream
(page 329)

royal blue, teal and aqua blue food colourings

DECORATIONS

3 x 300g (9½-ounce) packets mint leaves

41 clear coloured lollipops (as listed below)

10 clear blue rectangles

11 clear red flowers

11 clear green hearts

12 clear yellow hearts

1 black Jols lolly

1 packet chocolate freckles

Wacky Rabbit

Using paper pattern, cut face and ears from cake.

EQUIPMENT

deep 26cm x 36cm (10½-inch x 14½-inch) baking dish

40cm x 55cm (16-inch x 22-inch) rectangular cake board (page 334)

CAKE

3 x 470g (15-ounce) packets butter cake mix

3 quantities fluffy frosting (page 329)

black, blue and pink food colouring

200g (6½ ounces) ready-made white icing (page 329)

pure icing (confectioners') sugar, for dusting

DECORATIONS

1 black licorice strap

1 pink marshmallow

6 double-pointed toothpicks

2 milk bottles

2 black Skittles

Assemble the cake, cut-side down, to form rabbit.

1 Preheat oven to 180°C/350°F. Grease baking dish; line base and sides with baking paper, extending paper 5cm (2 inches) above sides.

2 Make cakes according to directions on packets; spread into dish. Bake about 1 hour. Stand cake in dish 5 minutes before turning, top-side up, onto wire rack to cool.

3 Level cake top; turn cake cut-side down. Using pattern from pattern sheet, cut out rabbit face and ears from cake. Secure cake pieces, cut-side down, on cake board to form rabbit, as pictured; secure with a little fluffy frosting.

4 Spread half the fluffy frosting over lower half of rabbit's face; build up frosting around cheeks to make full. Tint remaining frosting with black colouring to make grey; spread over top half of face and ears.

5 Knead ready-made icing on surface dusted with a little sifted icing sugar until icing loses its stickiness. Roll a quarter of the icing on surface dusted with sifted icing sugar into a 3mm (¹/₈-inch) thickness. Enclose remaining icing in plastic wrap; reserve. Using pattern, cut eyes from white icing; position on cake.

6 Tint half the reserved icing blue; roll on surface dusted with sifted icing sugar into a 3mm (¹/₈-inch) thickness. Using pattern, cut irises and mouth from blue icing; position on cake.

7 Tint remaining icing pink; roll on surface dusted with sifted icing sugar into a 3mm (¹/₈-inch) thickness. Using pattern, cut inner ears from pink icing; position on cake.

8 Cut licorice strap into thin strips; outline inner ears, eyes and mouth. Position marshmallow for nose.

9 Cut two 10cm (4-inch), two 9cm (3¾-inch) and two 8cm (3¼-inch) pieces from thinly sliced licorice. Insert a toothpick into one end of each licorice piece; position for whiskers.

10 Trim tops of milk bottles; using a little fluffy frosting, position for teeth. Position Skittles for pupils using a little fluffy frosting.

Spread frosting over lower half of face, making thicker around cheeks.

Use cardboard templates to cut eyes, ears and mouth from icing.

TIPS

While it's best to make the fluffy frosting on the day of the party, you can make it the day before; however, it will become crisp and lose its glossy appearance.

Draw the inner ear, mouth, eye and iris patterns onto cardboard, then use these templates to cut the shapes from the icing.

Be sure to remove toothpicks from the cake before cutting and serving.

Assemble cake on cake board, ready to be iced.

Use a fork to roughen chocolate butter cream on wombat.

Wobbly Wombat

Large and pudgy, and so absolutely adorable, everyone will fall in love with those big brown eyes. So much cuteness in such an easy cake.

1 Preheat oven to 180°C/350°F. Grease and flour pudding steamer, dolly varden pan, round cake pan and two holes of the muffin pan.

2 Make cakes according to directions on packets; pour ¼ cup of the cake mixture into each prepared muffin hole. Divide remaining cake mixture evenly between steamer and pans. Bake muffins about 15 minutes, pudding steamer cake about 20 minutes, round cake about 30 minutes and the dolly varden cake about 40 minutes. Stand cakes in pans 5 minutes before turning onto wire racks to cool. (Turn round cake and muffin cakes, top-side up, on rack to cool.)

3 Level tops of round and muffin cakes. Level large bases of steamer and dolly varden cakes. Brush cut-sides of cakes with some of the warmed jam.

4 To make wombat, join cut-sides of the steamer and round cake together; spread base of round cake with jam and join to the cut side of the dolly varden cake, as pictured. Cut muffins in half horizontally. Assemble wombat on cake board, as pictured; secure to board with a little butter cream.

5 Tint butter cream with brown colouring to make dark brown; spread all over cake. Using fork, roughen butter cream.

6 Position chocolate Melts on wombat for eyes; using a little butter cream, attach jelly beans for pupils. Cut After Dinner Mint in half for ears, position on cake. Position chocolate biscuit on cake for nose. Cut claws from licorice strap; position, as pictured.

EQUIPMENT

1.5-litre (6-cup)
pudding steamer
2.5-litre (10-cup)
dolly varden pan
deep 17cm (6¾-inch)
round cake pan
12-hole (⅓-cup/80ml)
standard muffin pan
30cm (12-inch) square
cake board (page 334)

CAKE

3 x 470g (15-ounce) packets
butter cake mix
½ cup (160g) apricot jam,
warmed, strained
2 quantities chocolate butter
cream (page 329)
brown food colouring

DECORATIONS

2 milk chocolate Melts
2 black jelly beans
1 square After Dinner Mint
1 Chocolate Monte biscuit
1 black licorice strap

Wally Whale

Unfortunately, Wally will be an endangered species at the party. Gently swirl the butter creams together for a marbled effect.

EQUIPMENT

deep 26cm x 36cm (10½-inch x 14½-inch) baking dish

40cm x 45cm (16-inch x 18-inch) rectangular cake board

(page 334)

CAKE

3 x 470g (15-ounce) packets butter cake mix

2 quantities butter cream

(page 329)

blue food colouring

DECORATIONS

½ cup (110g) white (granulated) sugar

1 black licorice strap

1 blue M&M

1 Preheat oven to 180°C/350°F. Grease baking dish; line base and sides with baking paper, extending paper 5cm (2 inches) above sides.
2 Make cakes according to directions on packets; spread into dish. Bake about 1 hour. Stand cake in dish 5 minutes before turning, top-side up, onto wire rack to cool.
3 Level cake top; turn cake cut-side down. Using pattern from pattern sheet, cut out whale; reserve leftover cake. Cut spout and flipper from reserved cake.
4 Position cake pieces, cut-side down, on cake board to form whale, as pictured; secure with a little butter cream. Discard any leftover cake pieces.
5 Tint half the butter cream blue; keep remaining butter cream plain. Using picture as a guide, spread whale's tummy with a little of the plain butter cream. Spread spout with a little of the blue butter cream.
6 Gently swirl the remaining blue and plain butter cream together to create a marbled effect. Carefully spread marbled butter cream over cake.
7 Place half the sugar and a little blue colouring in small plastic bag; rub until sugar is evenly coloured. Sprinkle blue sugar on and around the flipper, tail and tummy. Sprinkle remaining white sugar on spout.
8 Cut and position a thin strip of licorice strap for mouth. Cut eye from remaining licorice; position on cake. Secure blue M&M on licorice with a little butter cream.

Assemble whale on cake board, ready to ice.

Gently swirl the blue and plain butter creams together to create a marbled effect.

Francois ze Frog

I will zay thiz onlee once 'joyeux anniversaire!' – that's 'happy birthday'. Best to eat this cake, not kiss it, that'll be much more fun.

EQUIPMENT

deep 26cm x 36cm (10½-inch x 14½-inch) baking dish

40cm (16-inch) square cake board (page 334)

toothpick

piping bag fitted with 4mm (¼-inch) plain tube

CAKE

3 x 470g (15-ounce) packets butter cake mix

2 quantities butter cream (page 329)

green and red food colouring

DECORATIONS

14 brown Smarties

2 red Smarties

18 red frogs

18 green frogs

green and yellow ribbon

1 Preheat oven to 180°C/350°F. Grease baking dish; line base and sides with baking paper, extending paper 5cm (2 inches) above sides.

2 Make cakes according to directions on packets; spread into dish. Bake about 1 hour. Stand cake in dish 5 minutes before turning, top-side up, onto wire rack to cool.

3 Level cake top; turn cake cut-side down. Using pattern from pattern sheet, cut out frog's body and eyes from cake.

4 Assemble cake pieces on cake board, cut-side down, to form frog; secure with a little butter cream.

5 Reserve 2 tablespoons of the plain butter cream for eyes. Tint three-quarters of the remaining butter cream green; tint remaining butter cream red. Spread green butter cream all over cake.

6 Carefully place paper pattern on cake for eyes, face and front legs; using toothpick, mark outline on cake.

7 Spoon red butter cream into piping bag; pipe over marked outlines and around edge of frog. Pipe smile on face.

8 Spread plain butter cream on eyes; position brown Smarties for pupils and toes. Position red Smarties for nose; position red and green frogs around side of cake. Make single bow from ribbons; position bow under frog's chin.

Turn cake cut-side down. Position paper pattern, then cut frog's body and eyes from cake.

Assemble the cake pieces, cut-side down, to form frog; secure to the cake board with some butter cream.

Place patterns on cake for eyes, face and front legs; using a toothpick, mark outline on cake.

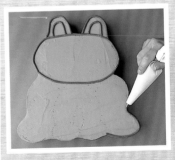
Place red butter cream into piping bag; pipe over marked outlines and around edge of frog.

Little Piggy

This little piggy went to a birthday party and had lots of fun, made lots of noise, and had lots of really, really yummy food.

Cut pig's face, feet and nose from cake.

Assemble the cake ready to ice.

EQUIPMENT

two deep 20cm (8-inch)
round cake pans
5cm (2-inch) round cutter
30cm (12-inch) round
cake board (page 334)

CAKE

1 x 470g (15-ounce) packet
butter cake mix
1 quantity butter cream
(page 329)
pink food colouring

DECORATIONS

8 yellow jelly snakes
1 red jelly snake
6 white marshmallows
purple, yellow and green
sugar sprinkles (see tip)
1 red Smartie
1 green Smartie
3 pink Smarties
2 purple-coated licorice allsorts
1 black licorice strap

1 Preheat oven to 180°C/350°F. Grease cake pans; line bases and sides with baking paper, extending paper 5cm (2 inches) above sides.
2 Make cake according to directions on packet; divide mixture evenly between pans. Bake cakes about 25 minutes. Stand cakes in pans 5 minutes before turning, top-side up, onto wire rack to cool.
3 Level tops of cakes; turn cakes, cut-side down. Using pattern from pattern sheet, cut pig's face and feet from one cake; using round cutter, cut nose from scraps.
4 Secure cake pieces, cut-side down, on cake board to form pig, as pictured; secure with a little butter cream. Discard any leftover cake.
5 Tint butter cream pink; spread all over cake.
6 Position yellow snakes for hair; position red snake for tail. Cut marshmallows in half; pinch ends gently into a point. Dip the marshmallow halves, cut-sides down, into coloured sugar sprinkles; position in hair to make flowers, as pictured. Secure red, green and one pink Smartie to flowers, as pictured, with a little butter cream.
7 Position remaining pink Smarties for nostrils and purple licorice allsorts for eyes. Cut pieces of licorice strap to make eyelashes; position on cake. Cut a thin strip of licorice for mouth.

TIP
To make your own
coloured sugar crystals.
place white table sugar in
a plastic ziptop bag with
a little colouring. Massage
the colouring through
the sugar until it's evenly
coloured.

TIP
Position frogs, lily pads and
flowers on jelly no earlier
than 1 hour before serving
or the frogs will dissolve.

NO FISH!

Using a small serrated knife and a tablespoon, scoop out a recess in the centre of the cake, about 4cm deep, leaving a 2cm border around the edges.

Frogs in a Pond

It's not that hard being green...there's a pond, plenty of water, lily pads and a rainbow connection...why, there's lots of fun to be had!

1 Preheat oven to 170°C/340°F. Grease baking dish; line base and sides with baking paper, extending paper 5cm (2 inches) above sides.
2 Make cakes according to directions on packets. Spread mixture into baking dish; bake about 1 hour. Stand cake in dish 10 minutes before turning, top-side up, onto wire rack to cool.
3 Make jelly according to packet directions; pour into shallow dish. Refrigerate about 1 hour or until jelly is the consistency of unbeaten egg whites.
4 Meanwhile, level cake top. Using pattern from pattern sheet, cut out pond. Using a small serrated knife and a tablespoon, scoop out a recess in the centre of the cake, about 4cm (1½ inches) deep, leaving a 2cm (¾-inch) border around the edges. Secure cake, cut-side up, on cake board with a little butter cream.
5 Tint butter cream green; spread over sides and top edge of cake, leave recess plain. When jelly is ready, pour into recess in cake; refrigerate until jelly is set.
6 Meanwhile, make frogs by securing jewelry beads to tops of flying saucer lollies with a little butter cream; secure choc drops to beads for eyes. To make lily pads, slice green licorice tube into thin rounds; using a small sharp knife, cut a "V" shape into each slice. Position frogs, lily pads and sugar flowers on set jelly.

EQUIPMENT

26cm x 35cm
(10¼-inch x 14-inch)
baking dish

20cm x 30cm (8-inch x 12-inch)
shallow pan

25cm x 30cm (10-inch x 12-inch)
rectangular cake board
(page 334)

CAKE

4 x 440g (14-ounce) packets
butter cake mix
(see 'mixing the cakes' page 345)

2 x 85g (3-ounce) packets
blue jelly crystals

1 x quantity butter cream
(page 329)

green food colouring

DECORATIONS

10 green candy jewelry beads

5 green flying saucer
lollies

10 brown choc drops

1 green licorice tube

5 pink and yellow
ready-made
sugar flowers

Octavius

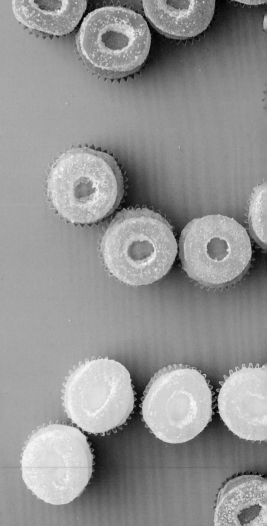

EQUIPMENT

20cm x 30cm (8-inch x 12-inch)
rectangular cake pan
5 x 12-hole (1-tablespoon/20ml)
mini muffin pans
60 mini muffin paper cases
(26 green, 20 yellow, 14 orange)
50cm (20-inch) square
cake board (page 334)

CAKE

2 x 470g (15-ounce) packets
butter cake mix

1½ quantities butter cream
(page 329)

green, orange and yellow
food colouring

DECORATIONS

2 x 300g (9½-ounce) packets
jelly fruit rings
200g (6½-ounce) packet small
jelly beans
2 blue mini M&M's
2 round peppermints
2 sour worms

1 Preheat oven to 180°C/350°F. Grease cake pan; line base and sides with baking paper, extending paper 5cm (2 inches) above sides.
2 Make one cake according to directions on packet. Spread mixture into pan; bake about 35 minutes. Stand cake in pan 5 minutes before turning, top-side up, onto wire rack to cool.
3 Line mini muffin pans with the paper cases. Make remaining cake according to directions on packet. Drop 2 level teaspoons of the mixture into each paper case; bake about 15 minutes. Stand cakes in pans 5 minutes before turning, top-side up, onto wire racks to cool.
4 Level top of large cake; turn cake cut-side down. Using pattern from pattern sheet, cut out head for octopus from cake. Secure head, cut-side down, on cake board with a little butter cream. Discard remaining cake.
5 Tint two-thirds of the butter cream green. Divide remaining butter cream equally into two small bowls; tint orange and yellow.
6 Spread two-thirds of the green butter cream all over top and sides of head; spread remaining green butter cream over tops of 26 cakes in green cases. Spread yellow butter cream over tops of 20 cakes in yellow cases. Spread orange butter cream over tops of remaining cakes. Using picture as a guide, position cakes on board to make tentacles; secure to board with a little butter cream.
7 Position colour-matched fruit rings on tops of small cakes.
8 Use jelly beans to outline head. Position 2 red fruit rings for eyes. Using a little butter cream, secure mini M&M's onto peppermints, place on top of red fruit rings. Position sour worms for mouth.

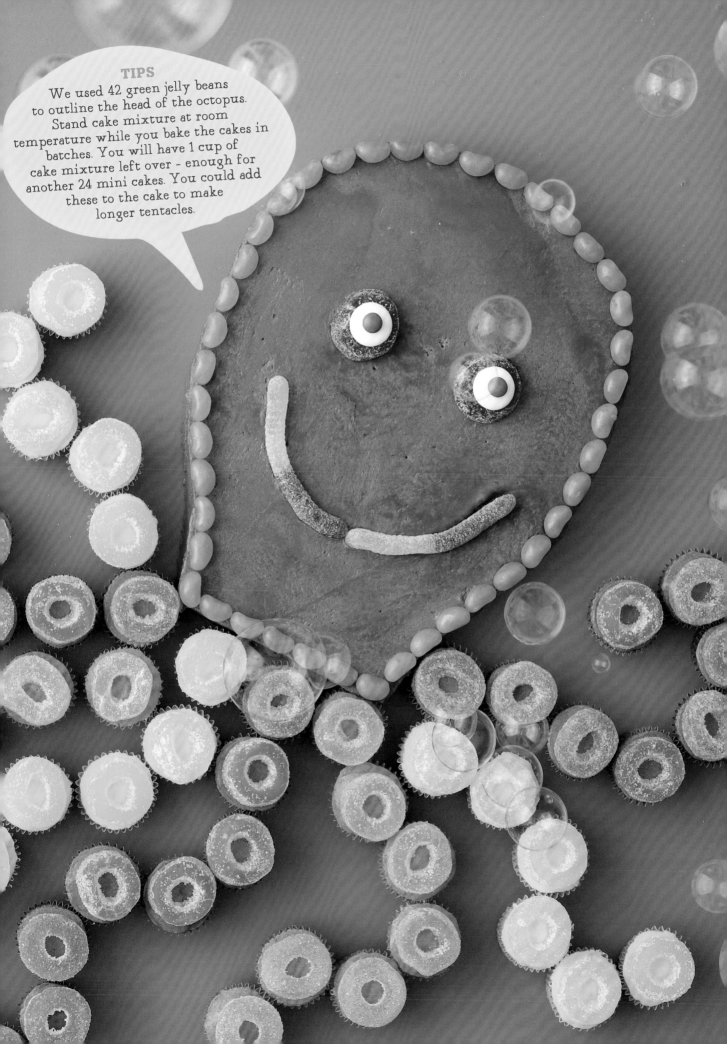

Roger Rabbit

Awound the wagged wocks woger wabbit wan...this little bunny
is a real cutie, a good cake for a first birthday party.

EQUIPMENT

three deep 20cm (8-inch)
round cake pans
40cm x 65cm (16-inch x 26-inch)
rectangular cake board
(page 334)

CAKE

2 x 470g (15-ounce) packets
butter cake mix
2 quantities butter cream
(page 329)
pink food colouring
2 cups (180g) desiccated
coconut

DECORATIONS

2 black Smarties
1 red Smartie
1 black licorice strap

1 Preheat oven to 180°C/350°F. Grease cake pans; line bases and sides with baking paper, extending paper 5cm (2 inches) above sides.
2 Make cakes according to directions on packets; divide mixture evenly into pans. Bake cakes about 30 minutes. Stand cakes in pans 5 minutes before turning, top-side up, onto wire rack to cool.
3 Level cake tops so they are the same height; turn cakes, cut-side down. Using pattern from pattern sheet, cut out rabbit's feet, paws and ears from one cake. Cut feet and paws in half, as pictured.
4 Cut each paw diagonally from narrow end to broad end to taper, discard other two pieces; cut 1cm (½-inch) from narrow ends of front feet, as pictured.
5 Secure cake pieces, cut-side down, on cake board to form rabbit, as pictured; secure with a little butter cream. Discard any leftover cake pieces.
6 Tint 1 tablespoon of the butter cream pink; leave the remaining butter cream plain.
7 Spread cake with plain butter cream; cover well with coconut. Spread pink butter cream in centre of ears. Place 2 tablespoons of coconut and a little pink colouring in small plastic bag; rub until coconut is evenly coloured. Sprinkle iced pink area with pink coconut.
8 Position black Smarties for eyes. Cut red Smartie in half, position on face for nose. Cut licorice strap into thin strips; position on face for whiskers, mouth, nose and claws.

Position paper pattern on cake, cut out ears, paws and feet.

Use a sharp knife to shape paws.

Cut rabbit's feet and paws in half.

Assemble cake ready to ice.

Snake, rattle & Roll

This cake is not at all difficult, however, it is time consuming flattening and positioning all those Mallow Bakes; but it's worth it.

EQUIPMENT

3 x 22cm (9-inch)
savarin pans
45cm (18-inch) square
cake board (page 334)

CAKE

2 x 470g (15-ounce) packets
butter cake mix
2 quantities butter cream
(page 329)
yellow food colouring

DECORATIONS

5 x 100g (3-ounce) packets
rainbow Mallow Bakes
2 strawberries and creams
1 red snake

1 Preheat oven to 180°C/350°F. Grease and flour savarin pans.

2 Make cakes according to directions on packets; divide mixture evenly among pans (see tips). Bake cakes about 25 minutes. Stand cakes in pans 5 minutes before turning onto wire racks to cool.

3 Level flat cake bases so cakes are the same height. Cut cakes into segments, as pictured. Assemble segments on cake board, cut-side down, to form snake. Cut both ends of one cake-quarter on the diagonal for head. Trim end piece of snake on the diagonal for tail.

4 Using rolling pin, flatten Mallow Bakes; divide into colours.

5 Tint butter cream yellow. Starting at tail of snake, spread butter cream over one segment; cover with slightly overlapping Mallow Bakes. Continue working in segments, connecting each segment with butter cream.

6 Attach snake's head to body with butter cream; spread remaining butter cream over head.

7 Position strawberries and creams for eyes; secure with a little butter cream. Make a cut into end of red snake; position for tongue.

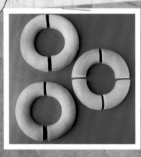

Place the cakes, cut-side down, then cut cakes into segments with a small serrated knife.

Assemble the segments on the cake board, cut-side down, then trim the tail piece on the diagonal.

Roll the Mallow Bakes to flatten then divide them into groups by their colour.

Starting at the tail end, cover a segment with butter cream then with coloured Mallow Bakes.

Working in sections, connect each of the segments with a little of the butter cream.

Attach the snake's head to the body with butter cream then continue with Mallow Bakes.

TIPS

Savarin pans are available at cookware shops. If you only have one savarin pan, pour a third of the cake mixture into the tin and bake it according to the recipe. The cake mixture will be fine if you can only bake one cake at a time.

You can flatten the Mallow Bakes a day ahead; store them in an airtight container.

Timothy Tiger

You need pinking shears, available from sewing and craft shops, to cut the tiger's stripes. You can use straight scissors, if you prefer.

EQUIPMENT

8cm x 25cm (3¼-inch x 10-inch) bar cake pan
two 20cm x 30cm (8-inch x 12-inch) rectangular cake pans
40cm (16-inch) square cake board (page 334)
pinking shears

CAKE

2 x 470g (15-ounce) packets butter cake mix
1½ quantities butter cream (page 329)
orange food colouring

DECORATIONS

2 white marshmallows
4 orange jubes
1 mint leaf
1 smooth black licorice strap

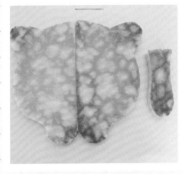

Cut out the head and nose of the tiger.

Cut through the nose at an angle using a sharp knife.

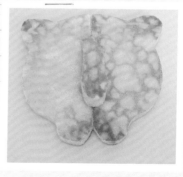

Assemble the cake pieces on cake board, ready to be iced.

1 Preheat oven to 180°C/350°F. Grease cake pans; line bases and sides with baking paper, extending paper 5cm (2 inches) above sides.
2 Make cakes according to directions on packets; spread 1½ cups of mixture into bar pan. Divide remaining mixture evenly between the rectangular pans. Bake bar cake about 25 minutes and rectangular cakes about 30 minutes. Stand cakes in pans 5 minutes before turning, top-side up, onto wire racks to cool.
3 Level cake tops so they are the same height; turn cakes, cut-side down. Place rectangular cakes side by side; using pattern from pattern sheet, cut out tiger's head. Cut out nose from bar cake. Cut nose at an angle; discard bottom piece of cake. Secure cake pieces, cut-side down, on cake board to form tiger, as pictured; secure with a little butter cream. Discard any leftover cake pieces.
4 Tint butter cream orange; spread all over tiger.
5 Flatten marshmallows with fingers; position on cake for eyes. Position trimmed jubes for tongue and eyebrows. Cut diamond shapes out of mint leaf, position for pupils.
6 Using pinking shears, cut tiger stripes and thin strips for eyes and nose out of licorice strap; position on cake.

Place steamer, upside down, on baking-paper-lined tray; remove steamer and plastic wrap.

Using ice magic, coat the nose and face.

Stand cake until chocolate is almost set, then use a sharp knife to trim away excess chocolate.

Working quickly, push chocolate biscuits into the ice-cream cake.

Spiky Echidna ice-cream cake

EQUIPMENT

2.25-litre (9-cup)
pudding steamer
25cm x 30cm (10-inch x 12-inch)
rectangular cake board
(page 334)

CAKE

3.5 litres (14 cups) choc-chip
ice-cream, softened
1 cream-filled chocolate
sponge finger, chilled

DECORATIONS

¾ cup (180ml) milk
chocolate Ice Magic
2 x 200g (6½-ounce) packets
chocolate finger biscuits
100g (3 ounces) dark eating
(semi-sweet) chocolate,
grated finely
2 green Smarties

1 Line pudding steamer with plastic wrap; press ice-cream into steamer. Cover with foil; freeze 3 hours or overnight.

2 Turn steamer upside down on baking-paper-lined tray. Remove steamer and plastic wrap from ice-cream.

3 Working quickly, trim 2cm (¾ inch) from sponge finger, position at base of ice-cream cake for nose. Using ice magic, coat nose and face in chocolate, as pictured; stand until chocolate is almost set. Using sharp knife, trim away any excess chocolate. (Return to freezer if necessary).

4 Working quickly, push finger biscuits into echidna's body; sprinkle grated chocolate between biscuits.

5 Using a little ice magic, secure Smarties to echidna for eyes.

6 Freeze echidna until ready to serve. Using egg slide, transfer echidna from baking paper to cake board.

TIP

Once the ice-cream softens
and melts slightly, it takes
up less space – that is why
3.5 litres of ice-cream fits into
the pudding steamer. Rub
the outside of the steamer
with a hot cloth to help
remove the cake.

Bush Buddies

These cakes would work well for an Australian-themed outback party: make one bush buddy for each guest.

EQUIPMENT

6-hole (¾-cup/180ml) texas muffin pan

1 texas muffin paper case

20cm (8-inch) square cake board (page 334)

CAKE

1 x 470g (15-ounce) packet butter cake mix

½ quantity fluffy frosting (page 329)

½ quantity butter cream (page 329)

black and brown food colouring

DECORATIONS

KOALA

1 Milk Arrowroot biscuit, halved crossways

1 white marshmallow, halved crossways

2 blue mini M&M's

1 small solid milk chocolate egg

3cm piece licorice strap, cut into a thin strip

COCKATOO

2 brown mini M&M's

1 triangular black jube, halved crossways

6 banana lollies

ECHIDNA

2 yellow mini M&M's

12 thin mint sticks, halved

1 chocolate malt stick, halved

WOMBAT

2 green mini M&M's

1 Clinker, halved crossways

5cm (2-inch) piece black licorice strap

TIPS

The cockatoo and koala will lose their gloss after an hour or so, as the frosting sets like a meringue. You will have a small amount of cake mixture left over – barely enough for one more cake.

1 Preheat oven to 180°C/350°F. Line one hole of the texas muffin pan with the paper case; grease three pan holes.
2 Make cake according to directions on packet. Pour ¹⁄₃ cup of the mixture into the paper case and greased pan holes; bake about 25 minutes. Stand cakes in pan 5 minutes before turning, top-side up, onto wire rack to cool.
3 Transfer half the fluffy frosting to a small bowl; use black colouring to tint frosting grey. Leave remaining frosting white. Tint the butter cream brown.

Koala Shape biscuit halves into rounded shapes for ears. Spread grey frosting over top of cake in paper case and over top and edges of both ears. Using picture as a guide, position ears on cake; top ears with marshmallow halves. Position remaining decorations to make koala's eyes, nose and mouth.

Cockatoo Level one cake top; turn cake cut-side down. Trim cake into a rounded oval shape. Spread white frosting over the cake. Using picture as a guide, decorate cake using the lollies for the cockatoo.

Echidna Level one cake top; turn cake cut-side down. Trim cake into a tear-drop shape. Spread brown butter cream over the cake. Using picture as a guide, decorate cake using the lollies for the echidna.

Wombat Level one cake top; turn cake cut-side down. Trim cake into a rounded oval shape. Spread brown butter cream over the cake. Using picture as a guide, decorate cake using the lollies for the wombat. Use a fork to mark frosting for a 'furry' look.

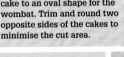

Use a small sharp, finely serrated knife to trim the cake to an oval shape for the wombat. Trim and round two opposite sides of the cakes to minimise the cut area.

Use a small sharp, finely serrated knife to trim the cake to a teardrop shape to make the echidna.

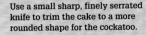

Use a small sharp, finely serrated knife to trim the cake to a more rounded shape for the cockatoo.

Clarissa the Cow

Clarissa the cow is out in the paddock, eating the flowers and generally getting into all kinds of mischief.

EQUIPMENT

26cm x 35cm (10¼-inch x 14-inch) baking dish

deep 30cm (12-inch) round cake pan

35cm (14-inch) round cake board (page 334)

2 bamboo skewers

CAKE

10 x 440g (14-ounce) packets butter cake mix
(see 'mixing the cakes' page 345)

2 quantities fluffy frosting
(page 329)

pink and brown food colouring

DECORATIONS

¼ cup (35g) white chocolate Melts

2 banana lollies

15cm (6 -inch) piece black licorice strap

2 white marshmallows

2 pink marshmallows

2 dark chocolate Bits

3 red tiny tots

1 clear red flower lollipop

1 mint leaf

1 Preheat oven to 170°C/340°F. Grease baking dish and cake pan; line bases and sides with baking paper, extending paper 5cm (2 inches) above sides.

2 Make cakes according to directions on packets – make the cake mixes in 4 batches so the mixture fits into the large bowl of an electric mixer – 6 packets go into the round pan (two batches of 3 mixes); and 4 packets go into the baking dish (2 batches of 2 mixes). Spread mixture into round pan; bake about 2 hours. Spread mixture into baking pan; bake about 1 hour. Stand cakes in pans for 10 minutes before turning, top-side up, onto wire racks to cool.

3 Level cake tops. Using pattern from pattern sheet, cut out cow's body, ears and legs from rectangular cake and head from round cake. Secure cow's body, cut-side down, to cake board with a little fluffy frosting. Secure head on top of body, cut-side down, with a little frosting. Position ears at top of head, secure with skewers.

4 Melt white chocolate Melts in small bowl over small saucepan of simmering water until smooth (don't let water touch base of bowl). Dip banana lollies into chocolate to coat, place on baking paper; stand until set.

5 Reserve 1½ cups frosting. Spread remaining frosting all over cake, except cow's udder. Divide reserved frosting into three small bowls; tint one bowl dark pink, one pale pink and one brown. Using picture as a guide, use brown frosting to make patches all over cow's body and one ear. Spread dark pink frosting over the udder and other ear. Spread pale pink frosting to create the cow's nose and mouth area. Position licorice for mouth.

6 Using picture as a guide, position white marshmallow for eyes; position and secure dark chocolate Bits on marshmallows to finish eyes. Position pink marshmallows for nose. Position chocolate-dipped banana lollies for horns on top of head. Secure tiny tots to cow's udder. Position lollipop and mint leaf at side of mouth.

Cedric Snake

Look into Cedric's hypnotic eyes, and you'll need all the power of a skilled snake charmer to break the trance and eat him up.

EQUIPMENT

two 20cm (8-inch) ring pans
30cm x 65cm
(12-inch x 26-inch)
rectangular cake board
(page 334)

CAKE

2 x 470g (15-ounce) packets
butter cake mix
1½ quantities butter cream
(page 329)

purple food colouring

DECORATIONS

2 x 350g (11-ounce) packets
jubes
2 green M&M's
black glossy decorating gel

1 Preheat oven to 180°C/350°F. Grease cake pans; line bases and sides with baking paper, extending paper 5cm (2 inches) above sides.
2 Make cakes according to directions on packets; divide mixture evenly into pans. Bake cakes about 35 minutes. Stand cakes in pans 5 minutes before turning, top-side up, onto wire racks to cool.
3 Cut both cakes in half. Secure cake pieces on cake board to form snake, as pictured; secure with a little butter cream. Discard any leftover cake pieces. Trim ends to form head and tail.
4 Tint butter cream purple; spread all over cake.
5 Using a sharp knife, cut jubes in half horizontally. Decorate snake with jubes. Trim one half of a red jube for forked tongue; position on cake.
6 Press green M&M's on cake for eyes. Using black decorating gel, pipe snake's eyes onto M&M's.

TIP
Use any soft jubes or jellies you like for the decorations. We preferred ones with very strong colours for a more striking effect.

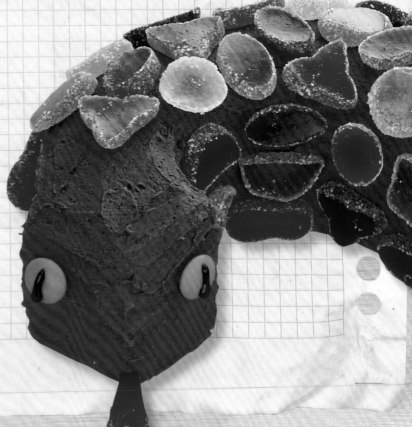

Cut both cakes in half;
assemble cake halves on board.

Use a sharp knife to shape
snake's head and tail.

Stella Stegosaur

Stegosaurus lived about 150 million years ago, though this one can be created the day before it's needed. So long as the weather's not hot, decorate the cake the day before and store it in a cool dry place.

EQUIPMENT

deep 26cm x 36cm
(10½-inch x 14½-inch)
baking dish

35cm x 45cm (14-inch x 18-inch)
rectangular cake board
(page 334)

CAKE

3 x 470g (15-ounce) packets
butter cake mix

1 quantity butter cream
(page 329)

green food colouring

DECORATIONS

8 square After Dinner Mints

3 x 125g (4-ounce) boxes
chocolate mint sticks

3 x 200g (6½-ounce)
packets mint leaves

12 Tic Tacs

1 red licorice
strap

1 Preheat oven to 180°C/350°F. Grease baking dish; line base and sides with baking paper, extending paper 5cm (2 inches) above sides.

2 Make cakes according to directions on packets; spread mixture into dish. Bake about 1 hour. Stand cake in dish 5 minutes before turning, top-side up, onto wire rack to cool.

3 Level cake top; turn cake cut-side down. Using pattern from pattern sheet, cut out stegosaur's shape. Secure cake, cut-side down, on cake board with a little butter cream.

4 Tint butter cream green; spread all over cake.

5 Cut After Dinner Mints in half diagonally; place mints along cake body so they are raised along the diagonal cut to look like armoured-plated spikes.

6 Cut mint sticks in graduated lengths; place in position along back so they follow the line of the spikes, longer in the centre, and shorter at the sides.

7 Starting at the tail, cover body and legs with slightly overlapping mint leaves. Using a sharp knife, cut about 10 mint leaves in half horizontally; place in position around neck.

8 To decorate face and feet, use Tic Tacs for claws, a thin piece of red licorice strap for mouth and a mint stick, thinly sliced, for eye and nose.

Use paper pattern to cut out cake.

Cut After Dinner Mints in half diagonally.

Using a sharp knife, cut mint leaves in half horizontally.

TIP
If the weather is hot, you can ice the cake and store it in the fridge overnight. Place the decorations on the morning of the party.

Buzzy Beehive

The worker bees have returned with honey for their queen. The cake can be completed two days ahead, so that's one less thing to worry about on the day of the party.

EQUIPMENT

dolly varden pan
30cm (12-inch) round
cake board (page 334) or
cake stand

CAKE

1½ x 470g (15-ounce) packets
butter cake mix
(see 'mixing the cakes' page 345)

½ cup (160g) apricot jam,
warmed, strained

yellow food colouring

DECORATIONS

1.5kg (3 pounds) ready-made
white icing (page 329)
pure icing (confectioners')
sugar, for dusting
1 ice-cream wafer
6 Milo Duos
black decorating gel

1 Preheat oven to 130°C/260°F. Grease and flour pan.

2 Make cakes according to directions on packets. Pour mixture into pan; bake about 1 hour. Stand cake in pan 5 minutes before turning onto wire rack to cool.

3 Level base of cake; secure cake, cut-side down, on cake board with a little warmed jam. Brush cake all over with jam.

4 Knead ready-made icing on surface dusted with a little sifted icing sugar until icing loses its stickiness; tint icing yellow. Roll icing into a rope shape about 1cm (½-inch) thick and long enough to reach around base of cake.

5 Repeat with remaining icing, stacking ropes up on the cake; keeping the icing joins at the back of the cake.

6 Tint a scrap of icing a darker shade of yellow; roll into a thin rope. Trim wafer into a rounded door shape. Brush around edge of wafer with jam; attach icing rope to door. Brush around door with a little jam; position door on hive.

7 Using picture as a guide, make bees using remaining icing scraps to shape heads and bodies, use Milo Duos for wings and black decorating gel to make eyes and markings. Attach bees to cake with a little jam.

Tint ready-made icing yellow; roll icing into a long rope and position around beehive.

Roll scraps of yellow icing into bee shapes; position Milo Duos for wings, pipe on stripes and eyes with black gel.

Butterfly Beauty

The butterfly is like a flower that flutters on a warm summer's breeze; the colours of this cake will brighten even the greyest day.

EQUIPMENT

two 20cm x 30cm (8-inch x 12-inch) rectangular cake pans

35cm x 40cm (14-inch x 16-inch) rectangular cake board (page 334)

toothpicks

CAKE

3 x 470g (15-ounce) packets butter cake mix

2 quantities butter cream (page 329)

violet, yellow, pink, green and blue food colouring

DECORATIONS

34 pink Smarties

26 blue Smarties

35g (1-ounce) jar snowflakes

15cm (6-inch) mauve chenille stick (pipe cleaner)

2 pink heart-shaped lollipops

1 Preheat oven to 180°C/350°F. Grease cake pans; line bases and sides with baking paper, extending paper 5cm (2 inches) above sides.

2 Make cakes according to directions on packets; divide mixture evenly into pans. Bake about 45 minutes. Stand cakes in pans 5 minutes before turning, top-side up, onto wire racks to cool.

3 Level cake tops so they are the same height; place cakes together, side by side, cut-side down. Using pattern from pattern sheet, cut out butterfly. Secure cake pieces, cut-side down, on cake board to form butterfly, as pictured; secure with a little butter cream. Discard any leftover cake pieces.

4 Using toothpicks, transfer markings on paper pattern onto cake.

5 Divide butter cream into three portions; tint one portion violet and one portion yellow. Divide remaining portion into three smaller portions; tint pink, green and blue.

6 Spread top and sides of cake with coloured butter creams, using markings on the cake as a guide.

7 Position Smarties around edges of different butter cream colours, decorate with snowflakes. Twist chenille stick to resemble antennae; position antennae and lollipops, as pictured.

Position paper pattern on cake, cut out butterfly using a sharp knife.

Use toothpicks to transfer butterfly markings from paper pattern onto the cake.

Spread different coloured butter creams on butterfly markings.

TIP
You will need to buy a 265g
(8-ounce) packet of small
lollipops for this recipe.

Clara Crocodile

You should never smile at a crocodile, or be taken in by her welcoming grin, but Clara looks friendly enough – maybe!

EQUIPMENT

two 20cm x 30cm
(8-inch x 12-inch)
rectangular cake pans

35cm x 60cm (14-inch x 24-inch) rectangular cake board
(page 334)

CAKE

3 x 470g (15-ounce) packets
butter cake mix

2 quantities butter cream
(page 329)

yellow and green
food colouring

DECORATIONS

30 small lollipops
8 yellow Smarties,
cut in half
1 large white marshmallow
1 black licorice strap
1 black jelly bean, cut in half

Position pattern on the cake ready to cut.

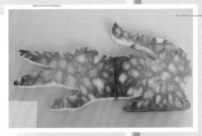

The cut cake, ready to be iced.

Place lollipops in small plastic bag; use a rolling pin to smash lollipops into shards.

To make eyelashes, cut licorice strap into small strips.

1 Preheat oven to 180°C/350°F. Grease cake pans; line bases and sides with baking paper, extending paper 5cm (2 inches) above sides.

2 Make cakes according to directions on packets; divide mixture evenly into pans. Bake about 35 minutes. Stand cakes in pans 5 minutes before turning, top-side up, onto wire racks to cool.

3 Level cake tops so they are the same height; turn cakes, cut-side down. Cut a 7cm (2¾-inch) piece off one end of one cake and assemble cakes, as pictured. Using pattern from pattern sheet, cut out crocodile. Position cake pieces, cut-side down, on cake board to form crocodile, as pictured; secure with a little butter cream. Discard leftover cake.

4 Tint ⅓ cup of the butter cream yellow; tint remaining butter cream green. Spread yellow butter cream over tummy of crocodile. Spread green butter cream over remaining cake.

5 Place lollipops into a small plastic bag; using end of a rolling pin, smash lollipops to create uneven sized shards; discard sticks. Shake broken lollipops through coarse sieve; discard fine powdered pieces. Sprinkle lollipop shards over crocodile's back and tail.

6 Position yellow Smarties for teeth. Trim marshmallow into eye shape; position on cake. To make eyelashes, cut small piece of licorice strap into a rectangle, then cut into thin strips, as pictured – do not cut all the way through the strap. Fan licorice, position above eye. Position jelly bean on marshmallow for iris.

7 Cut licorice into six strips for claws. Position three pieces on each foot.

Creepy Crawly Spider

EQUIPMENT

1.25-litre (5-cup)
pudding steamer

12-hole (⅓-cup/80ml)
standard muffin pan

deep 30cm (12-inch)
round cake pan

40cm (16-inch) round
cake board (page 334)

piping bag fitted with 4mm
(¼-inch) plain tube

piping bag fitted with a
medium fluted tube

10 toothpicks

CAKE

5 x 470g (15-ounce) packets
butter cake mix
(see 'mixing the cakes' page 345)

5 quantities butter cream
(page 329)

green, black and purple
food colouring

DECORATIONS

9 black bump chenille sticks

1 round licorice allsort

1 orange Skittle

5 red Crazy Bananas

1 Preheat oven to 180°C/350°F. Grease pudding steamer and one hole of muffin pan. Grease round cake pan; line base and side with baking paper, extending paper 5cm (2 inches) above sides.

2 Make cakes according to directions on packets; pour mixture into muffin hole and pudding steamer until each is three-quarters full. Bake muffin about 20 minutes and steamer cake about 45 minutes. Spread remaining mixture into round cake pan; bake cake about 1 hour. Stand all cakes in pans 5 minutes before turning, top-side up, onto wire racks to cool.

3 Level steamer and top of round cake. Secure round cake, cut-side down, on cake board with a little butter cream.

4 Tint three-fifths of the butter cream green; spread all over top and side of round cake.

5 Cut 30cm (12-inch) circle from baking paper; fold baking paper into eight equal segments. Position paper gently on cake; place one toothpick at centre of circle and one toothpick on the outside edge of cake at each segment. Using toothpick, score baking paper from centre of the cake to end of each segment, as pictured; remove paper and toothpicks.

6 Tint a quarter of the remaining butter cream black. Spoon into piping bag fitted with plain tube; using markings as a guide, pipe web over top and side of cake.

7 Position steamer cake, cut-side down, on round cake for spider's body, as pictured. Position muffin against body for spider's head.

8 Tint remaining butter cream purple; spread 2 tablespoons of the purple butter cream over head. Spoon remaining purple butter cream into piping bag fitted with fluted tube; pipe stars to cover spider's body, as pictured.

9 Bend eight chenille sticks to form spider legs; position on cake. Cut remaining chenille stick into quarters; position two pieces on cake for pincers.

10 Cut allsort in half; position on cake for eyes. Position Skittle on cake for nose, and Crazy Bananas for fangs.

Use a toothpick to score baking paper from centre of the cake to end of each segment marking.

Using the markings as a guide, pipe spider's web over top and side of the cake.

Position the steamer cake for spider's body and muffin for spider's head on web.

Spoon remaining purple butter cream into piping bag; pipe stars to cover spider's body.

Geraldine Giraffe

The tallest animal in the world keeps an eye out for hungry party animals who are on the prowl for a party feast.

1 Preheat oven to 180°C/350°F. Grease baking dish; line base and sides with baking paper, extending paper 5cm (2 inches) above sides.

2 Make cakes according to directions on packets; spread mixture into dish. Bake about 1 hour. Stand cake in dish 5 minutes before turning, top-side up, onto wire rack to cool.

3 Level cake top; turn cake cut-side down. Using pattern from pattern sheet, cut out body and head of giraffe. Secure cake pieces, cut-side down, on cake board to form giraffe; secure with a little butter cream. Discard any leftover cake pieces.

4 Tint butter cream orange spread all over cake.

5 Cut licorice strap into thin strips; position licorice around cake.

6 Cut roll-ups into three 30cm (12-inch) lengths. Layer the lengths of roll-ups together to make one thick length; cut thin strips into the layered roll-ups, but not all the way through, as pictured; position on giraffe for mane. Wrap some of the remaining roll-up around licorice to cover tail; cut end of roll-up to fray end. Secure tail with toothpick.

7 Cut some of the remaining licorice strap into thin strips, position on cake for ear and mouth. Cut licorice twist in half, position for horns. Cut jelly bean in half lengthways, position for nose. Cut chocolate bullet in half, position for eye. Cut licorice strap into a 1.5cm x 2cm (¾-inch x ¾-inch) rectangle, then cut into thin strips – do not cut all the way through the strap. Fan licorice, position above eye.

8 Melt chocolate (page 339); spread melted chocolate evenly over a piece of baking paper to make a 20cm (8-inch) square. When chocolate is almost set, cut into 2.5cm (1-inch) diamond shapes. When chocolate is completely set, gently lift diamonds off paper, position on giraffe.

EQUIPMENT

26cm x 36cm (10½-inch x 14½-inch) baking dish

35cm x 50cm (14-inch x 20-inch) rectangular cake board
(page 334)

toothpick with double-pointed head

CAKE

3 x 470g (15-ounce) packets butter cake mix

1½ quantities butter cream
(page 329)

orange food colouring

DECORATIONS

2 black licorice straps

2 x 75cm (30-inch) long pineapple and orange-flavoured Troppo Twist Fruit Roll-Ups reels

6cm (2½-inch) piece black licorice twist

1 black jelly bean

1 chocolate-covered licorice bullet

⅔ cup (100g) milk chocolate Melts

Position paper pattern on cake ready to cut out.

Layer the fruit roll-ups together to make one thick length.

Cut thin strips into the layered roll-ups to make giraffe's mane.

Cut licorice strap to make eyelashes, do not cut all the way through.

Use a ruler to cut the chocolate into diamond shapes.

Colin Caterpillar

Colin should be eaten before he undergoes a metamorphosis and changes into a giant butterfly! This cake is just the right size for small hands and its bright colours will keep little ones amused.

Trim four of the cakes, making each one slightly smaller than the previous one.

EQUIPMENT

two 6-hole (¾-cup/180ml) texas muffin pans

45cm x 80cm (18-inch x 32-inch) rectangular cake board
(page 334)

CAKE

2 x 470g (15-ounce) packets butter cake mix

2 quantities butter cream
(page 329)

orange, red, green and blue food colouring

4 cups (280g) shredded coconut

DECORATIONS

44 yellow jelly beans

2 brown Smarties

2 large round mints

1 black licorice strap

1 pink Fruit Stick or Musk Stick

1 yellow Fruit Stick

1 green Fruit Stick

2 yellow chenille sticks (pipe cleaners)

60 mini M&M's

TIP
You will need to buy
a 200g (6-ounce) packet
jelly beans and
a 35g (1-ounce) tube
mini M&M's
for this cake.

1 Preheat oven to 180°C/350°F. Grease muffin pans.
2 Make cakes according to directions on packets. Divide mixture evenly into pan holes; bake about 30 minutes. Stand cakes in pans 5 minutes before turning, top-side up, onto wire racks to cool.
3 Using small knife, trim four of the cakes for the end of the caterpillar's body, making each one slightly smaller than the previous one. Trim remaining cake tops into rounded shapes.
4 Divide butter cream among four bowls; tint orange, red, green and blue.
5 Spread each coloured butter cream over tops and sides of three cakes.
6 Place 1 cup coconut and a little orange colouring in a small plastic bag; rub until coconut is evenly coloured, gently press onto same coloured cake. Repeat with remaining coconut, colouring and cakes.
7 Assemble coconut-covered cakes on board to form caterpillar; secure with a little butter cream, if you like. Position jelly beans as feet.
8 Using a little butter cream, attach Smarties to mints for eyes; secure to cake with a little butter cream. Cut licorice strap into thin strip; secure on cake for mouth.
9 Thinly slice Fruit Sticks lengthways; position on cake for hair. Curl ends of chenille sticks, position on head for antennae. Scatter M&M's over top of remaining cakes.

TIP
If the marshmallows don't sit in place firmly when decorating the ear, secure them with toothpicks, but be sure to remove the toothpicks before serving.

Fifi the Poodle

Fifi is so grand, it's nothing but the best for her. After some preening and primping she's ready to be the star of the party.

1 Preheat oven to 180°C/350°F. Grease baking dish; line base and sides with baking paper, extending paper 5cm (2 inches) above sides.

2 Make cakes according to directions on packets; spread mixture into dish. Bake about 1 hour. Stand cake in dish 5 minutes before turning, top-side up, onto wire rack to cool.

3 Level cake top; turn cake cut-side down. Using pattern from pattern sheet, cut out poodle's body, paws and tail from cake.

4 Position cake pieces, cut-side down, on cake board to form poodle, as pictured; secure with a little butter cream.

5 Tint butter cream pink; spread all over cake.

6 Trim one licorice twist to 11cm (4½-inch); position on cake for tail. Trim another licorice twist to 8cm (3¼-inch); position on cake for ear. Trim remaining twists to 8cm (3¼-inch); position on cake for legs.

7 Using picture as a guide, decorate body and paws with Mallow Bakes. Decorate head, ear and tail with marshmallows.

8 Cut licorice strap into thin strips, position around outline of poodle's face; cut shorter pieces for eye and mouth. Trim 5mm (¼-inch) piece from licorice twist trimmings; position on cake for nose.

EQUIPMENT

26cm x 36cm (10½-inch x 14½-inch) baking dish

45cm x 50cm (18-inch x 20-inch) rectangular cake board (page 334)

CAKE

3 x 470g (15-ounce) packets butter cake mix

2 quantities butter cream (page 329)

pink food colouring

DECORATIONS

6 black licorice twists

200g (6½ ounces) white Mallow Bakes

275g (9 ounces) white marshmallows

1 black licorice strap

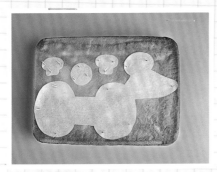

Turn cake cut-side down. Using the paper pattern, cut poodle's body, feet and tail from the cake.

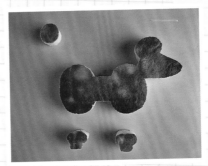

Assemble the cake pieces on cake board, cut-side down, to form poodle.

Jellyfish

The kids will love this smiling jellyfish - floating in blue jelly and with rainbow straps for tentacles, it is really eye catching.

EQUIPMENT

26cm x 36cm
(10½-inch x 14½-inch)
baking dish
35cm x 45cm
(14-inch x 17½-inch) large
shallow plastic tray

CAKE

2 x 470g (15-ounce)
packets butter cake mix
4 x 85g (3-ounce) packets
blue jelly crystals
1 quantity butter cream
(page 329)
green food colouring

DECORATIONS

1 white marshmallow,
halved crossways
1 egg shell, halved,
washed, dried
2 blue Smarties
9 rainbow straps
fish lollies
raspberries lollies
plastic coral

1 Preheat oven to 180°C/350°F. Grease baking dish; line base and sides with baking paper, extending paper 5cm (2 inches) above sides.

2 Make cakes according to directions on packets; spread mixture into dish. Bake about 1 hour. Stand cake in dish 5 minutes before turning, top-side up, onto wire rack to cool.

3 Dissolve jellies in large heatproof bowl using 3 cups (750ml) boiling water and 2½ cups (625ml) cold water. Refrigerate until just set.

4 Level cake top; turn cake cut-side down. Using pattern from pattern sheet, cut jellyfish shape from cake. Place in large shallow plastic tray.

5 Tint butter cream green; spread all over cake.

6 Cut two hollows into cake for jellyfish's eye sockets. Place marshmallow halves into each egg shell; top marshmallows with Smarties. Position eyes on cake.

7 Cut a blue strip from one rainbow strap; position on cake for jellyfish's mouth.

8 Using whisk or fork, break up jelly; spoon carefully into tray around the cake.

9 Position remaining rainbow straps as tentacles. Decorate with fish, raspberries and coral.

TIPS

You need a large shallow plastic tray to hold the cake and jelly. If it's non-plastic, line the tray with large sheets of plastic wrap. The cooked cake can be frozen for up to one month. Thaw the cake at room temperature for about six hours.

Jelly and cake can be completed and refrigerated, separately, a day ahead. Position cake, tentacles and decorations up to three hours ahead. Refrigerate if weather is hot.

Plastic coral is available from toy shops and pet stores.

TIP
This is a cute idea for a younger child, or for an older child who has a bird as a pet. If you like, make, or buy, a larger cake and fill it with enough birds to represent the child's age.

Baby Bluebirds

Bluebirds are the symbol of happiness, wealth, health, new births and springtime – that's a lot of positive support from a tiny bird.

1 Preheat oven to 180°C/350°F. Grease 3 holes of the muffin pan. Grease cake pan; line base and side with baking paper, extending paper 5cm (2 inches) above sides.

2 Make cake according to directions on packet. Drop 2½ level tablespoons of the mixture into greased muffin pan holes; bake about 20 minutes. Spread remaining mixture into round cake pan; bake about 30 minutes. Stand cakes in pans 5 minutes before turning, top-side up, onto wire racks to cool.

3 Cut a 15cm (6-inch) circle in the top of the large cake; hollow out to make a nest about 2cm (¾ inch) deep.

4 Stir two-thirds of the butter cream with the sifted cocoa powder in a small bowl until smooth. Tint remaining butter cream blue.

5 Spread chocolate butter cream all over top, side and hollow of birds' nest. Secure on cake board with a little butter cream.

6 Cut about half the biscuits in half; decorate nest with all of the biscuits and pieces of Flake.

7 Level small cake tops so they are the same height. Turn cakes cut-side down; trim cakes to give a rounded appearance. Spread rounded cake tops with blue butter cream. Position cakes in nest.

8 Using picture as a guide, position mini M&M's for birds' eyes. Cut beaks from chocolate Melts; place in position. Position sour worm in one bird's beak. Position mint leaves on side of nest.

EQUIPMENT

12-hole (¹/₃-cup/80ml) standard muffin pan
deep 20cm (8-inch) round cake pan
30cm (12-inch) round cake board (page 334)

CAKE

1 x 470g (15-ounce) packet butter cake mix
1½ quantities butter cream (page 329)
¼ cup (25g) cocoa powder
blue food colouring

DECORATIONS

200g (6½-ounce) packet chocolate finger biscuits
3 x 30g (1-ounce) Flake bars, broken into pieces
6 orange mini M&M's
4 dark chocolate Melts
1 sour worm, halved
2 mint leaves

Remove paper cases; turn cakes top-side down; use a small sharp, finely serrated knife to trim the cakes into rounded shapes.

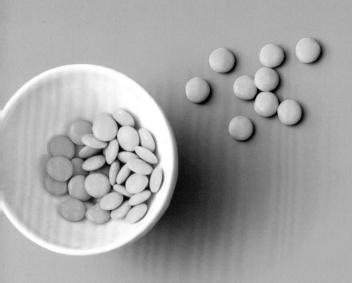

Secure cakes to board with a little butter cream.

Smiley Starfish

EQUIPMENT

6-hole (¾-cup/180ml)
texas muffin pan
7 x 12-hole (1-tablespoon/20ml)
mini muffin pans
1 yellow texas muffin
paper case
77 yellow mini muffin
paper cases
50cm (20-inch) square
cake board (page 334)

CAKE

1 x 470g (15-ounce) packet
butter cake mix
1 quantity butter cream
(page 329)
yellow food colouring

DECORATIONS

85g (3-ounce) packet
yellow jelly crystals
400g (12½-ounce) packet
Smarties
1 tablespoon orange sprinkles
5cm (2-inch) piece
black licorice strap
25 white Fizzers

1 Preheat oven to 180°C/350°F. Line texas muffin pan with texas paper case; line mini muffin pans with mini paper cases.

2 Make cake according to directions on packet. Drop ⅓ cup of mixture into texas paper case; bake about 25 minutes. Drop 2 level teaspoons of mixture into mini paper cases; bake about 15 minutes. Stand cakes in pans 5 minutes before turning, top-side up, onto wire rack to cool.

3 Divide butter cream into three small bowls; tint each with yellow colouring to give three shades (light, medium and dark yellow).

4 Spread light yellow butter cream over tops of 25 cakes; sprinkle lightly with the yellow jelly crystals; top each with a yellow Smartie.

5 Spread medium yellow butter cream over tops of 27 cakes; sprinkle lightly with orange sprinkles.

6 Spread dark yellow butter cream over the top of the large cake; position and secure on the board with a little butter cream. Use brown Smarties for eyes, and a small piece of licorice strap for the mouth.

7 Spread remaining dark yellow butter cream over tops of the remaining small cakes; top each with a Fizzer. Using picture as a guide, position and secure small cakes to the board with a little butter cream.

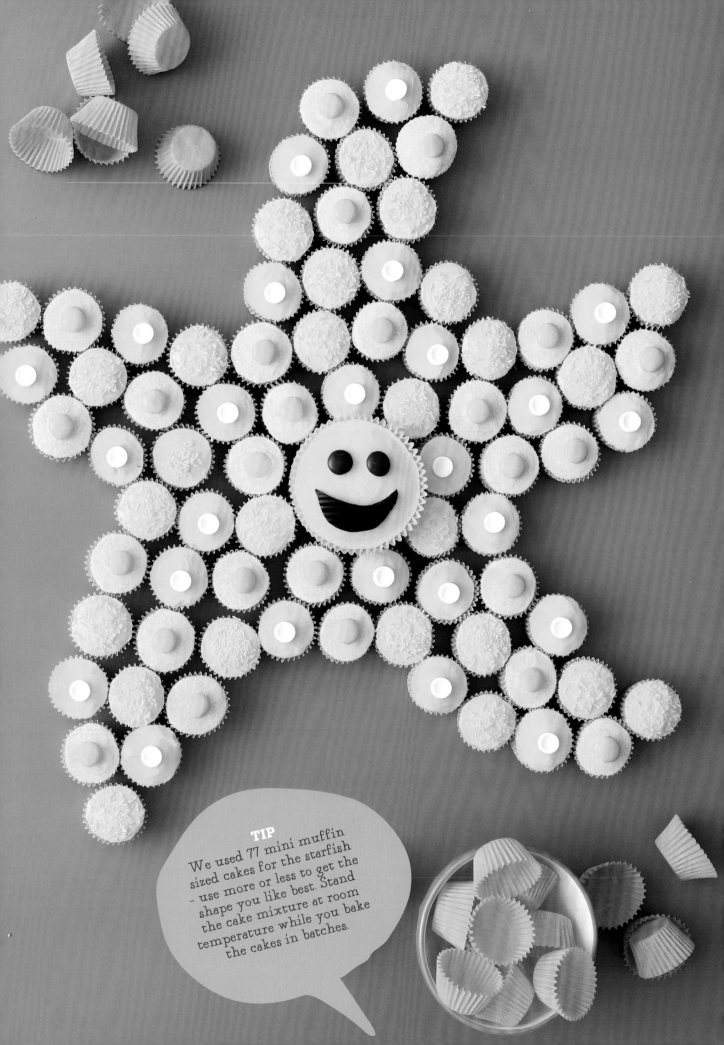

TIP

We used 77 mini muffin sized cakes for the starfish - use more or less to get the shape you like best. Stand the cake mixture at room temperature while you bake the cakes in batches.

Elsie the Fish

This is a good cake for a baby's first birthday...lovely pastel colours, and just a few small pieces that can easily be removed before serving.

1 Preheat oven to 150°C/300°F. Grease and lightly flour baking dish.

2 Make cakes according to directions on packets. Spread mixture into dish; bake about 50 minutes. Stand cake in dish 10 minutes before turning, top-side up, onto wire rack to cool.

3 Level cake top. Turn cake, top-side down. Using pattern from pattern sheet, cut out fish shape; secure cake on board with a little butter cream.

4 Tint butter cream aqua using green and blue colouring; spread butter cream all over cake.

5 Knead ready-made icing on surface dusted with a little sifted icing sugar until icing loses its stickiness. Tint half the icing orange; tint remaining icing purple. Roll both icings, separately, on surface dusted with a little icing sugar into a 3mm (⅛-inch) thickness.

6 Using pattern from pattern sheet, cut out shapes from icing. Using picture as a guide, position shapes on fish. Push chocolate Melts into side of cake. Use a slightly squashed marshmallow, cut-side up, and a Smartie for the eye, and two Smarties for lips. Use froot loops for bubbles, securing to board with a little butter cream.

EQUIPMENT

26cm x 35cm (10¼-inch x 14-inch) baking dish

30cm x 40cm (12-inch x 16-inch) rectangular cake board
(page 334)

CAKE

2 x 470g (15-ounce) packets butter cake mix

1½ quantities butter cream
(page 329)

green, blue, orange and purple food colourings

125g (4 ounces) ready-made white icing (page 329)

pure icing (confectioners') sugar, for dusting

DECORATIONS

8 white chocolate Melts

1 white marshmallow, halved

3 Smarties

5 Froot Loops

Ginger Neville

EQUIPMENT

deep 22cm (9-inch)
round cake pan
8cm x 25cm (3¼-inch x 10-inch)
bar cake pan
40cm (16-inch) round
cake board (page 334)
toothpick

CAKE

2 x 470g (15-ounce) packets
butter cake mix
2 quantities butter cream
(page 329)
orange food colouring

DECORATIONS

2 large white marshmallows
1 black licorice strap
1 giant blue Smartie, halved
8 x 15cm (6-inch) black
chenille sticks (pipe cleaners)
1 green bow

1 Preheat oven to 180°C/350°F. Grease cake pans; line bases and sides with baking paper, extending paper 5cm (2 inches) above sides.

2 Make cakes according to directions on packets. Divide mixture between pans so both mixtures are the same depth. Bake round cake about 50 minutes and bar cake about 25 minutes. Stand cakes in pans 5 minutes before turning, top-side up, onto wire rack to cool.

3 Using pattern from pattern sheet, and with cakes top-side up, cut ears and face from cakes.

4 Position cake pieces on cake board to form cat, as pictured; secure with a little butter cream.

5 Using toothpick, mark out centre stripe (triangle) between ears. Using a small serrated knife on the diagonal, trim about 1cm (½ inch) around edge of face.

6 Tint half the butter cream light orange. Tint half the remaining butter cream dark orange; leave remaining butter cream plain.

7 Spread light orange butter cream all over cake. Spread all but 1 tablespoon of the dark orange butter cream over ears and stripe.

8 Spread 1 tablespoon of the plain butter cream for tips of ears and inside stripe. Swirl remaining tablespoon of the dark orange butter cream and all of the remaining plain butter cream together for a marbled effect; dab over cat's cheeks to create fur.

9 Trim marshmallows into eye shapes; position on cake. Cut a small piece of licorice into thin strips to outline the eyes. Cut two small pieces of the licorice for eyelashes. Position Smarties in centre of eyes for irises.

10 Cut a small piece of the licorice for the nose and mouth. Position chenille sticks on cake for whiskers. Place bow under cat's chin.

Place the paper patterns on the cakes, then secure them with toothpicks to hold in place.

Using a small serrated knife on the diagonal, trim about 1cm off the edge of cat's face.

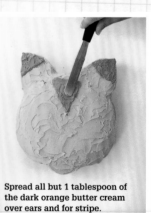

Spread all but 1 tablespoon of the dark orange butter cream over ears and for stripe.

Turn the cakes top-side down. Use a small sharp, finely serrated knife to trim the cakes into rounded shapes.

Pigs in Mud

The kids will be as happy as pigs in mud with this gorgeous cake and its muddy inhabitants having fun rolling around.

1 Preheat oven to 180°C/350°F. Grease four holes of the muffin pan. Grease cake pan; line base and side with baking paper, extending paper 5cm (2 inches) above side.

2 Make cakes according to directions on packets. Drop 2½ level tablespoons of the mixture into greased muffin pan holes; bake about 20 minutes. Spread remaining mixture into round pan; bake about 40 minutes. Stand cakes in pans 5 minutes before turning, top-side up, onto wire rack to cool.

3 Transfer a quarter of the butter cream to a small bowl; tint pink. Stir sifted cocoa powder into the remaining butter cream.

4 Level top of round cake; secure cake, cut-side down, on cake board with a little butter cream. Spread cake all over with chocolate butter cream. Press biscuits around side of cake.

5 Level tops of small cakes. Turn cakes cut-side down onto board. Trim cakes to give rounded shapes for pigs' bodies; spread pink butter cream all over cakes.

6 Cut and discard the small tip from each of the large marshmallows; secure marshmallows to bodies with a little butter cream to make pigs' heads. Secure brown mini M&M's to heads for eyes with a little butter cream.

7 Halve four Mallow Bakes. Pinch halves to make ears; position on heads with a little butter cream. Position one mallow bake below eyes for snout; secure with a little butter cream.

8 Curl each piece of the chenille stick; position for pigs' tails.

9 Using picture as a guide, position pigs in mud. Position remaining Mallow Bakes on one pig for legs. Trim tops from ice-cream cones, if required, then fill with sugar crystals; position on cake for troughs.

EQUIPMENT

12-hole (⅓-cup/80ml) standard muffin pan

deep 30cm (12-inch) round cake pan

40cm (16-inch) round cake board (page 334)

CAKE

2 x 470g (15-ounce) packets butter cake mix

2 quantities butter cream (page 329)

pink food colouring

½ cup (50g) cocoa powder

DECORATIONS

2 x 200g (12½-ounce) packets chocolate finger biscuits

4 large domed pink marshmallows

8 brown mini M&M's

12 pink Mallow Bakes

1 x 30cm (12-inch) pink chenille stick (pipe cleaner), quartered

2 square-based ice-cream cones

1 tablespoon yellow sugar crystals (page 338)

1 tablespoon blue sugar crystals (page 338)

Fishbowl Fun

Use the blue butter cream for water; make some ripples in the water, then spread the top of the cake with white butter cream.

Life really is like a fishbowl, especially with the wide-eyed stares this life-like cake will get from all the party guests.

EQUIPMENT

12-hole (1-tablespoon/20ml) mini muffin pan

deep 30cm (12-inch) round cake pan

35cm (14-inch) square cake board (page 334)

CAKE

2 x 470g (15-ounce) packets butter cake mix

1½ quantities butter cream (page 329)

blue, white, pink and yellow food colouring

DECORATIONS

pink sprinkles

yellow sprinkles

3 yellow triangular jubes, halved lengthways

2 red triangular jubes, halved lengthways

18 blue mini M&M's

150g (4½-ounce) packet rainbow choc-chips

10cm (4-inch) red sugar-coated bootlace

200g (6½-ounce) packet small jelly beans

4 mint leaves, cut into thin strips

1 x 15g (½-ounce) Flake bar, broken into pieces

1 Preheat oven to 180°C/350°F. Grease five holes of the mini muffin pan. Grease cake pan; line base and side with baking paper, extending paper 5cm (2 inches) above side.

2 Make cakes according to directions on packets. Drop 3 level teaspoons of the mixture into the greased mini muffin holes; bake about 15 minutes. Spread remaining mixture into round cake pan; bake about 40 minutes. Stand cakes in pans 5 minutes before turning, top-side up, onto wire rack to cool.

3 Level top of large cake; turn cake cut-side down. Using pattern from pattern sheet, cut fishbowl from cake; secure on cake board with a little butter cream.

4 Place two-thirds of the butter cream in a small bowl; tint blue. Place half the remaining butter cream in a small bowl; tint white. Place half the remaining butter cream in a small bowl; tint pink, tint remaining butter cream yellow.

5 Using picture as a guide, spread the blue butter cream over the top and sides of about three quarters of the cake to make water. Spread plain butter cream over the top of the cake.

6 Spread pink butter cream all over top and sides of two mini muffins; spread yellow butter cream all over top and sides of remaining cakes. Place pink and yellow sprinkles in separate small shallow bowls. Roll sides of pink muffins in pink sprinkles, roll sides of yellow muffins in yellow sprinkles; position on fishbowl. Trim jubes to resemble fins and tails; using matching colours, position jubes on cakes.

7 Using picture as a guide, use mini M&M's for bubbles. Using matching colours, decorate fish with rainbow choc-chips; use blue rainbow choc-chips for eyes. Use strips of red bootlace for mouths.

8 Decorate fish bowl with jelly beans, strips of mint leaves and pieces of Flake.

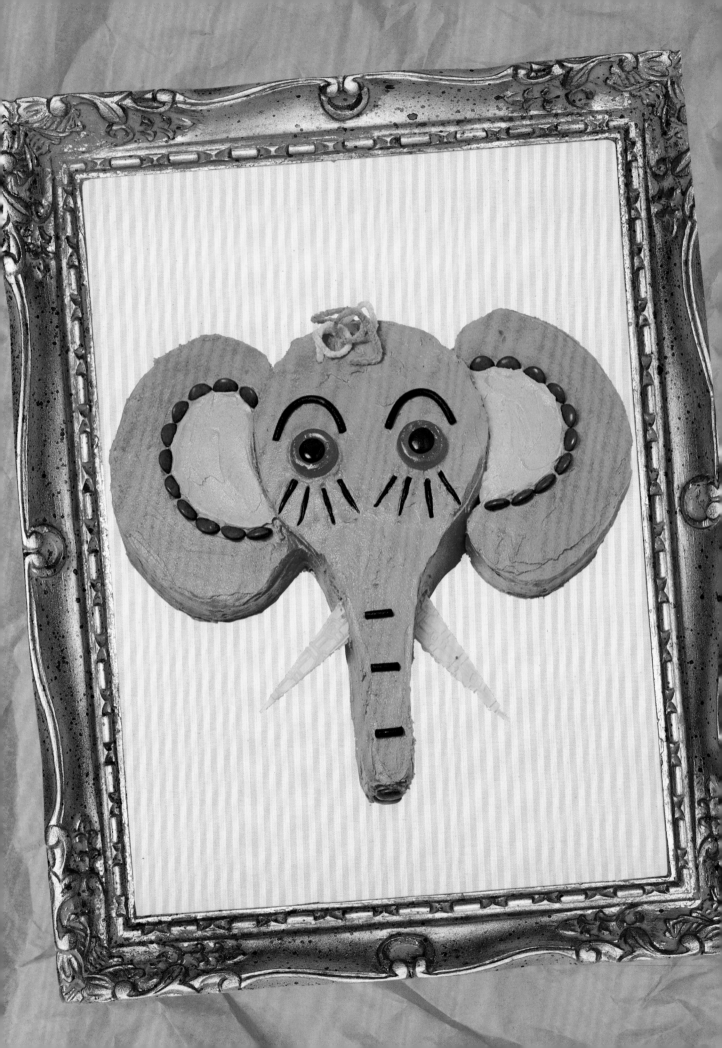

Cut head and trunk from the square cake.

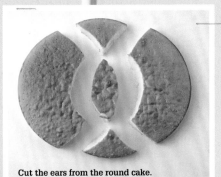

Cut the ears from the round cake.

Jungle Elephant

Elephants are the largest living land mammals and, not surprisingly, one of the noisiest, although your young guests may challenge that!

EQUIPMENT

deep 22cm (9-inch)
square cake pan
two deep 20cm (8-inch)
round cake pans
45cm x 50cm (18-inch x 20-inch)
rectangular cake board
(page 334)

CAKE

2 x 470g (15-ounce) packets
butter cake mix
1 quantity butter cream
(page 329)

pink food colouring

DECORATIONS

22 blue Smarties
2 red Life Savers
2 purple Skittles
1 black licorice strap
1 ice-cream wafer
2 x 30cm (12-inch) chenille
sticks (pipe cleaners)

1 Preheat oven to 180°C/350°F. Grease cake pans; line bases and sides with baking paper, extending paper 5cm (2 inches) above sides.
2 Make cakes according to directions on packets. Pour half the mixture into square pan; divide remaining mixture evenly into round pans. Bake the square cake about 35 minutes and the round cakes about 25 minutes. Stand cakes in pans 5 minutes before turning, top-side up, onto wire rack to cool. (Only one round cake is required for the elephant; the other can be frozen for later use.)
3 Level tops of cakes; turn cakes cut-side down. Using pattern from pattern sheet, cut elephant's face and trunk from square cake. Cut ears from round cake, as pictured. Secure cake pieces, cut-side down, on cake board to form elephant; secure with a little butter cream. Discard any leftover cake pieces.
4 Tint butter cream pink; reserve ½ cup for inner ears. Tint remaining butter cream dark pink. Spread dark pink butter cream over elephant's head, trunk and outer ears; spread pale pink butter cream inside ears.
5 Position 2 blue Smarties on end of trunk for nostrils; use remaining blue Smarties to outline ears. Position Life Savers and purple Skittles for eyes. Cut thin strips of licorice strip; position on cake for eyebrows, eyelashes and on trunk. Cut ice-cream wafer into long thin triangles, as pictured, to make tusks; make two slits in trunk, one on either side, insert tusks. Curl chenille sticks and position for hair.

Taffy Turtle

EQUIPMENT

6-hole (¾-cup/180ml) texas
muffin pan

8-hole (½-cup/125ml)
mini loaf pan

2.25-litre (9-cup)
pudding steamer

45cm (18-inch) square
cake board (page 334)

CAKE

2 x 470g (15-ounce) packets
butter cake mix

3 quantities butter cream
(page 329)

green and orange food
colouring

DECORATIONS

6 blue M&M's
2 round peppermints
4cm (1½-inch) strip red
licorice bootlace
3 yellow jelly fruit rings,
halved
22 orange fruit rings
33 green M&M's
28 blue mini M&M's

1 Preheat oven to 170°C/340°F. Grease one hole of the texas muffin pan; grease five holes of the mini loaf pan. Grease pudding steamer.

2 Make cakes according to directions on packets. Drop ⅓ cup of the mixture into the greased texas muffin pan hole; drop ⅓ cup of the mixture into the greased loaf pan holes. Bake cakes about 25 minutes. Stand cakes in pans 5 minutes before turning, top-side up, onto wire rack to cool.

3 Spread remaining mixture into pudding steamer; bake about 1 hour. Stand cake in pan 5 minutes before turning onto wire rack to cool.

4 Turn pudding cake large-side up; level top, turn cut-side down. Using pattern from pattern sheet, cut the hexagon shape from the centre of the pudding cake. Using picture as a guide, cut through the cake from each point of the hexagon.

5 Shape muffin into a rounded shape for head. Using paper pattern, cut two small and two large flippers from four of the loaf cakes. Shape tail from remaining loaf cake.

6 Tint three-quarters of the butter cream green; tint remaining butter cream orange. Spread green butter cream over the tops and sides of the body pieces. Using picture as a guide, assemble the cake, one piece at a time, from the hexagon centre outwards; secure pieces to cake board with a little butter cream as you go. Spread orange butter cream over top and sides of turtle's head, tail and flippers; secure to cake board, as pictured.

7 Secure a blue M&M onto each peppermint with a little butter cream; position on head for eyes. Shape and position red bootlace for turtle's mouth. Using picture as a guide, use decorations for the turtle's shell, flippers and tail.

Using paper pattern and a small sharp, finely serrated knife, cut a hexagonal shape from the centre of the pudding-shaped cake. Cut out the rest of the body shape by cutting pieces from each point of the hexagon outwards.

Using paper pattern for turtle's flippers, attach the pattern to one of the loaf cakes. Using a small sharp knife, cut out the flipper shape. Repeat with remaining loaf cakes to make four flippers.

Use a small sharp knife to trim the cake to a more rounded shape for the turtle's head.

TIP
There's plenty of cake for all the guests in this jigsaw-patterned turtle. We made the watery waves from pieces of felt, although paper would do just as well.

Sandcastle

Looks impressively like a sandcastle, thanks to the toasted desiccated coconut.

1 Preheat oven to 170°C/340°F. Grease square cake pan; line base and sides with baking paper, extending paper 5cm (2 inches) above sides. Grease two holes of the loaf pan and one hole of the texas muffin pan. Grease four holes of the standard muffin pan and nine holes of the mini muffin pan.

2 Make cakes according to directions on packets. Drop ¼ cup of the mixture into the greased holes of the loaf pan; drop ⅓ cup of the mixture into the greased hole of the texas muffin pan. Bake cakes about 25 minutes. Stand cakes in pans 5 minutes before turning, top-side up, onto wire rack to cool.

3 Drop 2½ level tablespoons of the mixture into the greased holes of the standard muffin pan. Bake cakes about 20 minutes. Drop 2 level teaspoons of the mixture into the greased holes of the mini muffin pan. Bake cakes about 15 minutes. Stand cakes in pans 5 minutes before turning, top-side up, onto wire rack to cool.

4 Spread remaining mixture into square pan. Bake about 50 minutes. Stand cake in pan 5 minutes before turning, top-side up, onto wire rack to cool.

5 Level all cake tops. Secure square cake, cut-side down, on cake board with a little butter cream. Tint butter cream pale yellow; spread over top and sides of the large cake. Sprinkle all over with the coconut, pressing into sides of cake.

6 Spread small cakes, one at a time, all over with butter cream then roll to cover in the coconut.

7 Assemble sandcastle by positioning four standard muffins in centre of the square cake; top with loaf cakes then texas muffin.

8 Position mini muffins on top of the castle and around the edge of the square cake to make turrets.

9 Using picture as a guide, position the decorations on the castle, securing with a little butter cream when necessary.

EQUIPMENT

deep 20cm (8-inch) square cake pan

8-hole (½-cup/125ml) mini loaf pan

6-hole (¾-cup/180ml) texas muffin pan

12-hole (⅓-cup/80ml) standard muffin pan

12-hole (1-tablespoon/20ml) mini muffin pan

30cm (12-inch) square cake board (page 334)

CAKE

2 x 470g (15-ounce) packets butter cake mix

1½ quantities butter cream (page 329)

yellow food colouring

2 cups (160g) desiccated coconut, toasted (see tips)

DECORATIONS

4 round jubes

4 oval jubes

17 small purple jelly beans, halved crossways

2 small orange jelly beans, halved crossways

2 round green lollipops

1 sour worm

2 jelly fruit rings

8 chocolate seahorses or shells (see tips)

1 foil-wrapped chocolate fish

paper flags

Wrap two 20cm ribbons around each skewer, securing with tape.

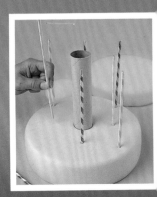

Score baking paper and icing with a toothpick to make eight markings.

Position one ribbon-wrapped skewer into each toothpick marking.

Carefully centre the shallow cake on skewers and cardboard cylinder.

Merry-go-Round

1 Preheat oven to 180°C/350°F. Grease one hole of muffin pan. Grease cake pans; line bases and sides with baking paper, extending paper 5cm (2 inches) above sides.

2 Make cakes according to directions on packets. Pour one-third of the mixture into one round pan, ½-cup mixture into greased muffin hole and remaining mixture into the other round pan. Bake muffin about 25 minutes, shallow cake about 30 minutes and deep cake about 50 minutes. Stand cakes in pans 5 minutes before turning, top-side up, onto wire rack to cool.

3 Level top of deep cake. Trim cardboard cylinder to 20cm (8 inches). Using sticky tape, secure two 20cm ribbons to one end of a skewer; wrap ribbon around skewer, as pictured. Secure other end with tape. Repeat with remaining 20cm ribbons and skewers. Tie 18cm ribbons around necks of horses.

4 Brush cakes all over with jam. Knead ready-made icing on surface dusted with a little sifted icing sugar until icing loses its stickiness; tint pink. Roll half the icing on surface dusted with sifted icing sugar until large enough to cover deep cake. Enclose remaining icing in plastic wrap; reserve.

5 Using rolling pin, lift icing over cake; smooth with hands, trim around base of cake. Position cake on cake board. Roll three-quarters of the reserved icing until large enough to cover shallow cake. Using rolling pin, lift icing over cake; trim around base. Position shallow cake on cardboard circle. Roll remaining icing until large enough to cover muffin. Using rolling pin, lift icing over muffin; trim around base of muffin.

6 Cut 22cm (9-inch) circle from baking paper; fold baking paper into eight equal wedges. Position paper on deep cake; using toothpick, score paper through to icing on wedge-shaped tracings at 1.5cm (¾-inch) and 5cm (2-inch) points from outside edge of cake, as pictured, to make eight markings. Discard paper.

7 Push cardboard cylinder through centre of deep cake to cake board. Insert one ribbon-wrapped skewer into each toothpick marking, making sure the skewers and cardboard cylinder are of the same height.

8 Stir egg white and sifted pure icing sugar together in small bowl until smooth. Brush cardboard cylinder all over with egg-white mixture; position 14 Fruit Sticks upright against cylinder. Decorate top of cylinder with fizzers.

9 Centre muffin on top of shallow cake; carefully centre shallow cake on top of skewers and cylinder. Using glue gun, secure one horse to each skewer; hold in place until secured.

10 Using egg-white mixture, decorate carousel with remaining Fruit Sticks and cachous. Use Fruit Stick trimmings to make stars; secure to cake using egg-white mixture.

EQUIPMENT

6-hole texas (¾-cup/180ml) muffin pan

two deep 22cm (9-inch) round cake pans

35cm (14-inch) round cake board (page 334)

glue gun

CAKE

3 x 470g (15-ounce) packets butter cake mix

¼ cup (80g) apricot jam, warmed, sieved

DECORATIONS

cardboard cylinder

sticky tape

16 x 20cm (8-inch) (6mm/¼ inch wide) assorted coloured ribbons

8 x 25cm (10-inch) long thick bamboo skewers, trimmed to 20cm (8 inches)

8 x 18cm (7¼-inch) (6mm/¼ inch wide) assorted coloured ribbons

8 small unpainted craftwood horses (see tip)

1.5kg (3 pounds) ready-made white icing (page 329)

pure icing (confectioners') sugar, for dusting

pink food colouring

22cm (9-inch) circle thick cardboard

1 egg white

1½ cups (240g) pure icing (confectioners') sugar

2 x 250g (8-ounce) packets Fruit Sticks

2 x 15g (½-ounce) packets Fizzers

2 x 15g (½-ounce) packets coloured cachous

Board Shorts

The grommets have gone a-surfing — even fussy teenage boys and girls will want to hang-10 with this cool pair of board shorts.

EQUIPMENT

26cm x 35cm (10¼-inch x 14-inch) baking dish
30cm x 40cm (12-inch x 16-inch) rectangular cake board (page 334)
bamboo skewer

CAKE

2 x 470g (15-ounce) packets butter cake mix
2 quantities butter cream (page 329)
turquoise and blue food colouring

DECORATIONS

90g (3 ounces) ready-made white icing (page 329)
pure icing (confectioners') sugar, for dusting
45cm (18-inch) length polyester cord
5 small yellow jelly beans, halved
33 small white jelly beans

1 Preheat oven to 150°C/300°F. Grease and flour baking dish.
2 Make cakes according to directions on packets. Spread mixture into dish; bake about 50 minutes. Stand cake in dish 10 minutes before turning, top-side up, onto wire rack to cool.
3 Level cake top; turn cake cut-side down. Using pattern from pattern sheet, cut out shorts. Secure cake, cut-side down, on cake board with a little butter cream. Tint butter cream turquoise using both food colourings; spread all over cake.
4 Knead ready-made icing on surface dusted with a little sifted icing sugar until icing loses its stickiness. Roll icing on surface dusted with sifted icing sugar into a 3mm (⅛-inch) thickness. Using pattern from pattern sheet, cut waistband and two pockets from icing. Use skewer to make two holes in centre of waistband; thread cord through holes and tie ends in a bow. Position waistband and pockets on shorts.
5 Using picture as a guide, make flowers on shorts using jelly beans.

Use a skewer to make holes for cord in waistband. Thread cord through holes.

TIP
Board shorts can be
completed a day before
the party.

TIPS
Cake can be made two days
ahead and kept refrigerated.
A fine serrated knife is best for
cutting this cake. If you prefer,
use glacé icing to decorate the cake,
you'll need 3 cups (480g) pure icing
(confectioners') sugar mixed
with about 2 tablespoons water;
tint pink with food colouring.

Coco Crackle Pop Cake

This delicious variation on a childhood favourite is sure to delight young and old alike.

EQUIPMENT

deep 20cm (8-inch) round cake pan

25cm (10-inch) round cake board (page 334) or cake stand

CAKE

5 x 53g (1½ ounces) Mars Bars, sliced thinly

250g (8 ounces) unsalted butter, chopped coarsely

⅔ cup (160ml) light corn syrup

10 cups (450g) Coco Pops

250g (8 ounces) ready-made white icing (page 329)

pure icing (confectioners') sugar, for dusting

pink food colouring

2 tablespoons apricot jam, warmed, strained

DECORATIONS

35 pink Mallow Bakes

35 white Mallow Bakes

candles

1 Grease cake pan; line base and side with baking paper, extending paper 5cm (2 inches) above side.

2 Stir Mars Bars, butter and syrup in medium heatproof bowl over medium saucepan of simmering water until smooth.

3 Place Coco Pops in large bowl; gradually stir in Mars Bar mixture. Spoon mixture into pan, in about four batches, pressing each batch down firmly. Refrigerate about 3 hours or until set.

4 Knead ready-made icing on surface dusted with a little sifted icing sugar until icing loses its stickiness. Tint icing pink. Secure cake on cake board with a little of the icing; brush top of cake with jam.

5 Roll icing on surface dusted with a little sifted icing sugar until large enough to cover top of cake generously. Lightly dust hands with icing sugar and, using picture as a guide, gently pull icing into shape over cake.

6 Position Mallow Bakes around base of cake. Position candles on cake.

Balls

Choose your game...sport-crazy kids will love these balls. The quantities given are enough to make six of any one type of ball, but there is enough cake mixture to make another three balls.

EQUIPMENT

6-hole (¾-cup/180ml) texas muffin pan
6 texas muffin paper cases (brown)

CAKE

1 x 470g (15-ounce) packet butter cake mix
½ quantity butter cream (page 329)
white food colouring

SOCCER BALL

white food colouring
1 black licorice strap

BASKETBALL

orange food colouring
black decorating gel

BASEBALL

white food colouring
red decorating gel

TENNIS BALL

yellow food colouring
85g (3-ounce) packet yellow jelly crystals
white decorating gel

SNOOKER BALL

green food colouring
50g (1½ ounces) ready-made white icing (page 329)
4.5cm (1¾-inch) round cutter
2 tablespoons icing (confectioners') sugar
black decorating gel

CRICKET BALL

red food colouring
white decorating gel

1 Preheat oven to 180°C/350°F. Line texas muffin pan with paper cases.
2 Make cake according to directions on packet. Drop $\frac{1}{3}$ cup of the mixture into each paper case; bake about 25 minutes. Stand cakes in pan 5 minutes before turning, top-side up, onto wire rack to cool.

Soccer ball Tint butter cream white; spread over cake tops. Using pattern from pattern sheet, cut 6 five-sided shapes and 30 small triangles from licorice. Using picture as a guide, position flat licorice pieces on cakes. Cut licorice into small strips, long enough to join flat licorice pieces.

Basketball Tint butter cream orange; spread over cake tops. Using picture as a guide, use black decorating gel to mark lines on cakes.

Baseball Tint butter cream white; spread over cake tops. Using picture as a guide, use red decorating gel to make dotted lines on cakes.

Tennis ball Tint butter cream yellow; spread over cake tops, sprinkle with jelly crystals. Using picture as a guide, use white decorating gel to mark lines on cakes.

Snooker ball Tint butter cream green; spread over cake tops. Knead ready-made icing on surface dusted with a little sifted icing sugar until icing loses its stickiness. Roll icing on surface dusted with sifted icing sugar into a 3mm ($\frac{1}{8}$-inch) thickness; using cutter, cut into six 4.5cm ($1\frac{3}{4}$-inch) rounds; position on cakes. Use black decorating gel to write numbers on the icing.

Cricket ball Tint butter cream red; spread over cake tops. Using picture as a guide, use white decorating gel to make a series of six broken lines down the centre of the cakes.

TIP
If making more than one type of ball, divide the butter cream into small bowls, so you can tint it the correct colour.

BIRTHDAY

HAPPY

To make umpire's chair, insert licorice strap into toothpicks.

Use melted chocolate to outline tennis racquets and strings.

Wrap strips of fruit roll-ups around racquet handles.

Tennis Court

TIP
Remove toothpicks from cake before cutting and serving.

1 Preheat oven to 180°C/350°F. Grease baking dish; line base and sides with baking paper, extending paper 5cm (2 inches) above sides.

2 Make cakes according to directions on packets. Spread mixture into dish; bake about 1 hour. Stand cake in dish 5 minutes before turning, top-side up, onto wire rack to cool.

3 Level cake top; secure cake, cut-side down, on cake board with a little butter cream. Tint butter cream brown; spread all over cake.

4 Knead ready-made icing on surface dusted with a little sifted icing sugar until icing loses its stickiness; tint blue. Roll icing on surface dusted with sifted icing sugar until large enough to cut out a 15cm x 32.5cm (6-inch x 13-inch) rectangle; carefully centre rectangle on cake.

5 Cut ribbon into 4 x 32.5cm (13-inch), 2 x 11.6cm (4¾-inch), 2 x 15cm (6-inch) and 1 x 17.4 cm (7-inch) lengths to make lines on tennis court. Brush backs of ribbons lightly with egg white; press onto court, as pictured. Secure net onto cake with toothpicks.

6 Melt dark chocolate and white chocolate, separately (page 339); cool slightly. Cut 4 x 10cm (4-inch) pieces from licorice strap. Pipe 'Happy Birthday' on two of the straps using white chocolate. Join remaining pieces to back of signs, along top edges, with dark chocolate. Outline with red licorice strips. Position on cake.

7 Draw four tennis racquets on baking paper; pipe dark chocolate for racquet frame. Pipe racquet strings with white chocolate. When set, peel off paper and wrap narrow strips of fruit Roll-Ups around racquet handles. Position on cake with small mints for balls.

8 To make umpire's chair, cut two 2cm (¾-inch) pieces of black licorice strap. Push two toothpicks through back of licorice seat, and attach the other piece of licorice for chair back, as pictured. Push another two toothpicks for front legs. Position chair on cake.

9 Place Mint Slice in one corner; attach two mint leaves with a little melted dark chocolate. Skewer remaining mint leaves with toothpicks; position along the back of the cake.

EQUIPMENT

deep 26cm x 36cm (10½-inch x 14½-inch) baking dish

35cm x 45cm (14-inch x 18-inch) rectangular cake board (page 334)

two small paper piping bags (page 338)

CAKE

3 x 470g (15-ounce) packets butter cake mix

1 quantity butter cream (page 329)

brown and blue food colouring

DECORATIONS

500g (1 pound) ready-made white icing (page 329)

pure icing (confectioners') sugar, for dusting

2m (2 yards) x 2mm (⅛-inch) wide white ribbon

1 egg white, beaten lightly

20cm (8 inches) netting

12 double-pointed toothpicks

½ cup (75g) white chocolate Melts

¼ cup (35g) dark chocolate Melts

3 black licorice straps

1 red licorice strap, cut into thin strips

1 fruit Roll-Up

8 small mints

1 Mint Slice biscuit

8 mint leaves

Smiley clock

Now is not the right occasion to teach your little ones how to tell the time: they'll be far too impatient to start eating.

EQUIPMENT

deep 26cm (10½-inch) round cake pan
35cm (14-inch) round cake board (page 334)
number chocolate mould
small paper piping bag (page 338)

CAKE

2 x 470g (15-ounce) packets butter cake mix
2 quantities butter cream (page 329)
yellow food colouring

DECORATIONS

250g (8 ounces) white chocolate Melts
purple food colouring
1 white marshmallow
2 google eyes
1 black licorice strap, cut into thin strips
2m (2 yards) x 6mm (¾-inch) wide purple ribbon
120 Smarties

1 Preheat oven to 180°C/350°F. Grease cake pan; line base and side with baking paper, extending paper 5cm (2 inches) above side.

2 Make cakes according to directions on packets. Spread mixture into pan; bake about 1 hour. Stand cake in pan 5 minutes before turning, top-side up, onto wire rack to cool.

3 Level cake top; secure cake, cut-side down, on cake board with a little butter cream.

4 Melt chocolate (page 339); tint chocolate purple. Pour chocolate into number mould. Tap moulds gently on bench to remove air bubbles; using palette knife, level chocolate across each number. Refrigerate mould about 10 minutes or until chocolate sets. To release numbers from mould, place sheet of baking paper slightly larger than mould on tray; holding mould upside down, tap one edge of the mould gently onto baking paper. Repeat process until numbers 1 to 12 have been made.

5 Spread remaining chocolate onto sheet of baking paper; allow to set. Cut two strips of chocolate, 2cm x 5.5cm (¾-inch x 2¼-inch). Trim edges of one end to a point to form clock hands.

6 Tint butter cream yellow, reserve 1 tablespoon of the butter cream; spread remaining butter cream all over cake.

7 Arrange chocolate numbers on cake. Split marshmallow in half horizontally; position top half in centre of cake for nose. Spoon reserved butter cream into piping bag; pipe around marshmallow.

8 Position chocolate hands on cake. Place eyes in position then cut and arrange licorice on cake for smile and eyelashes.

9 Secure ribbon around centre of cake; position Smarties above and below ribbon.

TIP
Make cupcakes from any leftover cake mixture.

Sam the Tool Man

Build it and they will come...and eat it with gusto. The toy tools are readily available from most toy stores.

1 Preheat oven to 180°C/350°F; grease pudding steamer.

2 Make cakes according to directions on packets. Pour mixture into steamer; bake about 50 minutes. Stand cake in steamer 5 minutes before turning onto wire rack to cool.

3 Level bottom of cake; secure cake, cut-side down, on cake board with a little butter cream.

4 Knead ready-made icing on surface dusted with a little sifted icing sugar until icing loses its stickiness. Roll icing on surface dusted with sifted icing sugar into a 3mm (⅛-inch) thickness. Cut hat peak from icing; mould around cake.

5 Tint butter cream blue; spread all over cake and hat peak.

6 Tint remaining ready-made icing yellow; roll three-quarters of the icing into a thick rope shape. Position around edge of hat.

7 Roll remaining icing on surface dusted with sifted icing sugar into a 3mm (⅛-inch) thickness; cut out name plaque. Position name and desired candy cake decorations on plaque using a little water; position plaque on hat.

8 Place assorted toy tools around cake.

EQUIPMENT

1.75-litre (7-cup) pudding steamer

45cm (18-inch) square cake board (page 334)

CAKE

2 x 470g (15-ounce) packets butter cake mix

1 quantity butter cream (page 329)

blue and yellow food colouring

DECORATIONS

200g (6½ ounces) ready-made white icing (page 329)

pure icing (confectioners') sugar, for dusting

candy cake decorations

assorted toy tools

Cut the hat's peak from the ready-made icing, then mould it around the front edge of the cake.

Tint butter cream blue, then spread it over the cake and hat peak with a palette knife.

Roll three-quarters of the yellow ready-made icing into a thick rope. Position rope around edge of hat.

Soccer Ball

Get the kids ready for the next world cup qualifier. This cake will surely encourage them to go outside and practise their ball skills.

1 Preheat oven to 150°C/300°F. Grease round pan; line base and side with baking paper, extending paper 5cm (2 inches) above side. Butter and flour pudding steamers.

2 Make 2 packets of cake mix according to directions on packets. Spread mixture into round pan; bake about 1¼ hours. Stand cake in pan 10 minutes before turning, top-side up, onto wire rack to cool.

3 Make remaining cakes according to directions on packets. Pour mixture evenly into pudding steamers; bake about 40 minutes. Stand cakes in pans 5 minutes before turning onto wire rack to cool.

4 Level round cake top; secure cake, cut-side down, on cake board with a little butter cream. Reserve 1 cup butter cream. Tint remaining butter cream green; spread all over round cake.

5 Place coconut and a few drops of green colouring in a plastic bag; rub until coconut is evenly coloured. Sprinkle coconut over cake.

6 Trim tops from pudding cakes to make flat. Using small serrated knife, trim cakes so they make a 14cm (4¾-inch) diameter ball when joined together; secure cakes together with a little butter cream. Spread butter cream all over ball.

7 Knead ready-made icing on surface dusted with a little sifted icing sugar until icing loses its stickiness. Roll two-thirds of the icing on surface dusted with sifted icing sugar into a 3mm (⅛-inch) thickness. Using hexagon pattern from pattern sheet, cut out 22 shapes. Tint remaining ready-made icing black; roll into a 3mm (⅛-inch) thickness on surface dusted with sifted icing sugar. Using pentagon pattern from pattern sheet, cut out 12 shapes. Using picture as a guide, secure shapes onto ball with a little water. Place ball on top of cake.

EQUIPMENT

deep 25cm (10-inch) round cake pan

two 2-litre (8-cup) pudding steamers

35cm (14-inch) round cake board (page 334)

CAKE

4 x 470g (15-ounce) packets butter cake mix
(see 'mixing the cakes' page 345)

2 quantities butter cream
(page 329)

green and black food colouring

DECORATIONS

1½ cups (120g) desiccated coconut

500g (1 pound) ready-made white icing (page 329)

pure icing (confectioners') sugar, for dusting

Trim the pudding cakes into round shapes to make soccer ball.

Cut out the hexagons and pentagons from the ready-made icing.

TIPS
You can make it easier on yourself by using a Styrofoam ball instead of a cake for the shape of the soccer ball. Position the soccer ball on the cake about an hour before the party. The ball and "field" cakes can be made two days ahead.

Using a small serrated knife, trim the tops of the cakes to make them more rounded.

When icing is large enough to cover the cake, carefully lift icing over cake using a rolling pin.

Up, up & Away

Balloons are essential at any party...the difference
here is that the guests can eat them as well!

EQUIPMENT

three deep 20cm (8-inch)
round cake pans
55cm (22-inch) round
cake board (page 334)

CAKE

3 x 470g (15-ounce) packets
butter cake mix
½ cup (160g) apricot jam,
warmed, strained

DECORATIONS

2.5kg (5-pound) ready-made
white icing (page 329)
pure icing (confectioners')
sugar, for dusting
pink, green and blue
food colouring
toothpicks
1m (1 yard) x 2cm (¾-inch)
wide pink ribbon
1m (1 yard) x 2cm (¾-inch)
wide blue ribbon
1m (1 yard) x 2cm (¾-inch)
wide green ribbon

1 Preheat oven to 180°C/350°F. Grease cake pans; line bases and sides with baking paper, extending paper 5cm (2 inches) above sides.
2 Make cakes according to directions on packets. Divide mixture evenly into pans; bake about 40 minutes. Stand cakes in pans 5 minutes before turning, top-side up, onto wire rack to cool.
3 Using small serrated knife, trim cake tops to make more rounded, as pictured. Brush warm jam all over cakes.
4 Knead ready-made icing on surface dusted with a little sifted icing sugar until icing loses its stickiness; tint one-third of the icing pink, one-third blue and the remaining third green. Wrap icing, separately, in plastic wrap.
5 Using pink icing, reserve a walnut-sized amount for balloon end; enclose in plastic wrap. Roll remaining pink icing on surface dusted with sifted icing sugar into circle large enough to cover one cake. Using rolling pin, lift icing over one cake; neatly trim excess icing from base of cake. Position cake on cake board. Using hands dusted with a little icing sugar, gently mould icing into balloon shape.
6 On surface dusted with a little icing sugar, make balloon end from reserved pink icing. Using toothpick or skewer, make creases in balloon end, as pictured. Gently push balloon end into balloon; attach to cake with a tiny dab of water. Carefully wrap ribbon around balloon end.
7 Repeat with remaining cakes, icing and ribbons.

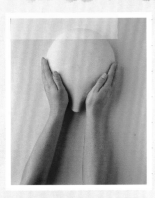

Dust your hands with icing sugar
then gently mould the icing into a
balloon shape.

On a surface dusted with icing
sugar, mould the balloon end from
the reserved icing.

Using a toothpick or skewer,
make small creases in the
underside of the balloon end.

Picture Perfect

This cake leaves no doubt who the star of the show is at this party. Use any lollies your child likes to decorate the cake.

EQUIPMENT

deep 22cm (9-inch)
square cake pan

35cm (14-inch) square
cake board (page 334)

CAKE

2 x 470g (15-ounce) packets
butter cake mix

2 quantities butter cream
(page 329)

DECORATIONS

11cm (4½-inch) square
photograph, laminated

1kg (2 pounds) mixed lollies

1 Preheat oven to 180°C/350°F. Grease cake pan; line base and sides with baking paper, extending paper 5cm (2 inches) above sides.
2 Make cakes according to directions on packets. Spread mixture into pan; bake about 1 hour. Stand cake in pan 5 minutes before turning, top-side up, onto wire rack to cool.
3 Level cake top; secure cake, cut-side down, on cake board with a little butter cream. Spread butter cream all over cake.
4 Centre photograph on cake.
5 Scatter mixed lollies all over cake; press lollies gently into butter cream to secure.

Carefully position photograph in centre of cake.

TIPS
You can use any photographic print you like, but remember to laminate it if you want it to remain after the cake is gone. Use a selection of your favourite lollies to decorate this cake.

TIP
Violet Crumbles can
be substituted with
Crunchie bars or any
other chocolate-coated
honeycomb.

ROAD WORKS
AHEAD

Construction Site

This cake is completely fail-safe...it doesn't matter a bit how it turns out underneath: the covering is all that counts.

1 Preheat oven to 180°C/350°F. Grease cake pan; line base and side with baking paper, extending paper 5cm (2 inches) above sides.

2 Make cakes according to directions on packets. Spread mixture into pan; bake about 1 hour. Stand cake in pan 5 minutes before turning, top-side up, onto wire rack to cool.

3 Using serrated knife, shape cake to make a pit and hill. Secure cake, top-side up, on cake board with a little butter cream. Tint butter cream yellow; spread all over cake.

4 Sprinkle cake with Violet Crumble. Place chocolate fruit and nuts around base of cake. Position toys on cake.

EQUIPMENT

deep 22cm (9-inch) round cake pan

30cm (12-inch) round cake board (page 334)

CAKE

2 x 470g (15-ounce) packets butter cake mix

2 quantities butter cream (page 329)

yellow food colouring

DECORATIONS

2 x 50g (1½-ounce) Violet Crumble bars, crushed

300g (9½-ounce) packet chocolate-covered fruit and nuts

1 road works sign

1 toy dump truck

2 toy construction workers

2 toy witches' hats

Turn cake cut-side down. Using the paper pattern, cut sheriff's badge from cake.

Using a piping bag, pipe the red butter cream around edges of sheriff's badge.

Pipe the birthday child's name onto sheriff's badge with the remaining red butter cream.

Howdy Sheriff

Howdy, Ma'am — this is just the cake for your favourite law-enforcement officer at a cowboy, or girl, themed party.

EQUIPMENT

deep 30cm (12-inch) square cake pan
35cm (14-inch) square cake board (page 334)
piping bag fitted with 4mm (¼-inch) plain tube

CAKE

3 x 470g (15-ounce) packets butter cake mix
2 quantities butter cream (page 329)
yellow and red food colouring

DECORATIONS

6 chocolate freckles
42 silver cachous

1 Preheat oven to 180°C/350°F. Grease cake pan; line base and sides with baking paper, extending paper 5cm (2 inches) above sides.

2 Make cakes according to directions on packets. Divide mixture evenly into pans; bake about 1¼ hours. Stand cake in pan 5 minutes before turning, top-side up, onto wire rack to cool.

3 Level cake top; turn cake cut-side down. Using pattern from pattern sheet, cut badge from cake. Secure cake, cut-side down, on cake board with a little butter cream.

4 Tint two-thirds of the butter cream yellow; spread all over cake.

5 Tint remaining butter cream red. Spoon into piping bag; pipe half the red butter cream around edges of badge.

6 Before butter cream dries, position freckles on badge. Using tweezers, decorate cake with cachous.

7 Pipe name onto cake with remaining red butter cream.

Make a hole in the side of a Twix Bar with a toothpick. Push one end of the mint leaf onto the toothpick, then stick into the hole in the Twix Bar. Push Twix into the top of the apple.

Apple Cake

No worms are hidden inside this delicious apple.

EQUIPMENT

deep 25cm (10-inch) round cake pan

35cm (14-inch) round cake board (page 334)

1 toothpick

CAKE

5 x 440g (14-ounce) packets butter cake mix
(see 'mixing the cakes' page 345)

1½ quantities butter cream
(page 329)

DECORATIONS

2 packets strawberry sour straps

2 rolls yellow fruit and cola wheels

6 coloured sugar-coated almonds

1 Twix Bar

1 mint leaf

1 Preheat oven to 170°C/340°F. Grease pan; line base and sides with baking paper, extending paper 5cm (2 inches) above sides.

2 Make cakes according to directions on packets. Spread mixture into pan; bake about 1½ hours. Stand cake in pan 10 minutes before turning, top-side up, onto wire rack to cool.

3 Level cake top; turn cake cut-side down. Using pattern from pattern sheet, cut out apple; secure cake, cut-side down, to cake board with a little butter cream. Spread butter cream all over cake.

4 Place a single sour strap on the side of the cake, making sure it touches the board; measure and cut the sour strap so that it lays about 2cm (¾ inch) over the top edge of the cake. Repeat with remaining sour straps. You will need about 30 pieces.

5 Unroll fruit and cola wheels; trim and position to cover the inside cut edge of the sour straps. Position almonds on cake for apple seeds.

6 Make a hole in the side of Twix Bar with toothpick. Push one end of the mint leaf onto the toothpick; push the toothpick into the hole in the Twix Bar. Push Twix Bar into top of the apple for stem.

Planter Box

EQUIPMENT	CAKE	DECORATIONS
20cm x 30cm (8-inch x 12-inch) rectangular cake pan	2 x 440g (14-ounce) packets butter cake mix	2m (6 feet) black licorice strap
35cm x 40cm (14-inch x 16-inch) rectangular cake board (page 334)	1 quantity butter cream (page 329)	5 pieces apple green licorice
wooden skewer	terracotta food colouring	12 mint leaves
toothpicks		25 flying saucer lollies (blue, yellow, pink, orange)
		5 blackberry lollies
		2 lollipops

1 Preheat oven to 170°C/340°F. Grease pan; line base and sides with baking paper, extending paper 5cm (2 inches) above sides.

2 Make cakes according to directions on packets. Spread mixture into pan; bake about 45 minutes. Stand cake in pan 10 minutes before turning, top-side up, onto wire rack to cool.

3 Level cake top; turn cake cut-side down. Using pattern from pattern sheet, cut out planter box; secure cake, cut-side down, to cake board with a little butter cream. Cut rim from cake; secure to top of planter box with a little butter cream.

4 Tint butter cream terracotta; spread all over cake.

5 Using picture as a guide, trim and position licorice strap to make the wrought iron pattern on planter box.

6 Slightly trim 3 apple licorice pieces to form 3 flower stems; secure to the cake board with a little butter cream. Secure 1 mint leaf at the side of each stem with a little butter cream.

7 Secure flying saucer lollies to cake board, above the stems, with a little butter cream, positioning them to make flower petals (use 5 flying saucers per flower). Secure a blackberry lolly to the centre of each flower with a little butter cream.

8 Cut remaining apple licorice into two 2cm/¾-inch pieces; carefully push the wooden skewer through the centre of each piece to make a hole. Push a lollipop stick through the hole in each piece of licorice; push the sticks into the top-edge of the planter box as far as they will go. Secure flying saucers to each lollipop with a little butter cream to make flowers. Secure a blackberry lolly to the centre of each flower with a little butter cream. Position remaining mint leaves in planter box to complete the flowers and leaves. (Insert toothpicks into the mint leaves to make it easier to position on cake, if necessary.)

Push a lollipop stick through the hole in each piece of licorice; push the sticks into the cake as far as they will go.

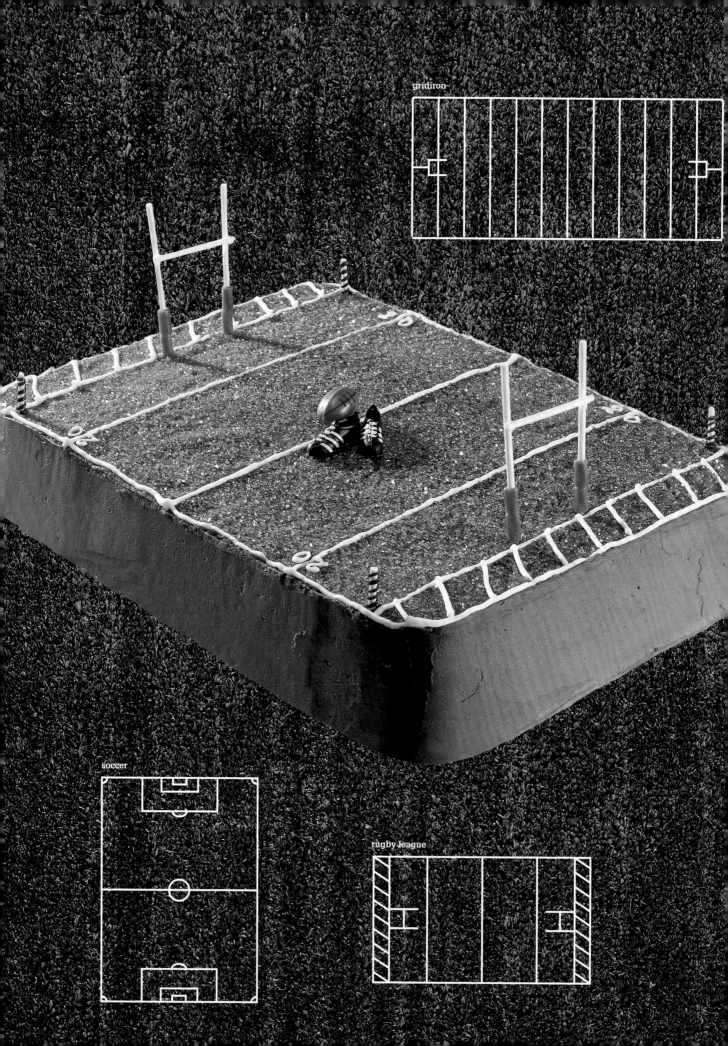

gridiron

soccer

rugby league

Fields of Play

This versatile cake can be used to make any number of sporting fields; just follow the markings on these two pages.

EQUIPMENT

deep 26cm x 36cm (10½-inch x 14½-inch) baking dish

35cm x 45cm (14-inch x 18-inch) rectangular cake board (page 334)

CAKE

3 x 470g (15-ounce) packets butter cake mix

1 quantity butter cream (page 329)

green food colouring

DECORATIONS

⅓ cup (75g) white (granulated) sugar

white and black glossy decorating gel

7 lollipop sticks

40cm (16-inch) red fruit Roll-Ups

assorted sporting toys

1 Preheat oven to 180°C/350°F. Grease baking dish; line base and sides with baking paper, extending paper 5cm (2 inches) above sides.

2 Make cakes according to directions on packets. Spread mixture into dish; bake about 1 hour. Stand cake in dish 5 minutes before turning, top-side up, onto wire rack to cool.

3 Level cake top; secure cake, cut-side down, on cake board, with a little butter cream. Tint butter cream green; spread all over cake.

4 Combine sugar and green colouring in small plastic bag; rub together until sugar is evenly coloured. Sprinkle top of cake with green sugar.

5 To decorate the rugby league field: using white decorating gel, pipe on field markings, using outlines as a guide. Pipe black decorating gel around lollipop sticks for corner posts. Wrap thin strips of red fruit Roll-Ups around lollipop sticks for goal posts.

6 Decorate with toy balls, equipment and goal posts, as desired.

rugby union

Australian rules

netball

Place the cake cut side down then, using the paper pattern, cut kite from cake.

Using toothpicks as a guide, spread coloured butter creams over the kite quadrants.

Roll icing until 3mm thick then, using flower cutters, cut clouds from icing.

Go fly a Kite

Kites used to be made from tree twigs, newspaper, string and tape. This one is more colourful, and certainly tastes much nicer.

EQUIPMENT

deep 26cm x 36cm (10½-inch x 14½-inch) baking dish

35cm x 45cm (14-inch x 18-inch) rectangular cake board (page 334)

4cm (1½-inch) and 5cm (2-inch) flower cutters

toothpicks

CAKE

3 x 470g (15-ounce) packets butter cake mix

2½ quantities butter cream (page 329)

yellow, red, green and orange food colouring

DECORATIONS

1 black licorice strap

50cm (20 inches) red ribbon

50cm (20 inches) purple ribbon

50cm (20 inches) orange ribbon

50cm (20 inches) green ribbon

1m (39 inches) rope

250g (8 ounces) ready-made white icing (page 329)

pure icing (confectioners') sugar, for dusting

1 Preheat oven to 180°C/350°F. Grease baking dish; line base and sides with baking paper, extending paper 5cm (2 inches) above sides.

2 Make cakes according to directions on packets. Spread mixture into dish; bake about 1 hour. Stand cake in dish 5 minutes before turning, top-side up, onto wire rack to cool.

3 Level cake top; turn cake cut-side down. Using pattern from pattern sheet, cut kite from cake. Secure cake, cut-side down, on cake board with a little butter cream.

4 Place two lines of toothpicks in cake, connecting opposing corners of kite, as pictured. Divide butter cream into four small bowls. Tint yellow, red, green and orange.

5 Using toothpicks as a guide, spread butter creams over top and side of kite quadrants; remove and discard toothpicks.

6 Cut licorice strap into thin strips; position around each coloured quadrant and edge of kite.

7 Using ribbons, tie bows onto rope and position at end of kite.

8 Knead ready-made icing on surface dusted with a little sifted icing sugar until icing loses its stickiness. Roll icing on surface dusted with sifted icing sugar into a 3mm (⅛-inch) thickness; using flower cutters, cut clouds from icing; position on board around kite.

Level the top of the muffin, then cut the end off to make the spout.

Watering Can

A cake for budding gardeners. Get the kids into the garden to play 'who can pick the most weeds', and 'what plant is that?'

EQUIPMENT

26cm x 35cm (10¼-inch x 14-inch) baking dish

6-hole (¾-cup/180ml) texas muffin pan

30cm x 40cm (12-inch x 16-inch) rectangular cake board (page 334)

CAKE

5 x 440g (14-ounce) packets butter cake mix
(see 'mixing the cakes' page 345)

1 quantity butter cream
(page 329)

blue and yellow food colouring

DECORATIONS

10 white chocolate Melts
3 rainbow sour straps
½ cup (135g) blue jelly beans

1 Preheat oven to 170°C/340°F. Grease baking dish; line base and sides with baking paper, extending paper 5cm (2 inches) above sides. Grease one hole of the muffin pan.

2 Make cakes according to directions on packets. Drop ½ cup mixture into greased muffin pan hole; bake muffin about 20 minutes. Spread remaining mixture into dish; bake about 1 hour. Stand cakes in pans 10 minutes before turning, top-side up, onto wire racks to cool.

3 Using pattern from pattern sheet, carefully cut out watering can from large cake; trim the cake scraps to make the neck of the spout. Slice top third off the muffin to level, then cut end third off muffin to make spout. Using picture as a guide, arrange cake pieces on cake board, securing with a little butter cream.

4 Tint ⅓ cup butter cream light blue. Tint remaining butter cream yellow. Using picture as a guide, spread handle with blue butter cream; spread yellow butter cream all over remaining cake.

5 Decorate watering can with chocolate Melts as polka dots. Position one rainbow sour strap to cover where the two coloured butter creams meet; trim remaining sour straps to cover the spout of watering can. Arrange jelly beans on board to look like water pouring out of the spout.

Stand square cake upright against bar cake on cake board, to make window and counter.

Sweet Shop

EQUIPMENT

8cm x 25cm (3¼-inch x 10-inch) bar cake pan

deep 20cm (8-inch) square cake pan

30cm (12-inch) square cake board (page 334)

small paper piping bag (page 338)

CAKE

2 x 470g (15-ounce) packets butter cake mix

1½ quantities butter cream (page 329)

pink food colouring

DECORATIONS

100g (3 ounces) white chocolate Melts

white cardboard

pink felt-tipped pen

1 packet candy sticks

1 black licorice strap

40g (1½-ounce) jar Bo Peep lollies

1 ice-block stick

non-toxic white paint

small artist's paintbrush

1 white marshmallow

2 small foil cases or foil milk-bottle tops

4 pink Mentos

1 Preheat oven to 180°C/350°F. Grease cake pans; line bases and sides with baking paper, extending paper 5cm (2 inches) above sides.

2 Make cakes according to directions on packets. Pour one-quarter of the mixture into bar pan, pour remaining into square pan. Bake bar cake about 30 minutes and square cake about 1 hour. Stand cakes in pans 5 minutes before turning, top-side up, onto wire rack to cool.

3 Level tops of cakes; turn cakes, cut-side down. Cut 1cm (½-inch) deep recess into square cake, leaving 1cm (½-inch) border. Cut 2.5cm (1-inch) wide, 1cm (½-inch) deep recesses on either end of the bar cake, as pictured. Stand square cake upright on cake board. Stand bar cake in front of it to represent front window and counter of shop; secure bar cake to cake board with a little butter cream.

4 Tint butter cream pink. Lie square cake flat; spread butter cream all over recess and border. Melt chocolate (page 339); spoon into piping bag, pipe 'Sweets Shop' in middle of recess. When chocolate is set, stand cake up again and position behind the counter; secure to cake board with a little butter cream. Spread remaining butter cream all over cake.

5 To make awning, draw stripes on the white cardboard with pink pen; cut a scalloped edge, then trim, fold and secure cardboard to front top edge of square cake, as pictured.

6 Decorate window edge and counter front with candy sticks; trim them to fit, as necessary. Use thin strips of licorice to trim awning and outline money drawer at front. Fill recesses in counter with Bo Peeps; position 2 purple Bo Peeps for money drawer handle.

7 To make scales, trim ends from the ice-block stick, paint it white (leave it unpainted, if you prefer); leave to dry. When dry, balance stick across white marshmallow, secure with a little butter cream. Trim two small foil cases or milk bottle tops and stick them at either end of the stick with a little glue or sticky tape. Fill with Mentos.

Dominoes

Use real dominos and get the party goers to build their own domino chain to topple at the end of the party.

EQUIPMENT

two 8cm x 26cm (3¼-inch x 10½-inch) bar cake pans

35cm x 50cm (14-inch x 20-inch) rectangular cake board
(page 334)

CAKE

½ x 470g (15-ounce) packet butter cake mix
(see 'mixing the cakes' page 345)

½ quantity butter cream
(page 329)

white food colouring

DECORATIONS

6cm (2½ inches) black licorice strap, cut into thin strips

2 x 35g (1-ounce) tubes mini M&M's

1 Preheat oven to 180°C/350°F. Grease cake pans; line bases and long sides with baking paper, extending paper 5cm (2 inches) above sides.
2 Make cake according to directions on packet. Drop ⅔ cup of mixture into each pan; bake about 20 minutes. Stand cakes in pans 5 minutes before turning, top-side up, onto wire rack to cool.
3 Cut strips of licorice strap into 16 x 3cm (1¼-inch) pieces. Tint butter cream white. Spread butter cream over tops of cakes; cut each cake crossways into eight 3cm-wide pieces. Secure cakes on board with a little butter cream.
4 Using picture as a guide, position licorice strips on cake pieces; decorate with mini M&M's before the butter cream sets.

Dinner Plate

EQUIPMENT

deep 28cm (11¼-inch)
round cake pan
6-hole (¾-cup/180ml)
texas muffin pan
thick wooden skewer

CAKE

7 x 440g (14-ounce) packets
butter cake mix
(see 'mixing the cakes' page 345)

DECORATIONS

1½ quantities butter cream
(page 329)
500g (1 pound) ready-made
white icing (page 329)
pure icing (confectioners')
sugar, for dusting
yellow food colouring

50 'top banana' flavoured
jelly belly jelly beans
15cm (6-inch) square piece
of aluminium foil
2 tablespoons apricot jam
warmed, strained
1 packet green Sixlets
5 orange Fruit Sticks

1 Preheat oven to 170°C/340°F. Grease round cake pan; line base and side with baking paper, extending paper 5cm (2 inches) above side. Grease 2 holes of the muffin pan.

2 Make cakes according to directions on packets. Drop ¼ cup of mixture into each greased muffin pan hole. Pour remaining mixture into round pan; bake small cakes about 25 minutes, bake large cake about 1¾ hours. Stand cakes in pans 10 minutes before turning, top-side up, onto wire rack to cool.

3 Level top of round cake; turn cake cut-side down. Trim round cake into a plate shape by making a 1cm (½-inch) deep recess in the centre of the cake and leaving a 3cm (1¼-inch) border. Try to manoeuvre the knife under the centre piece of cake so you can lift it out in a single piece (you will use this centre piece of cake to cut out the cutlets).

4 Place the cutlet pattern from the pattern sheet on the centre piece of cake; cut out 2 cutlets (if you couldn't lift the centre piece of cake out in one piece, and need to join pieces of cake to make the cutlets, join them with a little butter cream). Blend any leftover cake pieces into cake crumbs.

5 Secure plate-shaped cake on cake board with a little butter cream. Reserve ½ cup butter cream. Spread remaining butter cream all over plate cake; refrigerate cake about 30 minutes to allow butter cream to set.

6 Knead ready-made icing on surface dusted with a little sifted icing sugar until icing loses its stickiness. Roll icing on surface dusted with a little icing sugar until large enough to cover plate cake, allowing for the depth of the recess in the cake. Using a rolling pin, lift the icing onto the cake – don't stretch the icing. Dust hands with icing sugar; smooth icing over cake. Trim icing neatly around base of cake.

7 Reserve 1 tablespoon of the plain butter cream for 'potato'. Tint remaining butter cream yellow.

8 To make the corn cob, cut the top off one muffin; trim muffin into a cylindrical shape; spread with some of the yellow butter cream (leave the ends until after you position the jelly beans – so it's easier to ice the cake). Position the jelly beans around the cake. Spread butter cream over ends of the cake. Refrigerate about 30 minutes or until butter cream is set and the jelly beans are secured to the cake.

9 To make the potato, wrap the remaining muffin in the foil square; use a sharp knife to cut a cross in the centre of the top of the foil. Peel back the foil to expose the top of the 'potato' underneath. Secure potato to plate cake with a little butter cream. Dollop reserved plain butter cream on top of potato.

10 To make the crumbed cutlet, brush the cut out cutlet pieces all over with the warmed apricot jam; coat the cutlets with cake crumbs. Secure to the plate with a little butter cream.

11 Sprinkle green Sixlets onto plate for peas. Cut Fruit Sticks in half, then trim to resemble thinly sliced carrots; position on plate next to peas. Secure corn cob to plate with a little butter cream.

Trampoline

Trampolining has been a part of the Olympic Games since 2000. You're sure to win a medal with this cake.

EQUIPMENT

deep 22cm (9-inch) round cake pan
35cm (14-inch) round cake board (page 334)
ruler
toothpicks

CAKE

2 x 470g (15-ounce) packets butter cake mix
1 quantity butter cream (page 329)
green and yellow food colouring

DECORATIONS

3 x 250g (8-ounce) packets Fruit Sticks
500g (1-pound) ready-made white icing (page 329)
pure icing (confectioners') sugar, for dusting
18cm (7¼-inch) cardboard circle
4 x 60g (2-ounce) packets Chunky Raspberry Twisters
assorted small dolls

1 Preheat oven to 180°C/350°F. Grease cake pan; line base and side with baking paper, extending paper 5cm (2 inches) above side.

2 Make cakes according to directions on packets. Spread mixture into pan; bake about 1 hour. Stand cake in pan 5 minutes before turning, top-side up, onto wire rack to cool.

3 Level cake top; secure cake, cut-side down, on cake board with a little butter cream. Using ruler and toothpicks, mark a 17cm (6¾-inch) circle in centre of cake. Using markings as a guide, cut shallow recess into cake with a small serrated knife about 2.5cm (1-inch) deep. Remove and discard centre of cake; trim recess to neaten.

4 Tint butter cream green; spread all over cake.

5 Trim Fruit Sticks to the same height as cake; position around side of cake.

6 Knead ready-made icing on surface dusted with a little sifted icing sugar until icing loses its stickiness; tint icing yellow. Roll icing on surface dusted with sifted icing sugar into a 5mm (¼-inch) thickness. Using cardboard circle as a guide, cut circle from icing with sharp-pointed knife; position on cake to cover hollow. Enclose remaining icing in plastic wrap.

7 Cut Raspberry Twisters in half lengthways; cut halves into 2.5cm (1-inch) pieces. Trim edges of pieces on an angle; position on cake for springs.

8 On surface dusted with sifted icing sugar, roll reserved icing into a long 5mm (¼-inch) thick rope; position around outside top edge of cake. Position dolls as desired.

Using the markings as a guide, cut a shallow recess into the cake with a small serrated knife.

Tint the butter cream with green colouring; using a palette knife, spread all over the cake.

Using the cardboard circle as a guide, cut a circle from the icing with a sharp-pointed knife.

Cut Raspberry Twisters in half lengthways then into 2.5cm pieces; trim the edges on an angle.

Noughts & Crosses

A tactical game of blocking requiring great skill and, in this case, no end of cupcakes. It's also known as tic-tac-toe.

1 Preheat oven to 180°C/350°F. Line muffin pan with paper cases.

2 Make cake according to directions on packet. Drop 2½ tablespoons of mixture into each paper case; bake about 20 minutes. Stand cakes in pan 5 minutes before turning, top-side up, onto wire rack to cool.

3 Divide butter cream equally into two small bowls; tint one red and the other white.

4 Spread red butter cream over five cakes in red cases, and white butter cream over five cakes in white cases.

5 Use Musk Sticks to make noughts and crosses grid; secure to cake board with a little butter cream. Using picture as a guide, position cakes on board; secure with a little butter cream. Top white cakes with fruit rings for noughts; use Tic Tacs to make crosses on the red cakes.

EQUIPMENT

12-hole (¹/₃-cup/80ml) standard muffin pan

10 standard paper cases (5 red, 5 white)

30cm (12-inch) square cake board (page 334)

CAKE

1 x 470g (15-ounce) packet butter cake mix

½ quantity butter cream (page 329)

red and white food colouring

DECORATIONS

8 Musk Sticks

5 red fruit rings

18g (¾-ounce) packet white Tic Tacs

TIPS

You'll have about 1 cup of the cake mixture left over; make more noughts and crosses cakes for your guests.

This is a very easy birthday cake to make; it is suitable for boys and girls alike. You can make it in any colour you like.

Use the round cutter to mark and cut through the top of each cake to a depth of about 1.5cm. Carefully scoop out the cake and discard, making room for the "paint" to be poured into the hole.

Paint Pots

It doesn't matter if these pots tip over, nothing's going to spill. Tint the icing any colours you like, just make them bright.

EQUIPMENT

6-hole (¾-cup/180ml) texas muffin pan

6cm (2½-inch) round cutter

30cm x 40cm (12-inch x 16-inch) rectangular cake board (page 334)

CAKE

1 x 470g (15-ounce) packet butter cake mix

½ quantity butter cream (page 329)

1½ quantities glacé icing (page 329)

black, red, yellow, green, orange and blue food colouring

DECORATIONS

3 new artist's paint brushes

1 Preheat oven to 180°C/350°F. Grease texas muffin pan.

2 Make cake according to directions on packet. Drop ⅓ cup of mixture into each hole; bake about 25 minutes. Stand cakes in pan 5 minutes before turning, top-side up, onto wire rack to cool.

3 Level cake tops so they are the same height. Using round cutter, make an imprint in the top of each cake; scoop out cake to make a 1.5cm (¾-inch) deep hollow in each cake.

4 Tint butter cream black; spread all over side and top edge of each cake. Secure cakes on cake board with a little butter cream.

5 Divide glacé icing into five small bowls. Tint icing red, yellow, green, orange and blue.

6 Fill the hollow in each cake with one of the coloured icings. Position paint brushes as you like.

TIP

You'll have enough cake mixture left over to make another three paint pots if you like.

Parties for budding artists are popular - this cake will get them in the creative mood. Lollies could easily be hidden under the glacé icing.

Swimming Pool

Summertime....and the livin' is easy. Use blue jelly crystals if you think the green makes this pool look like it needs a good clean!

1 Preheat oven to 180°C/350°F. Grease cake pan; line base and side with baking paper, extending paper 5cm (2 inches) above sides.

2 Make cake according to directions on packet. Spread mixture into pan; bake about 50 minutes. Stand cake in pan 5 minutes before turning, top-side up, onto wire rack to cool.

3 Meanwhile, make jelly according to directions on packet; pour into a shallow container. Refrigerate until set.

4 Level cake top; secure cake, cut-side down, on cake board with a little butter cream. Cut a recess into the centre of the cake, about 2cm (¾-inch) in from the edge, and about 2.5cm (1-inch) deep. Remove and discard centre of cake; trim recess to neaten.

5 Spread chocolate butter cream all over edge and side of cake (but not into the hollowed-out area).

6 Position chocolate finger biscuits around side of cake, leaving an opening of about 5cm (2 inches) for ladder.

7 Use Musk Sticks and thin strips of licorice strap to make ladder; secure with butter cream, and toothpicks, if necessary. Position ladder on cake.

8 Paint stripes of food colouring onto Kool Mints to make beach balls; stand until set. Push 2 small dolls through the jelly rings to make children in rubber floats; spread a little butter cream on heads of dolls, dip in green sprinkles to make bathing caps. Secure 5cm (2-inch) pieces of jelly snakes together to make rubber mattress with a little butter cream, or toothpicks, if necessary.

9 Mash set jelly with a fork, spoon into the centre of the cake to represent water; position children, beach balls and umbrella in water.

EQUIPMENT

deep 20cm (8-inch) round cake pan
30cm (12-inch) round cake board (page 334)
toothpicks
new small artist's paint brush

CAKE

1 x 470g (15-ounce) packet butter cake mix
85g (3-ounce) packet lime jelly crystals
1 quantity chocolate butter cream (page 329)

DECORATIONS

300g (9½ ounces) chocolate finger biscuits
2 pink Musk Sticks
black licorice strap
assorted food colourings
3 Kool Mints
3 small baby dolls
2 jelly fruit rings
green sprinkles
3 jelly snakes
1 small paper umbrella

Using a small serrated knife, cut a recess into the cake, about 2cm in from the edge, and 2.5cm deep.

Remove and discard centre of cake.

Sandwich the two cakes together with a little blue butter cream.

Spread the cake with coloured butter creams.

Insert candy cane into centre of red icing ball to make drumstick.

Drum beat

We may all want to march to the beat of a different drum, but everyone will want a piece of this particular drum cake.

EQUIPMENT

two deep 20cm (8-inch) round cake pans

30cm (12-inch) round cake board (page 334)

CAKE

3 x 470g (15-ounce) packets butter cake mix

2 quantities butter cream (page 329)

blue and red food colouring

DECORATIONS

200g (6½ ounces) red licorice rope

8 white Kool Mints

70g (2½ ounces) ready-made white icing (page 329)

pure icing (confectioners') sugar, for dusting

2 x 12cm (4¾-inch) red and white striped candy canes

1 Preheat oven to 180°C/350°F. Grease cake pans; line bases and sides with baking paper, extending paper 5cm (2 inches) above sides.

2 Make cakes according to directions on packets. Divide mixture evenly into pans; bake cakes about 40 minutes. Stand cakes in pans 5 minutes before turning, top-side up, onto wire rack to cool.

3 Level cake tops. Tint two-thirds of the butter cream blue. Sandwich cut sides of cakes together with a little blue butter cream. Secure cake on cake board with a little butter cream.

4 Spread top of cake with plain butter cream, spread sides with blue butter cream.

5 Wrap some of the red licorice rope around base and top edge of drum (you may need to secure with toothpicks).

6 Cut remaining red licorice rope into four 14cm (5½-inch) lengths; place around side of drum, as pictured. Place Kool Mints in position.

7 Knead ready-made icing on surface dusted with a little sifted icing sugar until icing loses its stickiness; tint red. Dust hands lightly with icing sugar; roll ready-made icing into two balls for drumsticks, enclose in plastic wrap and stand about 1 hour until firm. Snap crook ends off candy canes, leaving about 12cm (4¾-inch) length of stick; insert broken ends into balls. Position drumsticks on top of cake just before serving.

TIPS
Be sure to remove toothpicks from cake before cutting and serving.

Raspberry straps, cut into strips, can be used instead of red licorice rope.

Vegetable Garden

This cute cake's a bit fiddly to make, but it looks so good – and you'll get plenty of 'wow's – that it's well worth the effort.

EQUIPMENT

26cm x 35cm (10½-inch x 14-inch) baking dish

30cm x 40cm (12-inch x 16-inch) rectangular cake board (page 334)

small paper piping bag (page 338)

wooden skewer

CAKE

4 x 440g (14-ounce) packets butter cake mix (see 'mixing the cakes' page 345)

1½ quantities butter cream (page 329)

leaf green food colouring

DECORATIONS

200g (6½-ounce) packet Lattice biscuits

6 x 30g (1-ounce) chocolate Flakes

1 cup (110g) Milo

¾ cup (60g) desiccated coconut

1 x green fruit and cola wheel

8 green choc mint balls

2 watermelon lollies

5 orange Fruit Sticks

18 ready-made green icing flowers

40 red rainbow choc chips

2 teaspoons yellow sugar pearls

15 Jaffas

1 Preheat oven to 170°C/340°F. Grease baking dish; line base and sides with baking paper, extending paper 5cm (2 inches) above sides.

2 Make cakes according to directions on packets. Spread mixture into baking dish; bake about 1 hour. Stand cake in dish 10 minutes before turning, top-side up, onto wire rack to cool.

3 Level cake top; secure cake, cut-side down, on cake board with a little butter cream.

4 Tint butter cream green with colouring; reserve 2 tablespoons of butter cream, spread remaining butter cream all over cake. Press lattice biscuits, side-by-side, around outside edge of cake.

5 Using picture as a guide, mark out the vegetable plot using five of the chocolate Flakes (cutting to fit as necessary). Spread Milo over cake, inside the flake border. Tint the coconut green (page 338); sprinkle over cake between edge of cake and flake border.

6 To make watermelon vine, unroll green fruit and cola wheel; position on cake. Position choc mint balls on either side of vine. Cut watermelon lollies into smaller segments and position near vine. Spoon reserved green butter cream into piping bag; pipe small leaves on edges of vine.

7 To make the carrots, trim each orange Fruit Stick diagonally into four 2cm (¾-inch) pieces. Using picture as a guide, push carrots in a row into cake; pipe a small leaf on top of each one with the green butter cream.

8 To make the strawberry patch, place 3 green flowers together; top each flower with 2-3 red rainbow choc chips. Make another 5 patches, about 5mm (¼-inch) apart.

9 To sow the seeds, use the skewer to make a line from one end of the garden to the other; sprinkle with the yellow sugar pearls.

10 To make the tomato vines, cut the remaining flake into 3 pieces (about 3cm tall and 5mm wide (1¼ inch x ¼ inch) to make tomato stakes; carefully push stakes into cake in a row evenly spaced apart. Position 5 jaffas around each stake; pipe a stem on each tomato and a few vines and leaves on each stake using a little green butter cream.

Pencil Case

School would be much more entertaining, and homework much more fun, if we could all have pencil cases as delicious as this one.

1 Preheat oven to 170°C/340°F. Grease pan; line base and sides with baking paper, extending paper 5cm (2 inches) above sides.
2 Make cakes according to directions on packets. Spread mixture into pan; bake about 50 minutes. Stand cake in pan 10 minutes before turning, top-side up, onto wire rack to cool.
3 Using a serrated knife, trim the cake top and edges into a slightly rounded 'pencil case' shape. Secure cake, rounded-side up, on cake board with a little butter cream.
4 Tint 2 tablespoons of the butter cream black. Tint remaining butter cream orange. Spread front edge of cake with black butter cream. Spread orange butter cream all over remaining cake.
5 Cut sour straps into squares. Using picture as a guide, position squares over top and sides of cake to make a 'chequered' pattern.
6 Unroll fruit and cola wheel; cut in half to make 2 long single strips. Outline black area of pencil case with the strips. Position Tic Tacs on black area to make zipper. Use candy letters to spell out name on cake. Secure all decorations to pencil case with a little butter cream as required.
7 Trim one end of each sherbet stick to look like a sharpened pencil; dip sharp end of pencils into same-coloured food colouring. Lay pencils in front of pencil case.

EQUIPMENT

20cm x 30cm (8-inch x 12-inch) rectangular cake pan
30cm x 40cm (12-inch x 16-inch) rectangular cake board (page 334)

CAKE

2 x 440g (14-ounce) packets butter cake mix
1 quantity butter cream (page 329)
black, orange, blue, red and yellow food colourings

DECORATIONS

160g (5-ounce) packet strawberry sour straps
1 red fruit and cola wheel
white-coloured Tic Tacs
ready-made candy letters
8 coloured sherbet sticks (2 each orange, red, yellow and blue colours)

Trim one end of each sherbet stick to look like a sharpened pencil.

Chessboard

Chess has long been considered the sport of kings and aristocrats. If you have a grandmaster in the making, this is the cake that will have the party in checkmate mode.

1 Preheat oven to 180°C/350°F. Grease cake pan; line base and sides with baking paper, extending paper 5cm (2 inches) above sides.

2 Make cake according to directions on packet. Spread mixture into pan; bake cake about 35 minutes. Stand cake in pan 5 minutes before turning, top-side up, onto wire rack to cool.

3 Level cake top and trim sides to make a square; secure cake, cut-side down, on cake board with a little butter cream. Spread butter cream evenly over top and sides of cake.

4 Knead ready-made icing on surface dusted with a little sifted icing sugar until icing loses its stickiness. Roll icing on surface dusted with sifted icing sugar until slightly larger than top of cake. Trim icing to fit top of cake exactly, carefully lift icing onto cake.

5 Cut licorice into 32 squares. Press licorice squares gently into icing to create chessboard. Cut four strips of licorice to cover each side of the cake. Position licorice around sides of cake.

6 Arrange chess pieces on cake.

EQUIPMENT

deep 22cm (9-inch) square cake pan
35cm (14-inch) square cake board (page 334)

CAKE

1 x 470g (15-ounce) packet butter cake mix
1 quantity butter cream (page 329)

DECORATIONS

500g (1 pound) ready-made white icing (page 329)
pure icing (confectioners') sugar, for dusting
2 black licorice straps
chess pieces

Trim sides of cake to make square.

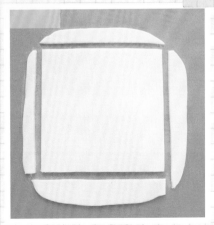

Trim icing to same size as cake top.

Bubble Bath

EQUIPMENT

14cm x 21cm (5½-inch x 8½-inch) loaf pan

20cm x 30cm (8-inch x 12-inch) rectangular cake board
(page 334)

CAKE

1½ x 470g (15-ounce) packets butter cake mix
(see 'mixing the cakes' page 345)

⅓ cup (110g) apricot jam, warmed, strained

1 quantity fluffy frosting
(page 329)

blue food colouring

DECORATIONS

1kg (2 pounds) ready-made white icing (page 329)

½ cup (80g) pure icing (confectioners') sugar

3 ice-cream wafers

4 Kool Mints

2 clear fruit rings

1 wooden toothpick

small duck candles

pearl balls

1 Preheat oven to 150°C/300°F. Grease and flour pan.

2 Make cakes according to directions on packets. Spread mixture into pan; bake about 1 hour 10 minutes. Stand cake in pan 5 minutes before turning, top-side up, onto wire rack to cool.

3 Level cake top; trim edges of cake to make a bath shape. Cut 2cm (¾-inch) deep hollow from cake with a small serrated knife, leaving a 2cm (¾-inch) border; brush cake all over with warmed jam.

4 Knead ready-made icing on surface dusted with a little sifted icing sugar until icing loses its stickiness. Roll icing on surface dusted with sifted icing sugar until large enough to cover whole cake. Carefully lift over top of cake, gently easing icing into hollow and around sides of bath. Dust hands with a little icing sugar and gently mould icing over cake. Trim excess icing away from base of bath.

5 Use remaining icing to make a 2cm (¾-inch) thick rope about 60cm (24 inches) long to go around the top edge of the bath. Secure rope to edge of bath with a little water. Dust hands with a little icing sugar and shape rope to make the rolled edge of the bath.

6 Roll some scraps of icing around Kool Mints to make feet for bath. Layer ice-cream wafers on top of each other with a little jam. Secure wafers on cake board with a little jam; centre cake on wafers (the wafers support the bath while giving it enough height so you can put the 'feet' under the bottom of the bath). Position Kool Mints to make feet for bath.

7 Tint fluffy frosting blue. Spoon frosting into bath.

8 Cut through one fruit ring. Gently push the toothpick about halfway through the fruit ring to make a tap. Push end of toothpick gently into cake. Halve remaining fruit ring to make tap handles; position on cake. Position candles and pearl balls in bath water.

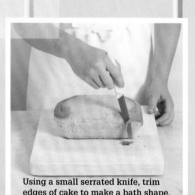

Using a small serrated knife, trim edges of cake to make a bath shape.

Cut a 2cm deep recess from cake for the 'bath water'.

Roll ready-made icing into a rope shape to make top edge of bath.

TIPS
The bath tub, feet and tap
(plus handles) can be completed up to
two days ahead of the party.
The water (fluffy frosting) is best made
about an hour before the party. The frosting
will lose its gloss after an hour or so.
Pearls balls, also known as pearlized balls, are
available from cake decorating
stores. Remove the toothpicks
from the cake before serving.

Chef's Hat

A party where the kids make their own party food...what a great idea! Get creative cooks into the kitchen for a fabulous, and fun-filled food feast. The head chef will love this cake.

1 Preheat oven to 160°C/325°F. Grease cake pan; line base and sides with baking paper, extending paper 5cm (2 inches) above sides.

2 Make cakes according to directions on packets. Pour mixture into pan; bake about 2 hours. Stand cake in pan 5 minutes before turning, top-side up, onto wire rack to cool.

3 Level cake top; turn cake cut-side down. Using pattern from pattern sheet, cut hat from cake. Secure cake, cut-side down, to cake board with a little fluffy frosting. Spread fluffy frosting all over cake.

4 Cut half the licorice strap into thin strips; use to outline hat and hat band. Cut remaining licorice strap into 1cm (½-inch) squares; position on cake to make a checkerboard hat band.

EQUIPMENT

deep 30cm (12-inch) square cake pan

30cm x 35cm (12-inch x 14-inch) rectangular cake board (page 334)

CAKE

5 x 470g (15-ounce) packets butter cake mix (see 'mixing the cakes' page 345)

1½ quantities fluffy frosting (page 329)

DECORATIONS

1 black licorice strap

TIPS

The chef of the day could have his or her name spelled out on the band of the hat using sweets or licorice. The cake can be made a day ahead, but the fluffy frosting is best made about an hour before the party, as it will lose its gloss after an hour or so, and will become more like a meringue. This cake requires a bit of patience, but is well worth the effort and looks impressive. A candy thermometer takes the guesswork out of the frosting; they are available from cookware shops and most major department stores.

Ice-cream Cones

They look so realistic, it's hard to believe these little cakes aren't really ice-creams. You may need to make more to feed any adults at the party.

EQUIPMENT

6-hole (¾-cup/180ml) texas muffin pan

CAKE

1 x 470g (15-ounce) packet butter cake mix
1 quantity butter cream (page 329)
1 tablespoon cocoa powder
pink food colouring
6 square-based ice-cream cones

DECORATIONS

40g (1½ ounces) dark chocolate Melts
hundreds and thousands chocolate sprinkles
2 red glacé cherries
1 teaspoon crushed unsalted peanuts
1 ice-cream wafer
5 white Choc Bits
1 wafer stick, halved

1 Preheat oven to 180°C/350°F. Grease texas muffin pan.
2 Make cake according to directions on packet. Drop ⅓ cup of the mixture into each hole; bake about 25 minutes. Stand cakes in pan 5 minutes before turning, top-side up, onto wire rack to cool.
3 Trim tops of cakes to make them into a dome shape as pictured.
4 Divide butter cream into three small bowls. Leave one bowl plain; stir sifted cocoa into another bowl. Tint remaining butter cream pink.
5 Using picture as a guide, spread the cakes with the different coloured butter creams.
6 Top each ice-cream cone with a cake. Melt chocolate (page 339); cool slightly before pouring over top of ice-cream top. Using picture as a guide, decorate the cones using decorations listed at left.

Turn the cakes, top-side down; use a small sharp serrated knife to trim the cakes into rounded shapes.

TIP
You will have enough cake mixture left over to make four more ice-cream cones if you like. Be careful handling the cones as they are a little top-heavy. If you like, fill the cones with lollies; the extra weight will stop the cones from toppling over. These ice-cream look-alikes will dazzle the party guests. Make one for each guest or arrange them on a long platter or board.

Spotto Yellow Punch Buggy

EQUIPMENT

26cm x 35cm (10½-inch x 14-inch) baking dish

30cm x 40cm (12-inch x 16-inch) rectangular cake board (page 334)

CAKE

4 x 440g (14-ounce) packets butter cake mix
see 'mixing the cakes' page 345)

1½ quantities butter cream
(page 329)

yellow food colouring

DECORATIONS

2 Wagon Wheels (48g)

6 yellow banana lollies

2 orange and yellow fruit and cola wheels

1 packet fruit-flavoured Mentos

1 white marshmallow

2 white flying saucer lollies

yellow sherbet

1 Preheat oven to 170°C/340°F. Grease baking dish; line base and sides with baking paper, extending paper 5cm (2 inches) above sides.

2 Make cakes according to directions on packets. Spread mixture into baking dish; bake about 1 hour. Stand cake in dish 10 minutes before turning, top-side up, onto wire rack to cool.

3 Level cake top; turn cake cut-side down. Using pattern from pattern sheet, cut out car; secure cake, cut-side down, on cake board with a little butter cream.

4 Tint butter cream bright yellow; spread butter cream all over cake. Secure wagon wheels to cake for wheels with a little butter cream. Position 3 banana lollies over each wheel for wheel arches (cutting to fit); cover with butter cream.

5 Unroll fruit and cola wheels; using picture as a guide, outline the car, windows and doors with the strips. Position Mentos on car to make flowers. Position marshmallow for headlight. Position flying saucer lollies for hub caps, secure with a little butter cream. Sprinkle sherbet over windows.

TIPS
The cutter we used was about 5cm (2 inches) deep, which made it easier to cut right through the cake. You could use a sharp pointed vegetable knife to cut out the cake rounds, cutting around the markings of the shorter cutter. Freeze the little round cakes first for about an hour to help prevent them from crumbling while icing.

Sunny Umbrella

Little ones will love this brightly-coloured cake. A deep cutter will cut the cake all the way through to make the handle pieces.

EQUIPMENT

deep 30cm (12-inch)
round cake pan
3cm (1¼-inch) round cutter
40cm (16-inch) square
cake board (page 334)

CAKE

1½ x 470g (15-ounce) packets
butter cake mix
(see 'mixing the cakes' page 345)

1½ quantities butter cream
(page 329)

yellow food colouring

DECORATIONS

hundreds & thousands
18 milk chocolate freckles
30cm (12-inches) yellow ribbon

1 Preheat oven to 180°C/350°F. Grease cake pan; line base and side with baking paper, extending paper 5cm (2 inches) above sides.

2 Make cakes according to directions on packets. Spread mixture into pan; bake about 45 minutes. Stand cake in pan 5 minutes before turning, top-side up, onto wire rack to cool.

3 Level cake top; turn cake cut-side down. Using pattern from pattern sheet, cut top of umbrella from cake. Secure cake, cut-side down, on cake board with a little butter cream. Reserve remaining cake.

4 Using 3cm (1¼-inch) round cutter, cut eight rounds from reserved cake to make the umbrella's handle.

5 Tint butter cream yellow; spread all over top, sides and scallops of the umbrella.

6 Working with one round of cake at a time, spread butter cream over the side of each round; roll the side in hundreds and thousands. Spread butter cream over tops of each round. Secure rounds on the cake board with a little butter cream; top with a freckle.

7 Decorate top of umbrella with remaining freckles and a bow.

Using paper pattern from pattern sheet, and a small sharp, finely serrated knife, cut out umbrella shape. Secure to cake board with a little butter cream. Reserve remaining cake.

Using a sharp metal 3cm-round cutter, cut out eight rounds from the reserved cake to make the umbrella's handle. We used a 5cm-deep cutter, to make cutting right through the cake easier.

Spread the sides (not the tops) of cakes with butter cream; roll the sides of the cakes in the hundreds & thousands, then ice the tops of the cakes.

Rugby Ball

We need rugby players for the next world cup, so get the kids out in the backyard practising their ball skills, then inside to eat the ball.

1 Preheat oven to 180°C/350°F. Grease dolly varden pans.

2 Make cakes according to directions on packets. Divide mixture evenly into pans; bake cakes about 1 hour. Stand cakes in pans 5 minutes before turning onto wire rack to cool.

3 Level large flat cake bases; cut a small section off the side of one cake to give a level base. Sandwich cakes together with a little butter cream then secure with a long skewer. Secure cake on cake board with a little butter cream. Spread remaining butter cream all over cake.

4 Using black decorating gel, pipe lines along length of ball, as pictured. Pipe an oval on top of cake; use white decorating gel to indicate stiches.

5 Using fruit Roll-Ups, make a green and yellow crest. Using black decorating gel, pipe desired message on crest; position crest on side of ball.

6 Cut six 4cm (1½-inch) lengths of red licorice strap; bend pieces into 'laces' and position on top of cake. Make a small pump hole with red licorice strap and position on cake. Sprinkle chocolate thins around base of ball.

EQUIPMENT

two 2.5-litre (10-cup capacity)
dolly varden pans

30cm x 40cm (12-inch x 16-inch)
rectangular cake board
(page 334)

CAKE

3 x 470g (15-ounce) packets
butter cake mix

2 quantities butter cream
(page 329)

1 long wooden skewer

DECORATIONS

black and white glossy
decorating gel

green and yellow fruit Roll-Ups

1 red licorice strap,
cut into thin strips

½ cup (100g) chocolate thins

Cut a small section off the side of one cake to give a level base.

Sandwich cakes with butter cream, then secure with a long skewer.

TIP
Be sure to remove skewer
from cake before cutting
and serving.

HAPPY
BIRTHDAY
TOM

Ferris Wheel

TIPS

Place this large cake on a small table covered with greaseproof blue plastic (or something that will tolerate the grease from the butter cream), and use cotton wool, or better still, persian fairy floss, to make some fluffy clouds. You'll have about 1 cup of the cake mixture left over; use it to make more small cakes for the party.

Ferris Wheel

No chance of this ferris wheel stopping halfway round. Such a quick and simple cake, made from cupcakes and Musk Sticks.

1 Preheat oven to 180°C/350°F. Grease four holes of the texas muffin pan. Line mini muffin pans with the paper cases.

2 Make cake according to directions on packet. Drop ⅓ cup of the mixture into greased holes of the texas muffin pan; bake about 25 minutes. Drop 2 level teaspoons of the mixture into each mini paper case; bake about 15 minutes. Stand cakes in pans 5 minutes before turning, top-side up, onto wire racks to cool.

3 Place a quarter of the butter cream in a small bowl; tint pink. Divide remaining butter cream equally into four small bowls; tint green, yellow, purple and orange.

4 Spread pink butter cream over small cakes. Position licorice strap at bottom of cake board for road; secure with a little butter cream.

5 Using picture as a guide, make the base for the ferris wheel with 14 small cakes; secure with a little butter cream. Cut a Musk Stick in half; use the halves as supports for the wheel. Position the remaining small cake for the centre of the wheel; top with Smartie. Position eight Musk Sticks for the spokes of the wheel.

6 To make the carriages, cut the large cakes in half crossways. Using picture as a guide, spread tops and sides of cakes with the coloured butter creams. Secure cakes on board with a little butter cream. Use trimmed Musk Sticks to complete the wheel.

7 Using picture as a guide, decorate carriages with trimmed pieces of sour straps, mini M&M's, little hearts, Bo Peep lollies and strips cut from the coloured layers of the licorice allsort. Secure lollies with tiny dabs of butter cream. Number the carriages using the decorating gel.

EQUIPMENT

6-hole (¾-cup/180ml) texas muffin pan

2 x 12-hole (1-tablespoon/20ml) mini muffin pans

15 mini muffin paper cases (red)

40cm x 50cm (16-inch x 20-inch) rectangular cake board (page 334), see tips

CAKE

1 x 470g (15-ounce) packet butter cake mix

1 quantity butter cream (page 329)

pink, green, yellow, purple and orange food colouring

DECORATIONS

40cm (16 inches) black licorice strap

250g (8-ounce) packet Musk Sticks

1 pink Smartie

4 red sour straps

35g (1-ounce) tube mini M&M's

35g (1-ounce) jar small ready-made icing hearts

40g (1½-ounce) jar Bo Peep lollies

1 licorice allsort

red decorating gel

Jewellery Box

EQUIPMENT

deep 20cm (8-inch)
square cake pan
20cm (8-inch) square
cake board (page 334)
30cm (12-inch) square
cake board (page 334)

CAKE

1 x 470g (15-ounce) packet
butter cake mix
pink food colouring
1 cup (320g) apricot jam,
warmed, strained

DECORATIONS

1kg (2 pounds)
ready-made
white icing (page 329)
pure icing (confectioners')
sugar, for dusting
10 ice-cream wafers
pearl cachous (dragees)
large and small silver
cachous (dragees)
square and round jubes
musk Life Savers
pink jelly buttons

1 Preheat oven to 150°C/300°F. Grease cake pan; line base and sides with baking paper, extending paper 5cm (2 inches) above sides.

2 Make cake according to directions on packet. Spread mixture into pan; bake about 50 minutes. Stand cake in pan 5 minutes before turning, top-side up, onto wire rack to cool.

3 Knead ready-made icing on surface dusted with a little sifted icing sugar until icing loses its stickiness; tint icing pink.

4 To make lid for the box, brush underside of smaller cake board with jam, brush a 5cm (2-inch) border over the covered side of the board. Stand and support board on its edge while preparing the covering. Roll a quarter of the icing on surface dusted with a little icing sugar, into a square large enough to cover the board and to cover the border underneath board. Place board, bottom-side down, onto icing, cut out the corners of the icing, as if covering a book with paper; gently fold the icing over to cover the border on the bottom of the board. Leave the lid to dry flat.

5 Level cake top; secure cake, cut-side down, on larger cake board with a little jam. Using small sharp knife, cut a neat square recess into cake, about 2cm (¾ inch) deep, leaving a 1cm (½-inch) border around the edges. Cut the centre piece of the cake into small squares, cut underneath each square of cake to remove them, as pictured. Brush cake all over with jam.

6 Roll remaining icing on surface dusted with a little sifted icing sugar into a square shape large enough to cover cake. Using rolling pin, lift icing over cake, allowing for depth of recess – don't stretch icing. Dust hands lightly with icing sugar; gently ease icing into corners and sides of recess and down sides of cake. Trim icing neatly around cake base.

7 Before icing sets, line base and sides of recess in box with wafers, cut with a sharp knife to fit. Make compartments for box; use small dabs of jam to hold wafers in place.

8 Using picture as a guide, make jewellery; use small dabs of jam to hold jewels in place and to make them easy to position.

9 Knead some scraps of ready-made icing together; shape into a small cylinder, cut out a heart-shaped handle for box lid, secure to lid with a little water or jam. When lid and handle are set and dry, position lid against box.

Cover the lid of the box as if covering a book.

Cut a recess from box for jewellery compartments.

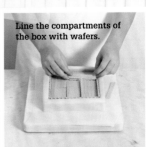
Line the compartments of the box with wafers.

Snakes & Ladders

An ancient Indian board game actually based on morality, where the ladders represent virtues and the snakes represent vices. No vices in this cake: if you don't want to slide down a snake, just eat it!

EQUIPMENT

3 x 12-hole (1/3-cup/80ml) standard muffin pans
36 paper cases (18 yellow, 18 red)
45cm (18-inch) square cake board (page 334)
small paper piping bag (page 338)

CAKE

2 x 470g (15-ounce) packets butter cake mix
2 quantities butter cream (page 329)
white, red and yellow food colouring

DECORATIONS

1 Killer Python
3 snakes (2 blue, 1 green)
4 x 25g (¾-ounce) Curly Wurly bars
4 Smarties

1 Preheat oven to 180°C/350°F; line muffin pans with paper cases.

2 Make cakes according to directions on packets. Drop 2½ level tablespoons of mixture into each paper case; bake about 20 minutes. Stand cakes in pans 5 minutes before turning, top-side up, onto wire rack to cool.

3 Place a quarter of the butter cream into small bowl; tint white. Divide remaining butter cream between two small bowls; tint red and yellow.

4 Spread red butter cream over tops of 18 cakes in yellow cases; spread yellow butter cream over tops of cakes in red cases.

5 Using picture as a guide, secure cakes on board with a little butter cream. Spoon white butter cream into piping bag; pipe numbers one to 36 on cakes.

6 Decorate cakes with killer python and snakes; use Curly Wurlys for ladders and Smarties for counters.

TIPS

Piping takes a little skill: practise on a flat surface before you pipe the numbers on the cakes. You can buy decorating gel for piping, but we found that the butter cream was easier to use. You'll have about 1 cup of the cake mixture left over, enough for about four more cakes.

TIPS
This cake is baked at a slightly higher temperature than other cakes in this book to encourage the mixture to 'dome' in the same way a cupcake does. The cake can be completed a day ahead of the party. Rather than make the sprinkles, cut coloured musk or Fruit Sticks into thin slices, similar to the giant donut on page 297

Giant Cupcake

You don't need one of those giant cupcake pans to make this cake – it's baked in an ordinary round cake pan.

1 Preheat oven to 180°C/360°F. Grease cake pan; line base and side with baking paper, extending paper 5cm (2 inches) above side.

2 Make cakes according to directions on packets. Spread mixture into pan; bake about 1 hour. Stand cake in pan 5 minutes before turning, top-side up, onto wire rack to cool.

3 To make sprinkles, knead ready-made icing on surface dusted with a little sifted icing sugar until icing loses its stickiness. Divide icing into three portions: tint yellow, blue and red. Lightly dust hands with icing sugar; roll icings, one at a time, into very thin ropes (cover icings not being used in plastic wrap so they don't dry out). Cut ropes into random lengths, leave to dry flat on baking paper.

4 Brush lollipop lightly with water, roll lollipop in sprinkles, stand upright to dry.

5 Using small sharp serrated knife, trim side of cake on an angle, to resemble the shape of a cupcake. Secure cake on cake board with a little butter cream.

6 To make paper patty case, spread side of cake lightly, but evenly, with butter cream. Fill medium piping bag with butter cream; using picture as a guide, pipe vertical stripes up side of cake about 1cm (½-inch) apart.

7 Tint remaining butter cream pink; fill large piping bag with butter cream. Starting from the outside edge of the cake, pipe a continuous swirl on top of the cake.

8 Decorate cake with lollipop and coloured sprinkles.

EQUIPMENT

deep 20cm (8-inch)
round cake pan
30cm (12-inch) round
cake board (page 334)
or cake stand
medium piping bag fitted
with medium plain tube
large piping bag fitted with
large fluted tube

CAKE

2 x 470g (15-ounce) packets
butter cake mix
yellow, blue, red and
pink food colouring
3 quantities butter cream
(page 329)

DECORATIONS

60g (2 ounces) ready-made
white icing (page 329)
pure icing (confectioners')
sugar, for dusting
1 red lollipop
red sugar sprinkles

Cricket Pitch

Player position seems to indicate only a handful of runs are needed before the end of the match. Budding cricketers will surely want a rematch before cutting into this fun cake.

EQUIPMENT

deep 31cm (12½-inch)
oval cake pan
40cm x 45cm (16-inch x 18-inch)
rectangular cake board
(page 334)

CAKE

3 x 470g (15-ounce) packets
butter cake mix
2 quantities butter cream
(page 329)

DECORATIONS

green, red and blue
food colouring
⅓ cup (75g) white
(granulated) sugar
9cm x 18cm (3¾-inch x 7¼-inch)
cardboard
3 teaspoons yellow
jelly crystals
toy cricket players and stumps

1 Preheat oven to 180°C/350°F. Grease cake pan; line base and side with baking paper, extending paper 5cm (2 inches) above side.
2 Make cakes according to directions on packets. Spread mixture into pan; bake about 1½ hours. Stand cake in pan 5 minutes before turning, top-side up, onto wire rack to cool.
3 Level cake top; secure cake, cut-side down, on cake board with a little butter cream.
4 Tint butter cream green, then carefully add a few drops of red and blue colouring to give a rich, deep green colour; spread butter cream all over cake.
5 Combine sugar and green colouring in small plastic bag; rub together until sugar is coloured green. Sprinkle top of cake with green sugar.
6 Cut 4cm x 15cm (1½-inch x 6-inch) rectangle from centre of cardboard. Place cardboard on cake; sprinkle yellow jelly crystals inside cardboard. Gently lift cardboard off cake.
7 Position players and stumps on top of cake.

Add green colouring to sugar; rub until evenly coloured.

Sprinkle top of cake with yellow jelly crystals.

TIPS

Mark the quilting on the bag before the icing becomes firm. Dots can be positioned on the cake before or after the icing has set. Be sure to remove the toothpicks before cake is served. This cake can be made two days ahead; position the handle just before the party.

Quilted handbag

Young fashionistas will love this trendy bag. Ready-made icing is quite forgiving — reroll it if you're not happy with the shape.

EQUIPMENT

two 14cm x 21cm
(5½-inch x 8½-inch) loaf pans
20cm x 30cm (8-inch x 12-inch)
rectangular cake board
(page 334) or cake stand
plastic ruler
3 strong wooden toothpicks
fine artist's paint brush

CAKE

3 x 470g (15-ounce) packets
butter cake mix
1 cup (320g) apricot jam,
warmed, strained

DECORATIONS

1kg (2 pounds) ready-made
white icing (page 329)
pure icing (confectioners')
sugar, for dusting
purple food colouring
1 yellow conversation heart
1 marshmallow rope

1 Preheat oven to 150°C/300°F. Grease loaf pans; line bases and sides with baking paper, extending paper 5cm (2 inches) above sides.

2 Make cakes according to directions on packets. Divide mixture evenly into pans; bake about 1¼ hours. Stand cakes in pans 5 minutes before turning, top-side up, onto wire rack to cool.

3 Knead ready-made icing on surface dusted with a little sifted icing sugar until icing loses its stickiness; tint icing mauve.

4 Trim cake tops to make them as flat as possible and the same depth.

5 Join cut sides of cakes with some of the warmed jam to form the handbag. Trim bottom of handbag to make it sit flat. Position cake, on trimmed side, on cake board. Brush cake all over with more jam.

6 Roll three-quarters of the icing on surface dusted with sifted icing sugar until large enough to cover cake. Using rolling pin, lift icing onto cake. Dust hands lightly with icing sugar; smooth icing over cake. Trim icing neatly around base of cake.

7 Starting from the centre of the back of the cake, use side of ruler to gently mark diagonal lines into icing before it sets.

8 Roll out remaining icing on surface dusted with sifted icing sugar. Using pattern from pattern sheet, cut out flap for handbag. Position flap on cake. Dab a tiny amount of jam on the front of the heart lolly, position on bag for clasp. Push one toothpick under the heart, through the cake to support the weight of the clasp.

9 Dust hands lightly with icing sugar, then roll icing scraps into tiny balls. Using the end of the paint brush, make tiny indents in the icing, where the quilting lines cross. Dab a tiny amount of water into each indent, gently push a ball of icing into each indent.

10 Cut marshmallow rope to length required for handle of bag, push a toothpick into each end of the rope, leaving about 1cm (½ inch) of toothpick exposed to push into the cake.

11 Position handle just before serving.

Little Cake Pops

Break store-bought cake into crumbs, mix with ready-made frosting, roll into balls, coat in chocolate and there you have it...a heap of cake pop party cakes and no need to cook anything!

EQUIPMENT

cardboard egg carton
18 ice-block sticks

CAKE

4 cups (340g) firmly packed cake crumbs
⅓ cup ready-made (creamy deluxe) vanilla frosting

DECORATIONS

375g (12 ounces) white chocolate Melts
blue food colouring
sprinkles

1 Combine cake crumbs and frosting in medium bowl. Roll tablespoons of mixture firmly into balls. Place balls on tray, freeze for 1 hour or refrigerate 3 hours or overnight.

2 Stir chocolate in medium heatproof bowl over medium saucepan of simmering water until smooth (do not allow water to touch bottom of bowl). Transfer one-quarter of the chocolate to a small bowl; tint blue.

3 Meanwhile, stab about 18 small holes about 5cm (2 inches) apart into egg carton. Dip the end of a ice-block stick into white chocolate, push stick about half-way into a ball of cake. Repeat with remaining sticks and balls of cake.

4 Swirl cake pops in white chocolate, stand pops upright in egg carton. Refrigerate until chocolate is set.

5 Re-melt blue chocolate if necessary, dip top of pop in blue chocolate, then dip into sprinkles before chocolate is set. Repeat with remaining cake pops and chocolate. Refrigerate pops until ready to serve.

TIPS

Cake pops can be made and kept in the fridge at least two days before the party. It might be necessary to re-melt the chocolate during the dipping process. Colour the chocolate and choose sprinkles to suit the theme of the party. Butter cake, fruit cake or mud cake are all good cakes to use for crumbs. The vanilla frosting is available from the baking aisle at major supermarkets.

Piano Player

It's 9am on a Saturday, and the party crowd's already here.
Birthday parties…it's about food, friends and making memories.

1 Preheat oven to 180°C/350°F. Grease cake pans; line bases and sides with baking paper, extending paper 5cm (2 inches) above sides.

2 Make cakes according to directions on packets. Pour a quarter of the mixture into bar pan; pour remainder into square pan. Bake bar cake about 30 minutes and square cake about 1 hour. Stand cakes in pans 5 minutes before turning, top-side up, onto wire rack to cool.

3 Cut 2.5cm (1-inch) slice off one side of square cake; cut one end off bar cake to make it the same length as square cake, reserve cut-off piece. Using round cutter, cut a circle from reserved cut-off piece of bar cake to make piano stool; cut a piece from base of stool so it is lower than keyboard, if necessary.

4 Secure cakes on cake board, as pictured, with a little butter cream. Spread piano and stool cakes all over with butter cream.

5 Cut chocolate into 5cm (2-inch) strips; position, top-side down, along keyboard, as pictured, to make white keys. Cut licorice strap into 4cm (1½-inch) lengths; place along keyboard, as pictured, to make black keys.

6 Trim ice-cream wafer to 4cm x 5cm (1½-inch x 2-inch) rectangle; press into piano to make music stand. Sheet music can be cut and pasted onto a small piece cardboard; position on music stand. Add candelabra and candles (or other small toy), if you like.

EQUIPMENT

8cm x 25cm (3¼-inch x 10-inch)
bar cake pan
deep 20cm (8-inch) square
cake pan
4cm (1½-inch) round cutter
30cm (12-inch) square
cake board (page 334)

CAKE

2 x 470g (15-ounce) packets
butter cake mix
1½ quantities chocolate butter
cream (page 329)

DECORATIONS

2 x 180g (5½-ounce) blocks
white eating chocolate
1 black licorice strap
1 ice-cream wafer
sheet music
small piece cardboard
toy candelabra and candles

Cut 2.5cm slice off one side of square cake; cut one end off bar cake to make it the same length as square cake. Using round cutter, cut a circle from cut-off piece of bar cake to make piano stool.

Assemble cakes on board to form piano.

Checkerboard

It's been around since 300BC... but it wasn't until 1952 that the first checkers programme was used by a computer.

1 Preheat oven to 180°C/350°F. Line mini muffin pans with the paper cases. Grease square cake pan; line base and sides with baking paper, extending paper 5cm (2 inches) above sides.

2 Make cakes according to directions on packets. Drop 2 level teaspoons of the mixture into each mini paper case; bake about 15 minutes. Stand cakes in pans 5 minutes before turning, top-side up, onto wire rack to cool.

3 Spread remaining cake mixture into square cake pan; bake about 1 hour. Stand cake in pan 5 minutes before turning, top-side up, onto wire rack to cool.

4 Level top of square cake; trim sides to a square shape. Secure cake, cut-side down, on cake board with a little butter cream.

5 Place a quarter of the butter cream in small bowl; tint black. Tint remaining butter cream red. Spread red butter cream over top and sides of square cake, and over the tops of 12 small cakes in red paper cases.

6 Spread black butter cream over tops of remaining small cakes.

7 Cut licorice straps into 32 squares. Using picture as a guide, press licorice squares gently onto butter cream to make a checkerboard. Cut four strips of licorice long enough to outline the cake. Position some of the cakes on the checkerboard.

EQUIPMENT

2 x 12-hole (1-tablespoon/20ml) mini muffin pans

24 mini muffin paper cases (12 red, 12 black)

deep 22cm (9-inch) square cake pan

35cm (14-inch) square cake board (page 334)

CAKE

1½ x 470g (15-ounce) packets butter cake mix
(see 'mixing the cakes' page 345)

1 quantity butter cream
(page 329)

black and red food colouring

DECORATIONS

2 black licorice straps

TIP
The hardest part of making this cake is getting the colours right. Use good quality colourings and you'll have no trouble.

My House

You could use one of those many pictures, drawn by your little Picasso and lovingly stuck on the fridge, to make the scene for the top of this cake instead of the house we've used here.

1 Preheat oven to 150°C/300°F. Grease pan; line base and sides with baking paper, extending paper 5cm (2 inches) above sides.
2 Make cakes according to directions on packets. Spread mixture into pan; bake about 1 hour. Stand cake in pan 10 minutes before turning, top-side up, onto wire rack to cool.
3 Level cake top; secure cake, cut-side down, on cake board with a little warmed jam. Brush cake all over with jam.
4 Knead ready-made icing on surface dusted with a little sifted icing sugar until icing loses its stickiness. Roll three-quarters of the icing on surface dusted with sifted icing sugar into a square large enough to cover cake. Using rolling pin, lift icing over cake. Dust hands lightly with icing sugar, smooth icing over cake; trim excess icing from base of cake.
5 Divide remaining icing into five portions; tint yellow, red, brown, green and light blue. Wrap each portion, separately, in plastic wrap. Roll each colour, one at a time, on surface lightly dusted with sifted icing sugar, until about 3mm (⅛-inch) thick.
6 Using picture as a guide, cut out simple shapes from icing using a small sharp knife. Add a tiny drop of blue colouring to the remaining light blue icing to tint it a darker shade of blue for the roof, windows and door. Position icing shapes on cake; secure with a little jam.

EQUIPMENT

deep 22cm (9-inch) square cake pan
30cm (12-inch) square cake board (page 334)

CAKE

1½ x 470g (15-ounce) packets butter cake mix (see 'mixing the cakes' page 345)
½ cup (160g) apricot jam, warmed, strained

DECORATIONS

1kg (2 pounds) ready-made white icing (page 329)
pure icing (confectioners') sugar, for dusting
yellow, red, brown, green and blue food colouring

TIP
Cake can be completed two days ahead of the party.

Sewing Machine

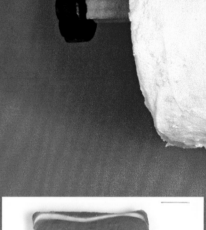

EQUIPMENT

deep 22cm (9-inch)
square cake pan

7cm (2¾-inch) round cutter

30cm (12-inch) square
cake board (page 334)

CAKE

1 x 470g (15-ounce) packet
butter cake mix

1 quantity butter cream
(page 329)

2 tablespoons cocoa powder

DECORATIONS

3 thick black licorice ropes

4 licorice allsorts

2 pink Musk Sticks

1 ice-cream wafer

toothpicks

thin cord

1 black Wine Gum

2 green Wine Gums

1 red Wine Gum

2 chocolate-coated
licorice bullets

1 Preheat oven to 180°C/350°F. Grease cake pan; line base and sides with baking paper, extending paper 5cm (2 inches) above sides.

2 Make cake according to directions on packet. Spread mixture into pan; bake about 30 minutes. Stand cake in pan 5 minutes before turning, top-side up, onto wire rack to cool.

3 Using pattern from pattern sheet, cut sewing machine pieces from cake (use round cutter to cut out circle). Stand circle on side; cut a 1cm (½-inch) piece off side of circle so it stands upright. Secure cake pieces on cake board with a little butter cream.

4 Combine ½ cup butter cream with sifted cocoa in small bowl; spread all over sewing machine base. Spread plain butter cream all over body and wheel of sewing machine.

5 To make cottonreel, secure 4cm (1½-inch) piece of thick licorice to two licorice allsorts, trim into rounded shape; position on top of sewing machine, as pictured. Trim piece of thick black licorice into pointed needle; press into cake. Position trimmed pink Musk Sticks, as pictured; split remaining licorice rope in half lengthways, position two pieces on cake as pictured. Wind coloured cord around cottonreel at top of machine, thread through and around licorice pieces, then thread through licorice needle (use toothpick to make hole in licorice).

6 Cut wafer into 5cm (2-inch) round circle; position as plate under the needle. Decorate sewing machine with remaining lollies.

Using pattern sheet, cut out sewing machine from cake.

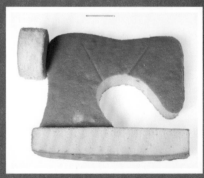

Assemble cake ready to ice.

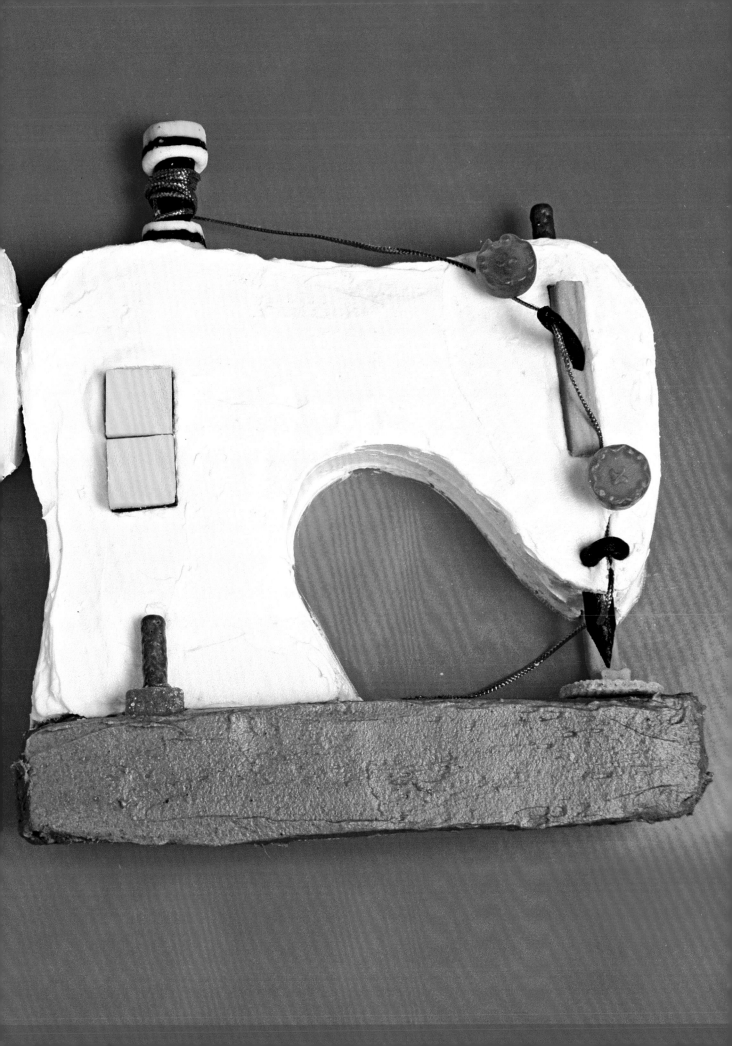

Candles

Birthday candles as a birthday cake...what a great idea.

EQUIPMENT

two 8cm x 17cm (3¼-inch x 6¾-inch) nut roll tins
30cm (12-inch) round cake board (page 334)
or plate

CAKE

2 x 470g (15-ounce) packets butter cake mix
⅓ cup (110g) apricot jam, warmed, strained
750g (1½ pounds) ready-made white icing (page 329)
2 cups (320g) pure icing (confectioners') sugar
yellow, pink and blue food colouring
1½ tablespoons water, approximately

DECORATIONS

3 small thin birthday candles

1 Adjust oven shelves to allow for the height of the nut roll tins. Preheat oven to 150°C/300°F. Grease and flour lids and inside of tins; place base lids on tins, position tins upright on oven tray.

2 Make cakes according to directions on packets. Divide mixture between tins; position lids on top. Bake rolls about 1 hour. Stand rolls in tins 10 minutes before removing lids; shake tins gently to release cakes onto wire rack to cool.

3 Level cake tops. Cut top off one cake at an angle; discard top. Cut one-third off remaining cake at an angle; keep both pieces of cake. Brush all three cakes all over with jam.

4 Knead ready-made icing on surface dusted with a little sifted icing sugar until icing loses its stickiness. Divide icing into three equal portions; tint yellow, pink and blue.

5 Roll three-quarters of each colour, one at a time, into a 5mm (¼-inch) thickness. Wrap yellow icing around shortest cake; trim away excess icing. Wrap pink icing around medium cake; trim away excess icing. Wrap blue icing around tallest cake; trim away excess icing.

6 Roll remaining icings, one at a time, into a 5mm (¼-inch) thickness. Cut an oval from each colour large enough to cover the tops of each cake; position ovals on tops of cakes.

7 Push candles through icing into centre of each cake until only the wicks are showing (you may need to trim the candles to fit). Secure cakes on cake board with a little jam.

8 Sift ½ cup of the icing sugar into small heatproof bowl, then stir in enough of the water to make a thick paste; tint yellow. Place bowl over small saucepan of simmering water (do not allow water to touch base of bowl); stir until icing is pourable. Working quickly drizzle icing over yellow cake to resemble melted wax.

9 Repeat step 8 to ice the remaining candles, using corresponding colours for the candles.

Cut the two cakes to make three candle cakes.

Use ready-made icing to ice cakes.

Push candles into cakes so only the wicks are showing.

Preparing sandwich cookies.

Choc-chip ice-cream sandwich

One of the largest ice-cream sandwiches ever made. The cookies can be made the day before, so there's no mad rush on party day.

EQUIPMENT

two deep 23cm (9¼-inch)
round cake pans
25cm (10-inch) round
cake board (page 334)
or serving plate

CAKE

4 litres (16 cups)
vanilla ice-cream
125g (4 ounces) unsalted
butter, softened
1 teaspoon vanilla extract
⅓ cup (55g) caster sugar
⅓ cup (55g) firmly packed
light brown sugar
1 egg
1 cup (150g) plain
(all-purpose) flour
¾ cup (110g) self-raising flour
½ cup (95g) dark Choc Bits
10 dark chocolate Melts

1 Line one cake pan with four layers of plastic wrap, extending plastic wrap 10cm (4 inches) over side of pan.
2 Working quickly, spoon ice-cream into pan, pressing down firmly and smoothing surface. Fold plastic wrap over ice-cream to enclose. Freeze 3 hours or overnight until firm.
3 Remove ice-cream from pan, still wrapped in plastic; place on oven tray. Return to freezer.
4 Preheat oven to 150°C/300°F. Grease both cake pans.
5 Beat butter, extract and sugars in small bowl with electric mixer until light and fluffy. Add egg; beat until combined. Transfer mixture to large bowl; stir in sifted flours then choc Bits.
6 Divide dough in half; press one half over base of one pan. Press remaining half over base of second pan, leaving a 1cm (½-inch) gap around edge of dough; push chocolate Melts onto top of dough.
7 Bake cookies about 20 minutes. Stand cookies in pans 20 minutes before turning, top-side up, onto wire racks to cool.
8 Place plain cookie on cake board; top with ice-cream cake then choc-topped cookie. Serve immediately.

TIPS
Ice-cream cake and cookies
can be prepared one day ahead.
Store cookies in an airtight
container. Use regular ice-cream
for best results; high or low
fat ice-creams are not suitable.
Assemble cake just before
serving. Use a serrated knife
to cut the cake.

Hopscotch

Remember the days in the old school yard when the boys played marbles and the girls played hopscotch?

EQUIPMENT

20cm x 30cm (8-inch x 12-inch)
rectangular cake pan
20cm x 50cm (8-inch x 20-inch)
rectangular cake board (page 334)
small paper piping bag
(page 338)

CAKE

1 x 470g (15-ounce) packet
butter cake mix
2½ quantities butter cream
(page 329)

blue, green, yellow
and pink food colouring

DECORATIONS

165g (5-ounce) packet
Mini Musks

1 Preheat oven to 180°C/350°F. Grease cake pan; line base and long sides with baking paper, extending paper 5cm (2 inches) above sides.

2 Make cake according to directions on packet. Spread mixture into pan; bake about 35 minutes. Stand cake in pan 5 minutes before turning, top-side up, onto wire rack to cool.

3 Place a fifth of the butter cream into a small bowl; leave plain. Place a third of the remaining butter cream into a small bowl; tint blue. Divide remaining butter cream equally into three small bowls; tint green, yellow and pink.

4 Level cake top; turn cake cut-side down. Trim cake to 14cm x 28cm (5½-inch x 11¼-inch). Using pattern from pattern sheet, cut 'home' from cake. Cut remaining cake into eight 7cm (2¾-inch) squares.

5 Using picture as a guide, spread some of the green butter cream over tops and sides of two hopscotch squares; repeat with yellow, pink and blue butter cream. Spread remaining blue butter cream over top and sides of 'home' cake. Secure cakes on cake board with a little butter cream.

6 Spoon plain butter cream into piping bag. Pipe around edges of each hopscotch square and 'home' cake. Using picture as a guide, use Mini Musks to make 'home' and the numbers one to eight.

Cutting strips to size.

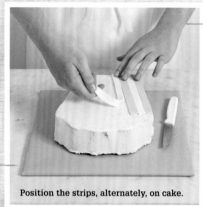

Position the strips, alternately, on cake.

Box of Popcorn

The oldest popcorn ever found was discovered in the "Bat Cave" of central New Mexico. It's believed to be over 5000 years old.

1 Preheat oven to 150°C/300°F. Grease pan; line base and sides with baking paper, extending paper 5cm (2 inches) above sides.

2 Make cakes according to directions on packets. Spread mixture into pan; bake about 1 hour. Stand cake in pan 10 minutes before turning, top-side up, onto wire rack to cool.

3 Level cake top to make cake about 5cm (2 inches) high; turn cake cut-side down. Using pattern from pattern sheet, cut out popcorn box. Secure cake, cut-side down, on cake board with a little butter cream. Spread butter cream all over cake.

4 Knead ready-made icing on surface dusted with a little sifted icing sugar until icing loses its stickiness. Divide icing in half. Leave one half white; wrap in plastic wrap. Tint remaining icing blue; roll on surface dusted with sifted icing sugar into a 3mm ($\frac{1}{8}$-inch) thickness. Cut into long 1.5cm-thick ($\frac{3}{4}$-inch) strips; cover with plastic wrap. Repeat making strips using the white icing.

5 Using picture as a guide, position strips along sides and top of cake, trimming and tapering slightly to fit the bottom of the popcorn box. Roll out scraps of white icing. Cut icing into a 3cm x 5cm ($1\frac{1}{4}$-inch x 2-inch) rectangle. Position on box with a little butter cream; write child's name with writing icing.

6 Press popcorn gently onto butter cream up to an hour before serving.

EQUIPMENT

deep 23cm (9$\frac{1}{4}$-inch)
square cake pan
30cm (12-inch) square
cake board (page 334)
ruler

CAKE

2 x 470g (15-ounce) packets
butter cake mix
1 quantity butter cream
(page 329)
blue food colouring

DECORATIONS

500g (1 pound) ready-made
white icing (page 329)
pure icing (confectioners')
sugar, for dusting
blue writing icing
1$\frac{1}{2}$ cups (15g) popped popcorn

Footy jumper

Ice this cake in your child's favourite footy team's colours.

1 Preheat oven to 180°C/350°F. Grease baking dishes; line bases and sides with baking paper, extending paper 5cm (2 inches) above sides.
2 Make cakes according to directions on packets. Divide mixture evenly into dishes; bake cakes about 1 hour. Stand cakes in dishes 5 minutes before turning, top-side up, onto wire rack to cool.
3 Using serrated knife, level cake tops so they are the same height. Trim one long edge of each cake so cakes sit closely together. Turn cakes, cut-side down. Using pattern from pattern sheet, cut out half the jumper, turn pattern over and repeat with other cake.
4 Assemble cake pieces on cake board, cut-side down, to form footy jumper; discard any remaining cake. Secure cake pieces to board with a little butter cream.
5 Tint butter cream yellow; spread all over cake. Cut and position fruit Roll-Ups for jumper colours, as pictured.
6 To make 'Happy Birthday' and number plaques, draw outlines of a 4.5cm x 16cm (1¾-inch x 6½-inch) rectangle and 5.5cm (2¼-inch) circle on baking paper. Melt chocolate (page 339); tint blue. Spread chocolate within the circle and rectangle outlines. When chocolate is almost set, trim edges of rectangle with a sharp knife; use the round cutter to trim circle, peel off paper.
7 Using black decorating gel, pipe on plaques. Carefully lift and position plaques on cake. Press candy letters onto sleeves of jumper, as desired.

EQUIPMENT

two deep 26cm x 36cm (10½-inch x 14½-inch) baking dishes
40cm x 60cm (16-inch x 24-inch) rectangular cake board (page 334)
5.5cm (2¼-inch) round cutter

CAKE

4 x 470g (15-ounce) packets butter cake mix
(see 'mixing the cakes' page 345)

2 quantities butter cream
(page 329)

yellow food colouring

DECORATIONS

4 x 75cm (30-inch) long fruit Roll-Ups reels
⅔ cup (100g) white chocolate Melts
blue food colouring
black glossy decorating gel
blue and yellow candy letter decorations

Turn cake cut-side down. Using pattern sheet, cut out footy jumper from cake.

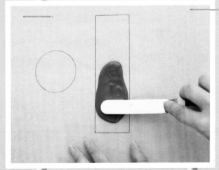

Draw markings on baking paper; turn paper over. Spread melted chocolate into markings.

When chocolate is almost set, use a sharp knife to trim edges of rectangle. Use the round cutter to cut out the circle.

Rocking horse

While not as old as the Trojan horse used by the Greeks, this cake certainly has the looks of an antique rocker.

1 Preheat oven to 180°C/350°F. Grease cake pan; line base and sides with baking paper, extending paper 5cm (2 inches) above sides.

2 Make cake according to directions on packet. Spread mixture into pan; bake about 30 minutes. Stand cake in pan 5 minutes before turning, top-side up, onto wire rack to cool.

3 Cut 4cm (1½-inch) wide strip from long edge of cake at base, as pictured. Cut this strip into three even-sized pieces; cut a small wedge from one third, as pictured, for the ears, the larger wedge makes the head. Cut another wedge from the next third of cake; the small wedge makes the nose, the larger wedge makes the neck where it joins the body. Cut about one third off the end of the remaining piece of cake; the larger piece forms the top part of the neck, reserve the small piece. Cut a 4cm (1½-inch) wide strip from each end of the cake for the legs. Cut a slightly curved piece from the top of the long side of the large piece of cake, to give the curve of the back of the horse. Reserve cake cut-offs.

4 Position cakes on cake board, as pictured, to form horse shape; secure to board with a little butter cream, using reserved cake cut-offs to fill gaps between legs and body.

5 Tint butter cream red; spread all over cake. Sprinkle coconut all over cake.

6 Position Smarties on cake for saddle and feet. Push potato straws into cake for horse's neck, mane and tail.

7 Cut jubes to represent eyebrow and part of eye; secure a black Smartie to eye with a little butter cream, secure yellow mini M&M for pupil with a little butter cream. Cut red jelly fruit ring for mouth.

8 Use thin strips of licorice strap to make stirrup and bridle; decorate with silver cachous. Position coathangers, stacked two on top of each other, at base of rocking horse, to make rocker.

EQUIPMENT

20cm x 30cm (8-inch x 12-inch)
rectangular cake pan

40cm x 50cm (16-inch x 20-inch)
rectangular cake board
(page 334)

CAKE

1 x 470g (15-ounce) packet
butter cake mix

1 quantity butter cream
(page 329)

red food colouring

DECORATIONS

2 cups (80g) shredded coconut

2 x 50g (1½-ounce)
packets Smarties

1 large packet potato straws

2 round green jubes

1 yellow mini M&M

1 red jelly ring

1 black licorice strap

silver cachous

4 wooden coathangers,
hooks removed

Cut cake shapes from large cake.

Position cakes on board ready to ice.

Giant Donut

You're going to need a pretty big mug to dunk this donut!

1 Preheat oven to 150°C/300°F. Grease and flour savarin pan.

2 If you only have one savarin pan, use two packets of the cake mix to make one cake according to directions on packets. Spread mixture into pan; bake cake about 50 minutes. Stand cake in pan 5 minutes before turning onto wire rack to cool. Repeat with remaining packet cake mixes to make the second cake in cleaned savarin pan.

3 Cut Musk Sticks into thin strips, then into 1cm (½-inch) lengths.

4 Using a serrated knife, trim the flat bases on both cakes so they are level; spread cut surfaces with warmed jam. Place one cake, jam-side up, on cake board; place remaining cake, jam-side down, on top of the other cake.

5 To make icing, sift icing sugar into large heatproof bowl and stir in enough water to make a stiff paste; tint pink. Place bowl over large saucepan of simmering water, stir icing until smooth and of a pouring consistency (don't let water touch base of bowl – if it overheats it will crystallise, and you will have to start again).

6 Quickly pour the icing as evenly as possible over the cake, avoid using a spatula if possible. Decorate with sprinkles immediately before the icing sets.

TIPS

Bake one cake at a time, unless you have access to two savarin pans. Have the sprinkles close by for decorating, as this icing sets rapidly after it has been warmed. If you're not happy with the icing, leave it to set completely, then snap or lift off any ugly pieces on the cake or the board. The cakes can be made and assembled one day ahead. Ice the cake up to an hour before serving.

Guitar

No one will want to pick this guitar up and smash it...it's much too tasty for that. Cutting and icing the cake can be a little fiddly.

EQUIPMENT

8cm x 25cm
(3¼-inch x 10-inch)
bar cake pan
deep 20cm (8-inch)
square cake pan
deep 22cm (9-inch)
square cake pan
40cm x 80cm
(16-inch x 32-inch)
rectangular cake board
(page 334)

CAKE

2 x 470g (15-ounce) packets
butter cake mix
1 quantity butter cream
(page 329)
⅓ cup (35g) cocoa powder

DECORATIONS

1 black licorice strap
1 ice-cream wafer
2 pink Musk Sticks
thin black elastic
1 thick licorice twist
6 round yellow lollipops
1m (3 feet) x 5cm (2 inch)
wide ribbon

1 Preheat oven to 180°C/350°F. Grease cake pans; line bases and sides with baking paper, extending paper 5cm (2 inches) above sides.

2 Make cakes according to directions on packets. Pour mixture into pans, so that all mixtures are the same level; bake bar cake about 30 minutes and square cakes about 40 minutes. Stand cakes in pans 5 minutes before turning, top-side up, onto wire rack to cool.

3 Assemble the three cakes, as pictured, placing bar cake in centre at end of smaller square cake. Make two slits in top of each side of smaller square cake, as pictured, to halfway through cake; cut off these four small pieces (you will need only two cut-out pieces for the guitar). Place a cut-out piece on either side of larger square cake 4cm (1½ inches) up from bottom.

4 Using pattern from pattern sheet, cut out guitar. Position cake pieces, cut-side down, on cake board to form guitar, as pictured; secure with a little butter cream. Discard any leftover cake pieces.

5 Combine ½ cup of butter cream with ¼ cup of the sifted cocoa in small bowl; using picture as a guide, spread all over neck and sound hole. Combine remaining butter cream with remaining 1 tablespoon of sifted cocoa in medium bowl; spread over remaining cake.

6 Outline sound hole with a thin strip of licorice strap, as pictured. Position thin strips licorice strap across neck of guitar.

7 Cut wafer in half lengthways, cut away two corners of each half; press wafer halves firmly into position, one to form bridge, the other at base of neck, as pictured.

8 Cut each Musk Stick into three pieces; secure a piece of elastic on each piece Musk Stick for strings. Press Musk Sticks well into top of neck, as pictured. Press a piece of licorice twist firmly over elastic ends at base of guitar to hold the strings steady.

9 Position lollipops at top of neck to make tuning knobs; slip ends of ribbon under cake to make strap.

Assemble the three cakes; make two cuts on each side of smaller square cake halfway through the cake – cut off these small pieces, reserve two of the pieces.

Place the two reserved pieces on either side of larger square cake, towards the bottom. Using the pattern sheet, cut out guitar shape.

Bales of Hay

While it is cute, it's best to serve this to older children as the small noodles can be a choking hazard for younger children.

EQUIPMENT

deep 22cm (9-inch)
square cake pan
25cm (10-inch) square
cake board (page 334)

CAKE

3 x 440g (14-ounce) packets
butter cake mix
1 quantity butter cream
(page 329)
yellow food colouring

DECORATIONS

6 rainbow sour straps
8 x 25g (¾-ounce) packets
ready-to-eat noodles
toy chickens

1 Preheat oven to 170°C/340°F. Grease pan; line base and sides with baking paper, extending paper 5cm (2 inches) above sides.

2 Make cakes according to directions on packets. Spread mixture into pan; bake about 1½ hours. Stand cake in pan 10 minutes before turning, top-side up, onto wire rack to cool.

3 Level cake top; trim cake into three 5cm x 10cm (2-inch x 4-inch) rectangles. Using a small serrated knife cut 'V'-shaped indents into the middle of each piece of cake.

4 Tint butter cream pale yellow; spread all over cakes.

5 Break noodles into pieces; roll cakes firmly in broken noodles until covered all over.

6 Cut the red stripes off the rainbow straps. Using picture as a guide, trim and position red straps around the hay bales. Secure two hay bales, side-by-side, on cake board with a little butter cream. Position remaining hay bale on top. Decorate with toy chickens.

Using a small serrated knife cut 'V'-shaped indents into the middle of each piece of cake.

Using the markings as a guide, cut a deep hollow into the cake with a small serrated knife.

Spread the chocolate butter cream over the cake, then fill the hollow with coins and rainbow choc-chips.

Swirl the chocolate around the inside of the steamer until it is evenly coated.

When set, use a hot cloth to briefly rub bowl to remove the shell.

Party Piñata

Let the birthday child break open the chocolate piñata shell with the toy hammer.

EQUIPMENT

deep 15cm (6-inch) round cake pan
30cm (12-inch) round cake board (page 334)
ruler
toothpicks
2.25-litre (9-cup) pudding steamer

CAKE

1 x 470g (15-ounce) packet butter cake mix
1 quantity chocolate butter cream (page 329)

DECORATIONS

23 large chocolate coins
19 medium chocolate coins
13 small chocolate coins
150g (4½ ounces) rainbow choc-chips
½ teaspoon vegetable oil
450g (14½ ounces) milk chocolate Melts
50g (1½ ounces) milk eating chocolate
35g (1-ounce) tube mini M&M's
250g (8-ounce) packet M&M's
toy hammer

1 Preheat oven to 180°C/350°F. Grease cake pan; line base and side with baking paper, extending paper 5cm (2 inches) above side.
2 Make cake according to directions on packet. Pour mixture into pan until three-quarters full; bake about 45 minutes. Stand cake in pan 5 minutes before turning, top-side up, onto wire rack to cool.
3 Secure cake on cake board with a little butter cream. Using ruler and toothpicks, mark 11cm (4½-inch) circle in centre of cake. Using markings as a guide, cut a deep hollow into the cake with a small serrated knife.
4 Spread chocolate butter cream all over cake; allow to set, then fill hollow with coins and half of the rainbow choc-chips.
5 To make chocolate shell: grease pudding steamer with oil; place bowl in freezer 10 minutes. Melt chocolate Melts (page 339); pour the melted chocolate into pudding steamer; swirl chocolate to coat inside of steamer evenly. Continue swirling until chocolate begins to set and stops flowing around the steamer; try to keep the chocolate a uniform thickness, particularly at the top edge. Stand until chocolate is almost set. Freeze until chocolate sets completely.
6 Carefully place pudding steamer with set chocolate shell over cake; using a hot cloth, briefly rub outside of bowl. Chocolate shell will slip from bowl to completely enclose cake.
7 Melt milk chocolate; secure remaining rainbow choc-chips and M&M's to outside of chocolate shell with chocolate. Allow to set.

TIP
If there is enough cake mix left over, you can make some mini cupcakes and hide them under the piñata.

Press 4cm round cutter down through centre of cake as far as it will go; with a sharp knife, cut away cake from around outside of cutter, remove cutter, leaving a small round attached to top of loaf cake.

Press 5cm round cutter further down into cake, cut away cake from around outside of cutter to make second round.

Jack in the Box

EQUIPMENT

14cm x 22cm (5½-inch x 9-inch) loaf pan

4cm (1½-inch) round cutter

5cm (2-inch) round cutter

25cm (10-inch) square cake board (page 334)

CAKE

1 x 470g (15-ounce) packet butter cake mix

1 quantity butter cream (page 329)

red and blue food colouring

DECORATIONS

1 ice-cream cone

hundreds and thousands

coloured paper

1 black licorice strap

2 brown mini M&M's

1 yellow mini M&M

1 red licorice strap

2 ice-cream wafers

8 green Fruit Sticks

300g (9½-ounce) packet raspberry lollies, halved

2 tablespoons apricot jam, warmed, strained

1 Preheat oven to 180°C/350°F. Grease cake pan; line base and sides with baking paper, extending paper 5cm (2 inches) above sides.

2 Make cake according to directions on packet. Spread mixture into pan; bake about 50 minutes. Stand cake in pan 5 minutes before turning, top-side up, onto wire rack to cool.

3 Trim cake until all sides are straight; stand cake on one end. Press 4cm round cutter down through centre of cake as far as it will go; with a sharp knife, cut away cake from around outside of cutter, remove cutter, leaving a small round attached to top of loaf cake. Press 5cm round cutter further down into cake, cut away cake from around outside of cutter to make second round.

4 Trim rounds into rounded shapes to make head and shoulders, leave top flat. Secure cake to cake board with a little butter cream.

5 Reserve ¼ cup butter cream. Tint half the remaining butter cream red; tint remaining half blue.

6 Spread plain butter cream over head and shoulders. Spread front, top and back of box with red butter cream; spread remaining two sides of box with blue butter cream.

7 Spread pointed end of ice-cream cone with plain butter cream; coat with hundreds and thousands, position on top of clown's head. Cut coloured paper to make collar, press into position. Wrap thin strip of licorice strap around bottom of clown's shoulders. Position brown mini M&M's for eyes; position yellow mini M&M for nose, and a thin strip of red licorice for mouth.

8 Press wafers upright into top back edge of cake to form lid. Split Fruit Sticks in half lengthways; secure to all edges of box and lid with butter cream.

9 Brush raspberry lolly halves with a little jam, coat in hundreds and thousands; position on cake, as pictured, to decorate sides of box.

Numbers

One

The first birthday party is usually an occasion for the parents to celebrate getting, relatively unscathed, through the first year!

EQUIPMENT

12-hole (¹/₃-cup/80ml) standard muffin pan
6 standard paper cases (blue)
3.5cm (1½-inch) and 6.5cm (2¾-inch) wide duck-shaped cutters
new small artist's paint brush
20cm x 50cm (8-inch x 20-inch) rectangular cake board
(page 334)

CAKE

½ x 470g (15-ounce) packet butter cake mix
(see 'mixing the cakes' page 345)

½ quantity butter cream
(page 329)

yellow, orange and blue food colouring

DECORATIONS

100g (3-ounce) ready-made white icing (page 329)
pure icing (confectioners') sugar, for dusting
6 blue rainbow choc-chips

1 Preheat oven to 180°C/350°F. Line six holes of the muffin pan with paper cases.

2 Make cake according to directions on packet. Drop 2½ level tablespoons of mixture into each paper case; bake about 20 minutes. Stand cakes in pan 5 minutes before turning, top-side up, onto wire rack to cool.

3 Knead ready-made icing on surface dusted with a little sifted icing sugar until icing loses its stickiness; tint yellow. Roll icing on surface dusted with sifted icing sugar into a 3mm (⅛-inch) thickness. Using cutters, cut two large ducks and five small ducks from the icing. Brush one side of a large duck sparingly, but evenly, with water. Gently press the other large duck onto the damp surface.

4 Using the paint brush and orange food colouring, paint an orange beak on each side of the mother duck's head. Gently press a blue rainbow choc-chip into the icing to make an eye. Lay mother duck flat on a baking-paper-lined tray to dry. Paint beaks and position eyes on ducklings; dry on tray with mother duck.

5 Tint butter cream blue; spread over tops of cakes. Position cakes on cake board to resemble the number 1; secure with a little butter cream. Position mother duck and ducklings on cakes.

TIPS
Make a duckling-topped cake for each small guest - even though they might not be eating the cakes they'll love the look of them. Make sure the ducks are completely dry and firm. The drying time will depend on the weather: if it's wet or humid, it could take overnight. The ducklings will take less time to dry than the mother duck.

Cut out cake using paper pattern.

Insert toothpicks into base of leaves.

Taller at Two

1 Preheat oven to 180°C/350°F. Grease cake pans; line bases and sides with baking paper, extending paper 5cm (2 inches) above sides.

2 Make cakes according to directions on packets. Divide mixture between pans so both mixtures are the same depth. Bake rectangular cake about 35 minutes and bar cake about 25 minutes. Stand cakes in pans 5 minutes before turning, top-side up, onto wire rack to cool.

3 Level cake tops so cakes are the same height; turn cakes, cut-side down. Using pattern from pattern sheet, cut out cake, as pictured. Assemble cake pieces on cake board, cut-side down, to form the number 2; secure cake to board with a little butter cream.

4 Tint three-quarters of the butter cream orange; spread all over cake.

5 Place sugar and yellow colouring in small plastic bag; rub until sugar is evenly coloured. Sprinkle over cake.

6 Combine remaining butter cream and sifted cocoa in small bowl. Dollop teaspoons of butter cream onto cake, flatten with back of spoon to resemble giraffe markings.

7 Cut licorice strap into thin strips; position strips to outline cake and mouth.

8 Cut marshmallow in half, discard one half; place green allsort on top of remaining half. Pipe dot with blue decorating gel on allsort to complete eye; position on head.

9 Insert toothpicks into base of mint leaves; press into head for ears. Position biscuits next to mint leaves to resemble horns.

EQUIPMENT

20cm x 30cm (8-inch x 12-inch) rectangular cake pan

8cm x 25cm (3¼-inch x 10-inch) bar cake pan

35cm x 45cm (14-inch x 18-inch) rectangular cake board (page 334)

CAKE

2 x 470g (15-ounce) packets butter cake mix

2 quantities butter cream (page 329)

orange and yellow food colouring

¼ cup (25g) cocoa powder

DECORATIONS

¼ cup (55g) white (granulated) sugar

1 black licorice strap

1 white marshmallow

1 green licorice allsort

blue glossy decorating gel

2 double-pointed toothpicks

2 mint leaves

2 chocolate finger biscuits

Three

Three-year-olds love nursery rhymes, and even though the mice are clearly not blind they're having fun finding the cheese.

EQUIPMENT

12-hole (¹/₃-cup/80ml)
standard muffin pan
11 standard paper cases
1.5cm (¾-inch) round cutter
35cm x 45cm (14-inch x 18-inch)
rectangular cake board
(page 334)

CAKE

1 x 470g (15-ounce) packet
butter cake mix
1 quantity butter cream
(page 329)

yellow and pink food colouring

DECORATIONS

60g (2 ounces) ready-made
white icing (page 329)
pure icing (confectioners')
sugar, for dusting
2 large marshmallows, halved
5 white marshmallows, halved
35g (1-ounce) tube mini M&M's
3 pink Mallow Bakes, halved
1 white Mallow Bake, halved
1m (1 yard) length black
licorice bootlace

1 Preheat oven to 180°C/350°F. Line 11 holes of the muffin pan with paper cases.

2 Make cake according to directions on packet. Drop 2½ level tablespoons of the mixture into each paper case; bake about 20 minutes. Stand cakes in pan 5 minutes before turning, top-side up, onto wire rack to cool.

3 Divide butter cream into four small bowls; tint one bowl yellow, and tint remaining bowls various shades of pink (light, medium, dark).

4 Spread yellow butter cream over four cakes. Using picture as a guide, spread pink butter cream over remaining seven cakes.

5 Knead ready-made icing on surface dusted with a little sifted icing sugar until icing loses its stickiness; tint yellow. Roll icing on surface dusted with sifted icing sugar into a 3mm (¹/₈-inch) thickness. Cut out 2 x 5cm (2-inch) squares from icing. Using 1.5cm round cutter, cut a few circles from the squares to give the look of swiss cheese; cut each square into two triangles. Position cheese triangles on yellow cakes.

6 Using picture as a guide, position marshmallow halves for ears and mini M&M's for eyes. Position Mallow Bake halves for noses. Cut 28 x 1cm (½-inch) pieces from licorice bootlace; use these to make whiskers. Secure cakes to board with a little butter cream to resemble the number 3. Cut 7 x 10cm (4-inch) pieces from licorice bootlace to make tails; push into cakes.

TIPS

You'll have 1 cup of the cake mixture left over - use it to make more cakes for your guests. We used the mouse traps as a prop in the photo; it's best not to use them at a children's party because of safety concerns.

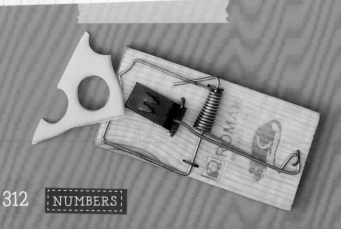

Four Racing Cars

1 Preheat oven to 180°C/350°F. Grease cake pan; line base and sides with baking paper, extending paper 5cm (2 inches) above sides.

2 Make cakes according to directions on packets. Spread mixture into pan; bake about 40 minutes. Stand cake in pan 5 minutes before turning, top-side up, onto wire rack to cool.

3 Level cake top; turn cake, cut-side down. Cut cake into three even strips, as pictured. Leave centre strip whole; cut remaining strips into three segments, as pictured.

4 Assemble cake pieces on cake board, cut-side down, to form the number 4; secure to board with a little butter cream.

5 Tint butter cream red; spread all over cake.

6 Knead ready-made icing on surface dusted with a little sifted icing sugar until icing loses its stickiness; reserve a walnut-sized amount of icing for road markings, enclose in plastic wrap.

7 Knead black colouring into remaining icing to make a grey colour; roll until 3mm (⅛-inch) thickness. Using sharp knife, cut a 6.5cm x 28cm (2¾-inch x 11¼-inch) rectangle, a 6.5cm x 15cm (2¾-inch x 6-inch) rectangle and a 6.5cm x 8cm (2¾-inch x 3¼-inch) rectangle; position on cake for roads.

8 Roll reserved white icing into thin cord; cut into two 6.5cm (2¾-inch) pieces and one 27cm (10¾-inch) piece; secure to cake, with tiny dabs of water, for road markings.

9 Secure Tic Tacs to roads with tiny dabs of water to mark lanes. Cut licorice strap into fourteen 1cm (½-inch) pieces and one 13cm (5¼-inch) piece; position on cake to form rail tracks. Position cars and road signs on cake, as desired; secure with a little butter cream.

EQUIPMENT

20cm x 30cm (8-inch x 12-inch) rectangular cake pan
40cm (16-inch) square cake board (page 334)

CAKE

2 x 470g (15-ounce) packets butter cake mix
1½ quantities butter cream (page 329)
red and black food colouring

DECORATIONS

250g (8 ounces) ready-made white icing (page 329)
pure icing (confectioners') sugar, for dusting
19 Tic Tacs
1 black licorice strap
4 chocolate cars
assorted mini road signs

Turn cake cut-side down. Using a serrated knife, cut the cake into three even strips.

Leave the centre strip whole; cut the two remaining strips into segments, as pictured.

Assemble the cake pieces on the board to form the number four; discard remaining cake pieces.

Five Meringue Grubs

EQUIPMENT

oven tray

8cm x 25cm (3¼-inch x 10-inch) bar cake pan

20cm (8-inch) ring pan

30cm x 45cm (12-inch x 18-inch) rectangular cake board

(page 334)

MERINGUE GRUBS

1 egg white

¾ cup (165g) caster (superfine) sugar

¼ teaspoon cream of tartar

2 tablespoons boiling water

large piping bag fitted with 1cm (½-inch) plain tube

coloured sprinkles

10 coloured cachous

CAKE

1 x 470g (15-ounce) packet butter cake mix

1½ quantities butter cream

(page 329)

pink food colouring

DECORATIONS

36 mini pink Musk Sticks

36 love hearts

1 green Fruit Stick

11 mint leaves

1 Preheat oven to 120°C/250°F. Line oven tray with baking paper.

2 To make meringue grubs: Combine egg white, sugar, cream of tartar and the boiling water in small heatproof bowl. Bring a small saucepan of water to the boil; reduce heat to a simmer. Place bowl with egg whites over saucepan, taking care that the water does not touch the base of the bowl. Beat egg-white mixture with electric mixer about 7 minutes or until the sugar is dissolved and stiff peaks form. Remove bowl from heat; spoon egg-white mixture immediately into piping bag. Pipe five grubs onto oven tray. Top grubs with coloured sprinkles; position cachous on grubs for eyes. Bake about 30 minutes or until grubs are dry to touch; cool.

3 Increase oven to 180°C/350°F. Grease cake pans; line bases and sides with baking paper, extending paper 5cm (2 inches) above sides.

4 Make cake according to directions on packet. Divide mixture between pans so both mixtures are the same depth. Bake cakes about 25 minutes. Stand cakes in pans 5 minutes before turning, top-side up, onto wire rack to cool.

5 Level cake tops so they are the same height; turn cakes, cut-side down. Cut bar cake in half widthways; cut ring cake, as pictured.

6 Assemble cake pieces on cake board, cut-side down, to form the number 5; secure to board with a little butter cream.

7 Tint butter cream pink; spread all over cake.

8 Position meringue grubs on cake; decorate sides of cake with Musk Sticks and love hearts. Thinly slice fruit stick lengthways; position on cake for stems. Using a sharp knife, cut mint leaves in half horizontally to make leaves; cut a few 'nibbles' out of a leaf or two. Position leaves on cake.

Using a piping bag, pipe five grubs onto an oven tray lined with baking paper.

Cut bar cake in half widthways; cut the ring cake into small segments, as pictured.

Assemble the cake pieces on the cake board to form the number five; discard remaining cake pieces.

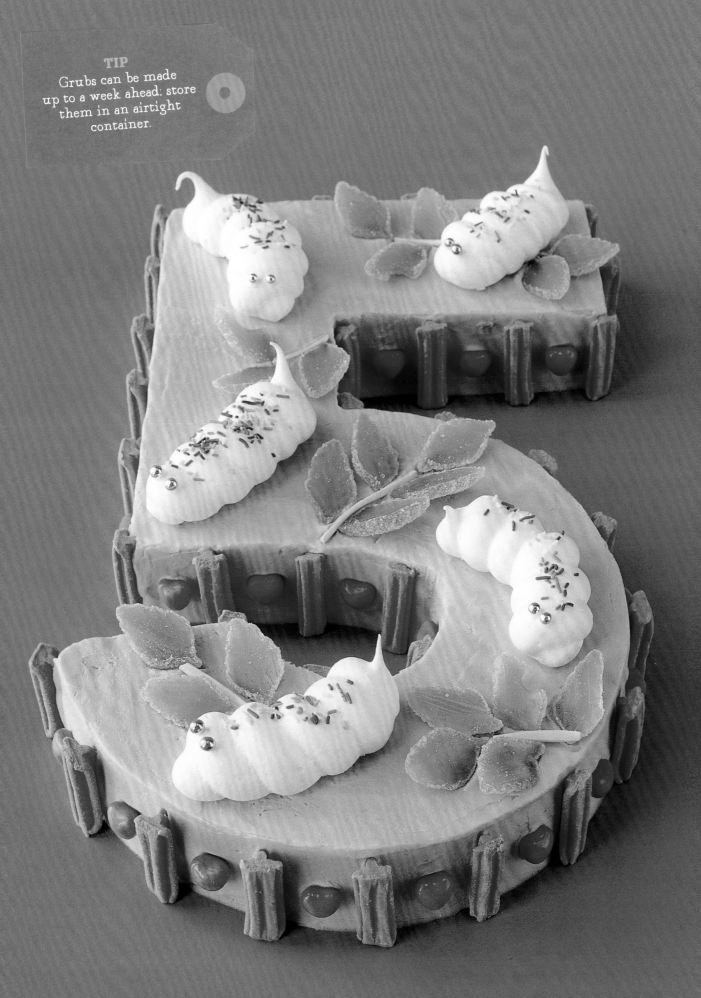

TIP
Grubs can be made
up to a week ahead; store
them in an airtight
container.

TIP
You'll have ¾ cup of the
cake mixture left over,
enough for another three cakes.
Many children like gardening,
so take-home treats could be
small gardening tools.

Six

Fun for little kids who like to garden, so think about a garden-based party theme. Having the kids running around outside is much more fun.

1 Preheat oven to 180°C/350°F. Line muffin pan with paper cases.

2 Make cake according to directions on packet. Drop 2½ level tablespoons of mixture into each paper case; bake about 20 minutes. Stand cakes in pan 5 minutes before turning, top-side up, onto wire rack to cool.

3 Tint half the butter cream green. Divide remaining butter cream between two small bowls; tint one bowl blue. Stir the sifted cocoa into the remaining butter cream.

4 Spread each butter cream over the tops of cakes, matching the colour of the paper cases with the colour of the butter cream. Sprinkle brown-coloured cakes with crushed chocolate biscuits.

5 Using picture as a guide, assemble cakes on cake board to resemble the number 6; secure cakes with a little butter cream. Use the Curly Wurly to make a trellis; intertwine the snakes to resemble vines. Decorate with mint leaves and icing flowers.

6 Decorate brown cakes with jelly-filled strawberries and mint leaves. Using the end of a teaspoon, make a small hole in two of the brown cakes; gently push one end of the sour worms into the holes.

7 Cut coloured layers of the licorice allsorts into the shape of a shovel, bucket and watering can; position on blue cakes. Position butterflies and ladybirds on the cakes.

EQUIPMENT

12-hole (¹⁄₃-cup/80ml) standard muffin pan

12 standard paper cases (5 green, 4 brown, 3 blue)

40cm x 50cm (16-inch x 20-inch) cake board (page 334)

CAKE

1 x 470g (15-ounce) packet butter cake mix

1 quantity butter cream (page 329)

green and blue food colouring

1 tablespoon cocoa powder

DECORATIONS

2 plain chocolate biscuits, crushed

25g (¾-ounce) Curly Wurly bar

5 green jelly snakes, heads removed

11 mint leaves, halved lengthways

9 ready-made icing flowers

4 jelly-filled strawberries

2 sour worms

5 licorice allsorts

2 ready-made icing butterflies

2 foil-wrapped chocolate ladybirds

Use the handle of a teaspoon to make a small hole in the top of the cake. Push the sour worms into the cake, as pictured.

Seven
Choc-crackle Spiders

Leave one bar cake whole, cut the other into two pieces, as pictured.

Assemble cake pieces on cake board, cut-side down, to form the number 7.

Twist four chenille sticks together at centre; bend the ends to make spider legs.

EQUIPMENT

two 12-hole (1 tablespoon/20ml) mini muffin pans

two 8cm x 25cm (3¼-inch x 10-inch) bar cake pans

30cm x 50cm (12-inch x 20-inch) rectangular cake board (page 334)

piping bag fitted with 2mm (⅛-inch) plain tube

CAKE

1 x 470g (15-ounce) packet butter cake mix

1 quantity butter cream (page 329)

orange and black food colouring

CHOC-CRACKLE SPIDERS

1 cup (35g) Rice Bubbles

1 cup (70g) shredded coconut

1 tablespoon cocoa powder

1 tablespoon icing (confectioners') sugar mixture

100g (3 ounces) dark eating (semi-sweet) chocolate, melted

30g (1-ounce) butter, melted

DECORATIONS

28 x 15cm (6-inch) black chenille sticks (pipe cleaners)

14 Skittles

1 To make choc-crackle spiders: combine rice bubbles, coconut, sifted cocoa and icing sugar in medium bowl. Using fork, mix in chocolate and butter. Spoon level tablespoons of mixture into mini muffin pan holes. Refrigerate about 1 hour or until spiders have set.

2 Preheat oven to 180°C/350°F. Grease bar cake pans; line bases and sides with baking paper, extending paper 5cm (2 inches) above sides.

3 Make cake according to directions on packet. Divide mixture evenly between pans; bake cakes about 25 minutes. Stand cakes in pans 5 minutes before turning, top-side up, onto wire rack to cool.

4 Level cake tops so they are the same height; turn cakes cut-side down. Cut one cake into two pieces, as pictured. Secure cake pieces, cut-side down, on cake board with a little butter cream to form the number 7.

5 Tint three-quarters of the butter cream orange; spread all over cake. Tint remaining butter cream black; spoon into piping bag, pipe spider webs onto cake and cake board.

6 Twist four chenille sticks together at centre; bend ends to make spider legs. Position legs on cake; top with one spider body.

7 Using leftover butter cream, attach Skittles onto spider for eyes; pipe a little black icing on Skittles for pupils. Repeat with remaining chenille sticks, spider bodies, black butter cream and Skittles (see tips).

TIPS

Chocolate and butter can be melted together over hot water or in a microwave oven on HIGH (100%) for about 1 minute.

This recipe makes 24 choc-crackle spiders, however, the decorations are for the 7 spiders for the cake. Serve the extras as an accompaniment or, if you have extra chenille sticks and Skittles, make more spiders to decorate the cake board, or give one spider to each guest.

Eight

Put that old train set to good use. Many grown-up train enthusiasts still revert to their childhood at the sight of a model railway.

EQUIPMENT

26cm x 35cm
(10½-inch x 14-inch)
baking dish
50cm (20-inch) round
cake board (page 334)
piping bag fitted with 2mm
(⅛-inch) plain tube

CAKE

2 x 470g (15-ounce) packets
butter cake mix
2 quantities butter cream
(page 329)

yellow food colouring
1 teaspoon cocoa powder

DECORATIONS

1 toy train
3 lollipops
flags

1 Preheat oven to 150°C/300°F. Grease and flour baking dish.
2 Make cake according to directions on packet. Spread mixture into baking dish; bake about 50 minutes. Stand cake in dish 10 minutes before turning, top-side up, onto wire rack to cool.
3 Level cake top; turn cake, cut-side down. Using pattern from pattern sheet, cut number eight from cake. Position cake, cut-side down on cake board.
4 Reserve ½ cup butter cream. Tint remaining butter cream yellow; spread all over cake.
5 Stir sifted cocoa into reserved butter cream; spoon into piping bag. Using picture as a guide, pipe chocolate butter cream onto cake to make train tracks. Position train, lollipops and flags on cake.

Nine

Little girls will love this pretty cake in pale orange.
It's simple to make, and really easy to decorate.

EQUIPMENT

26cm x 35cm (10½-inch x
14-inch) baking dish
30cm x 40cm (12-inch x
16-inch) rectangular
cake board (page 334)

CAKE

2 x 470g (15-ounce) packets
butter cake mix
1 quantity fluffy frosting
(page 329)

orange food colouring

DECORATIONS

2 x 130g (4-ounce) packets
candy jewellery

1 Preheat oven to 150°C/300°F. Grease and flour baking dish.
2 Make cakes according to directions on packets. Spread mixture into dish; bake about 50 minutes. Stand cake in dish 10 minutes before turning, top-side up, onto wire rack to cool.
3 Level top of cake; turn cake cut-side down. Using pattern from pattern sheet, cut number 9 from cake.
4 Secure cake, cut-side down, on cake board with a little fluffy frosting.
5 Tint frosting pale orange; spread all over cake. Using picture as a guide, position candy jewellery on cake.

TIPS
To keep the glossy finish
to the frosting, the cake
needs to be frosted about
an hour before the party.
The frosting soon dries
out to resemble cooked
meringue.

Ten

Double digits at last! This cake is colour galore. When cutting the jubes, frequently dip the knife in hot water, then dry before cutting to stop the jubes from sticking to the knife.

1 Preheat oven to 170°C/340°F. Grease pans; line bases and sides with baking paper, extending paper 5cm (2 inches) above sides.
2 Make one cake according to directions on packet. Spread mixture into bar pan; bake bar cake about 40 minutes. Stand cake in pan 10 minutes before turning, top-side up, onto wire rack to cool.
3 Make remaining three cakes according to directions on packets. Spread mixture into round pan; bake about 1½ hours. Stand cake in pan 10 minutes before turning, top-side up, onto wire rack to cool.
4 Level cake tops so they are the same height. Using pattern from pattern sheet, cut out pattern for round cake. Trim bar cake into number '1', as pictured. Secure cakes to cake board with a little butter cream.
5 Tint butter cream pale yellow; spread all over cakes.
6 To decorate sides of cakes, measure the height of the cakes and use scissors to trim sour straps to lengths of the same height. Position the trimmed sour straps around the sides of cakes.
7 Using scissors, cut jubes in half; position, cut-side up, on tops of cakes, overlapping slightly, to cover completely.

EQUIPMENT

deep 25cm (10-inch) round cake pan
8cm x 25cm x 7cm (3¼-inch x 10-inch x 2¾-inch) bar cake pan
45cm (18-inch) square cake board (page 334)

CAKE

4 x 440g (14-ounce) packets butter cake mix
(see 'mixing the cakes' page 345)

2 quantities butter cream
(page 329)

yellow food colouring

DECORATIONS

3 x 160g (5-ounce) packets rainbow sour straps
2 x 350g (11-ounce) packets jubes

Cake recipes

If you want to make your own cakes, these recipes will all bake at similar temperatures, times, and in the same pan sizes as the packet mix cakes suggested in each recipe. One quantity of each of these cake recipes is equivalent to one 470g (15-ounce) packaged cake mix.

BASIC BUTTER CAKE

125g (4 ounces) butter, softened
½ teaspoon vanilla extract
¾ cup (165g) caster (superfine) sugar
2 eggs
1½ cups (225g) self-raising flour
½ cup (125ml) milk

Preheat oven. Grease (and line) pan(s). Beat butter, extract and sugar in small bowl with electric mixer until light and fluffy. Beat in eggs, one at a time. Stir in sifted flour and milk, in two batches. Bake as directed.

To marble a butter cake, place portions of cake mixture in three bowls then tint each with the desired colours. Drop spoonfuls of mixture into pan(s), alternating colours, then swirl together with a skewer for a marbled effect.

GLUTEN-FREE BUTTER CAKE

100g (3 ounces) butter, softened
1 cup (150g) gluten-free self-raising flour
½ cup (110g) caster (superfine) sugar
¼ cup (60ml) milk
1 egg
1 egg white

Preheat oven. Grease (and line) pan(s). Beat butter in small bowl with electric mixer until changed to a paler colour. Sift flour and 2 tablespoons of the sugar together. Beat flour mixture and milk into the butter, in two batches, until combined. Beat egg and egg white in small bowl with electric mixer until thick and creamy. Gradually add remaining sugar, beating until sugar dissolves. Gradually pour egg mixture into flour mixture with motor operating on a low speed; beat only until combined. Bake as directed.

CARROT CAKE

½ cup (125ml) vegetable oil
2 eggs
¾ cup (110g) self-raising flour
½ cup (110g) firmly packed brown sugar
2 teaspoons mixed spice
1½ cups (360g) firmly packed coarsely grated carrot

Preheat oven. Grease (and line) pan(s). Combine oil, eggs, sifted flour, sugar and spice in medium bowl; stir in carrot. Bake as directed.

GLUTEN-FREE CARROT CAKE

1 cup (125g) soy or besan (chickpea) flour
¾ cup (110g) 100% corn cornflour (cornstarch)
2 teaspoons gluten-free baking powder
1 teaspoon bicarbonate of soda (baking soda)
2 teaspoons mixed spice
1 cup (220g) firmly packed brown sugar
1 cup (120g) coarsely chopped roasted walnuts
1½ cups (360g) coarsely grated carrot
½ cup (125ml) extra light olive oil
½ cup (120g) sour cream
3 eggs

Preheat oven. Grease (and line) pan(s). Sift flour, cornflour, baking powder, soda and spice into large bowl; stir in sugar, nuts and carrot. Stir in combined oil, sour cream and eggs. Bake as directed.

WHITE CHOCOLATE MUD CAKE

165g (5 ounces) butter, chopped
100g (3 ounces) white eating chocolate, chopped coarsely
⅔ cup (160ml) milk
1⅓ cups (295g) caster (superfine) sugar
1 cup (150g) plain (all-purpose) flour
⅓ cup (50g) self-raising flour
1 egg

Preheat oven. Grease (and line) pan(s). Combine butter, chocolate, sugar and milk in medium saucepan; stir over low heat until smooth. Cool 30 minutes. Whisk in sifted flours, then egg. Bake as directed.

DARK CHOCOLATE MUD CAKE

225g (7 ounces) butter, chopped
360g (11½ ounces) dark chocolate, chopped coarsely
¾ cup (165g) firmly packed brown sugar
¾ cup (180ml) water
1 cup (150g) plain (all-purpose) flour
¼ cup (35g) self-raising flour
2 tablespoons cocoa powder
2 eggs

Preheat oven. Grease (and line) pan(s). Combine butter, chocolate, sugar and the water in medium saucepan; stir over low heat until smooth. Cool 30 minutes. Whisk in sifted flours and cocoa then eggs. Bake as directed.

QUICK CHOCOLATE CAKE

1⅓ cups (200g) self-raising flour
½ cup (50g) cocoa powder
125g (4 ounces) butter, softened
½ teaspoon vanilla extract
1¼ cups (275g) caster (superfine) sugar
2 eggs
⅔ cup (160ml) water

Preheat oven. Grease (and line) pan(s). Sift flour and cocoa into medium bowl, add remaining ingredients; beat on low speed with electric mixer until ingredients are combined. Increase speed to medium; beat about 3 minutes or until mixture is smooth and changed to a lighter colour. Bake as directed.

Icing recipes

BUTTER CREAM

Basic butter cream is also called vienna cream: the flavour can be varied by adding any extract or essence you like.

125g (4 ounces) unsalted butter, softened
1½ cups (240g) icing (confectioners') sugar
2 tablespoons milk

Beat butter in small bowl with electric mixer until as white as possible. Gradually beat in half the sifted icing sugar, milk, then remaining icing sugar.
Chocolate variation Sift ⅓ cup (35g) cocoa powder in with the first batch of icing sugar.

GLACÉ ICING

2¼ cups (360g) icing (confectioners') sugar
¼ cup (60ml) water, approximately
food colouring

Sift icing sugar into medium heatproof bowl, stir in enough water to give a firm paste. Colour as desired. Stir the paste over medium saucepan of hot water (the water should not touch the bottom of the bowl) until icing is spreadable; do not overheat. The bottom of the bowl should feel warm (not hot) to the touch. Use immediately. (Also see page 339.)

FLUFFY MOCK CREAM FROSTING

2 tablespoons milk
⅓ cup (80ml) water
1 cup (220g) caster (superfine) sugar
1 teaspoon powdered gelatine
2 tablespoons water, extra
250g (8 ounces) unsalted butter, softened
1 teaspoon vanilla extract

Combine milk, the water and sugar in small saucepan; stir syrup over low heat, without boiling, until sugar is dissolved. Sprinkle gelatine over the extra water in a cup, add to pan; stir syrup until gelatine is dissolved. Cool to room temperature. Beat butter and extract in small bowl with electric mixer until it is as white as possible. While motor is operating, gradually pour in cold syrup, in a thin steady stream; beat until light and fluffy. Mixture will thicken more on standing. (Also see pages 336-337).

ROYAL ICING

1½ cups (240g) pure icing (confectioners') sugar
1 egg white
½ teaspoon lemon juice

Sift icing sugar through very fine sieve. Lightly beat egg white in a small bowl with an electric mixer; add icing sugar, a tablespoon at a time. When icing reaches firm peaks, use a wooden spoon to beat in the juice. Royal icing must be kept covered, either with a well wrung out wet cloth then plastic wrap, or with the plastic wrap pressed onto the surface of the icing. Royal icing develops a crust when it's left open to the air – this usually makes the icing unusable, particularly for piping.

FLUFFY FROSTING

1 cup (220g) caster (superfine) sugar
⅓ cup (80ml) water
2 egg whites

Combine sugar and the water in small saucepan; stir with a wooden spoon over high heat, without boiling, until sugar dissolves. Boil, uncovered, without stirring, about 3 to 5 minutes or until syrup is slightly thick, but not coloured. If a candy thermometer is available, the syrup will be ready when it reaches 114°C (240°F). When the syrup is thick, remove the pan from the heat, allow the bubbles to subside then test the syrup by dropping 1 teaspoon into a cup of cold water. The syrup should form a ball of soft sticky toffee. The syrup should not be changed in colour; if it has, it has been cooked for too long and you will have to discard it and start again. While the syrup is boiling, and after about four minutes, beat the egg whites in a small bowl with an electric mixer until stiff; keep beating (or the whites will deflate) until syrup reaches the correct temperature. When syrup is ready, allow bubbles to subside then pour a very thin stream onto the egg whites with mixer operating on medium speed. If the syrup is added too quickly to the egg whites the frosting will not thicken. Continue beating and adding syrup until all syrup is used. Continue to beat until frosting stands in stiff peaks (frosting should be barely warm). For best results, frosting should be applied to a cake on the day it is to be served. While you can frost the cake the day before, the frosting will become crisp and lose its glossy appearance, much like a meringue. (Also see page 337).

READY-MADE WHITE ICING

Ready-made icing is available from cake-decorating suppliers and supermarkets. There are several brands available. This is very easy to use. Break off as much icing as you need; re-wrap remaining icing to exclude the air or a crust will develop, which will spoil the smooth texture of the icing. Knead the piece of icing on a surface lightly dusted with sifted icing sugar. If colouring the icing, start working tiny amounts of the colouring through the icing. The icing should be smooth and free from stickiness. Only work with small amounts of icing at a time as the air will dry it out. Cover any rolled-out icing with plastic wrap. To cover a cake with ready-made icing, follow the steps on page 336.

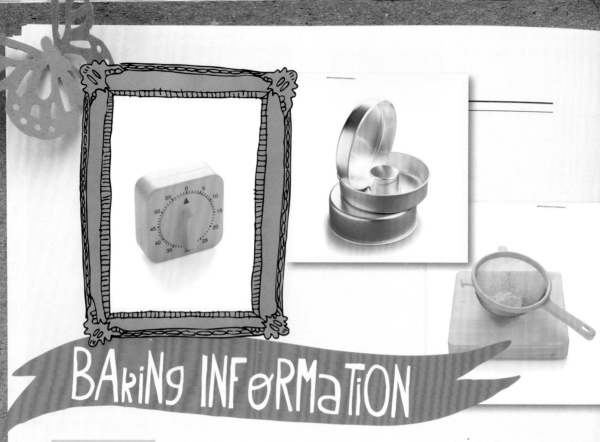

BAKING INFORMATION

CAKE PANS

There's a vast array of cake pans available from chain stores, supermarkets, cookware, and homeware shops, and also from shops that specialise in cake decorating supplies. Price is a guide to quality when it comes to cake pans; if you buy wisely and look after the pans, they should last a lifetime. Cake pans are made from many different materials – uncoated aluminium, which is our favourite, are becoming increasingly difficult to find. There are metal pans with non-stick coating, which still need greasing, scratch easily and tend to make baked goods develop a heavy crust (decrease the oven temperature to compensate for this). Heavy good-quality tin pans bake cakes well, but usually work better if the goods are baked at a slightly lower temperature than normal. Inexpensive cake pans made from thin flimsy tin are not a good investment as they tend to twist and buckle, often after the first time they're used.

Silicone pans are also available; cakes baked in these develop a light crust, which is sometimes a good thing. Muffins and cupcakes work particularly well in these pans.

PACKET OR HOME MADE CAKES

Unbaked cake mixtures (both packet and homemade) will tolerate standing at a cool room temperature for at least an hour before baking. We have used cakes made from packet mixes throughout this book for consistency of size and baking times. While, we used 440g and 470g (14oz and 15oz) packets, there are other sizes available and they will all work with our recipes. If you want to make your own cakes, choose any of the recipes on page 328; they will all bake at similar temperatures, times, and in the same pan sizes as the packet mix cakes suggested in each recipe. One quantity of any of the cake recipes is equivalent to one 470g packaged cake mix.

BEATING PACKET MIXES

It's important to beat the packet mixes properly using an electric mixer – not a food processor or blender. We found a stand-alone mixer gave us the best results, simply because it's easier to let the machine do the work rather than holding a hand-held mixer (there is a tendency to under-beat the mixture using one of these). Also, it's important to beat the packet mixes enough to develop the volume of the mixture. Have the ingredients to be added at room temperature for the best results, start the mixer at a low speed to incorporate the ingredients, then gradually increase the speed to medium. As a rule, one packet of cake mix fits into a small bowl, two or three packets into a medium bowl, and four packets into a large bowl. The beaters should always be well down in the mixture to create volume.

BAKING

The oven temperatures in this book are for conventional ovens; for fan-forced ovens, decrease the temperature by 10-20 degrees. Fan-forced ovens should bake everything that is being cooked in the oven evenly, however, some domestic ovens have hot spots. If you need to bake cakes on two oven racks, it will be necessary to change the positions of the cakes about halfway through the baking time. It's fine to cook more than one cake on the same rack, but the cake pans shouldn't touch each other, the sides of the oven or the closed oven door. It's usually a good idea to change the positions of the cake pans on the same rack, too. Allow for the cake to rise when positioning racks before the oven is preheated. As a guide, cakes should be baked in the centre of the oven, towards the lower half of the oven. If the oven is loaded with cakes of varying sizes, they might take a little longer to bake than our recipes indicate.

MEASURING CAKE QUANTITIES

To achieve the same results as we did for the cakes in this book, it's important to measure the mixture accurately into the correct-sized cake pans. Often there is some cake mixture left over, just use it to make more cakes for the party. Some of the cakes in this book require half-packets of cake mixture to be used; make the whole cake then use half the mixture, as indicated by the recipe, and use the remaining mixture to make additional patty or cupcakes for the party.

FOOD COLOURINGS

Use good-quality colourings for the best results; they will 'hold' the colour in the icing. Some of the inexpensive liquid colourings will fade or darken the icing on standing. Icings or frostings based on butter are the most difficult to colour as butter is yellow, so any colour will be affected by the base colour. This is why it's important to beat the butter until it's as white as possible. We found unsalted butter to work (and taste) the best. Fluffy frosting and royal icing are the easiest to colour, because they're white to begin with. Coloured icings can change on standing, particularly if you're using liquid colourings. If possible (it's not with fluffy frosting), colour a small portion of the icing to the shade you want, keep it airtight, and let it stand for a few hours before colouring the whole batch.

Pans & equipment

1. SWISS ROLL PAN
Choose a straight-sided metal dish that has a solid flat base. Trim the cake's corners and sides if necessary before cutting into the shape required. A baking pan is a similar shape to a swiss roll pan, however, its sides are at least 5cm (2 inches) in height, or more.

2. CHOCOLATE MOULDS, ICE-CREAM SCOOP & CANDY THERMOMETER
We used plastic chocolate moulds, there are many types available – all good. A candy thermometer is handy to have in the kitchen, it takes the guess-work out of making sure sugar syrups reach the correct temperature.

3. SAVARIN PAN
These are available from specialty cookware shops and are made from aluminium. They are available in a number of sizes.

4. PATTY & MUFFIN PANS
There are many shapes and sizes available in cookware shops department stores, supermarkets etc. The pans are made from a variety of materials, including those with a non-stick coating, aluminium, tin and silicone.

5. PATTY CASES
A wide variety of colours, patterns and sizes are available from supermarkets, cookware shops, chain stores and cake decorating suppliers. They can be made from paper in varying thicknesses and quality, also from foil and silicone.

6. LOAF PAN & NUT ROLL TINS
Loaf pans come in a wide variety of sizes and are made from many different materials. Nut roll tins are made from tin and are available from cookware shops.

7. DOLLY VARDEN PAN & METAL PUDDING STEAMER
Both are made from aluminium. Cakes made in these pans need to be baked at a lower than normal oven temperature to make sure the cake mixtures cook through in the centre.

8. PIPING BAGS & TUBES
Plastic piping bags and tubes are available from supermarkets; fabric piping bags are available from cookware shops and cake decorating suppliers. Piping tubes are available in plastic and metal, in a wide variety of shapes and sizes.

9. DEEP ROUND CAKE PANS
Use pans made from aluminium or good-quality tin. Cake pans that have a non-stick coating can be used, but cakes baked in these pans should be baked at a slightly lower temperature than those baked in aluminium or good-quality tin pans.

10. SKEWERS, STRAWS & FLORISTS' WIRE
Florists' wire is used for supporting shapes made from icing, it is available from craft shops and cake decorating suppliers. Wooden skewers and strong plastic straws can be used for supporting cake tiers, trim them to the correct length.

11. DEEP SQUARE CAKE PANS
We used pans made from aluminium or good-quality tin. Some cakes look better if they're baked in sharp-cornered pans such as those pictured. Tin conducts oven heat quickly, so bake cakes at a slightly lower temperature than if using an aluminium cake pan.

12. CUTTERS
We used a variety of different-sized and -shaped metal cutters in this book. Plastic cutters can be used, but they don't cut as neatly as those made from metal.

1.

6.

4.

2.

10.

7.

11.

5.

9.

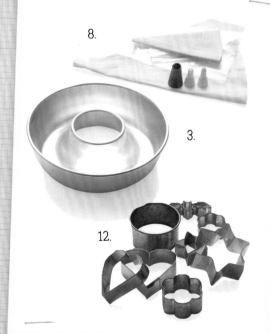

8.

3.

12.

2 mm

Covering a square cake board
Cut the covering paper about 5cm (2 inches) larger than the board, place the board, top-side down on the back of the paper. Use tape or glue to stick the paper to the board. If the paper is thick, cut the corners out of the paper as if covering a book.

Covering a round cake board
Cut the covering paper about 5cm (2 inches) larger than the board, place the board, top-side down on the back of the paper. Snip the paper border, on an angle, all the way around. Fold each snipped piece of paper over onto the board; tape or glue the paper onto the board.

Greasing cake pans Melted butter, applied evenly with a pastry brush, is the best method of greasing a cake pan, particularly those cake pans that are patterned, or are of an unusual shape.

Flouring a greased cake pan
We have indicated when to grease and flour cake pans. Refrigerate the greased pan for a few minutes to set the butter. Sprinkle the buttered area with flour, turn and tap the pan until the pan is floured evenly, then tap the pan over the sink or bin, to get rid of the excess flour.

Lining for a round cake pan (1)
Cut a strip of baking paper, long enough to encircle the inside of the pan and overlap slightly, plus about an extra 7cm (2¾ inches) to allow for the fold over at the base of the pan and for the paper to extend above the side of the pan. Fold about 2cm (¾-inch) of the paper over, then snip the paper, on an angle up to the fold.

Lightly grease the inside of the pan (2), to hold the lining paper in place, position the snipped paper around the side of the pan. Using the base of the pan as a guide, trace around the base of the pan. Cut out the round of paper, cutting slightly inside the marked circle. Position the paper in the pan.

Lining rectangular or square cake pans Cut strips of baking paper long enough to cover base and sides of the lightly greased cake pan, sometimes only one strip of paper is necessary. Always extend the paper over the sides of the pan by about 5cm (2 inches).

Using patterns Trace the pattern from the pattern sheet provided onto paper, cut out the shape. Secure the pattern to the cake – usually the bottom of the cake – with toothpicks to hold the pattern firmly in place.

Levelling cakes Most cakes need to have their tops cut off to make the cakes sit flat on a cake board or plate. Use a large sharp serrated knife to do this.

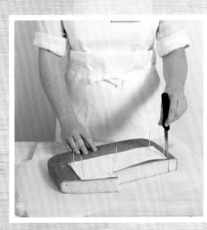

Cutting out the cake Use a small sharp serrated knife to cut carefully around the pattern. Hold the knife upright for the best results.

Preparing cakes for decorating Most of the cakes in this book are turned top-side down for decorating. There are just a few decorated top-side up, for a domed effect. Recipes will indicate when to position the cake on a cake board or plate.

Brushing the cake with jam Use warmed, sieved jam (we like apricot, but use whatever jam you like) to brush over the surface of the cake, when recipes indicate this is necessary. Be particular about brushing the jam evenly and thoroughly over any cut surfaces on the cake. If the cake is fresh and crumbly, freeze it for an hour or so to make the job easier.

Step-by-step

Rolling out ready-made icing
Use a rolling pin to roll the icing to the correct size and thickness. Roll icing on a surface lightly dusted with a little sifted icing sugar. Use the rolling pin to lift the icing over the cake.

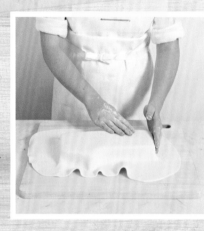

Smoothing ready-made icing
Using hands, dusted with a little icing sugar, gently mould and smooth the icing around the shape of the cake. Make sure the icing feels like it is clinging to the jam on the cake.

Trimming ready-made icing
Use a small sharp pointed knife to carefully trim away the excess icing from around the edge of the cake. Scraps of icing will keep well for months if they're wrapped tightly in plastic wrap to exclude the air.

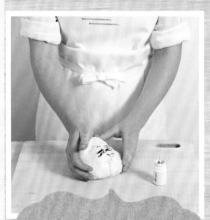

Colouring ready-made icing
Use good-quality food colourings for best results. Always start with a tiny dab of the colouring, and work it through the icing with your fingers. Determine the depth and strength of the colouring before adding any more.

Cutting shapes from ready-made icing Use a rolling pin to roll the icing to the correct thickness on a surface dusted with a little sifted icing sugar. Use sharp cutters to cut out shapes. Dry shapes on baking paper until firm, or apply directly to the icing on the cake while still soft.

Making fluffy mock cream (1)
Beat the softened butter in a small bowl – so that the beaters are well down into the butter – until the butter is as white as possible.

Adding syrup to fluffy mock cream (2) Gradually add the room temperature syrup in a thin steady stream to the butter while the motor is operating.

Preparing cake for decorating If the cake is very fresh, freeze it for a few hours, or refrigerate it overnight. Using a metal spatula, apply a very thin layer of butter cream evenly over the cold cake, don't worry if crumbs become mixed with this layer of butter cream. If necessary, refrigerate or freeze the cake to set the butter cream 'undercoat'.

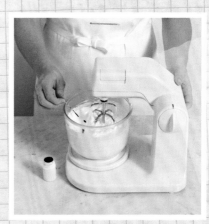

Applying the final coating of butter cream Spread the final layer of butter cream evenly over the 'undercoat'. If the cake feels firm, by-pass the undercoat and simply apply the final layer of butter cream to the cake.

Making fluffy frosting Beat the egg whites until stiff towards the end of the syrup's cooking time; keep beating the egg whites while the syrup reaches the correct temperature. Gradually add the hot syrup to the beating egg whites in a thin steady stream. Beat the frosting until firm peaks form.

Colouring fluffy frosting This frosting should be coloured by beating the colouring into the frosting just before the frosting is to be used. This frosting does not stand well, it should be made and used quite quickly, as it sets on standing.

Step-by-step

Making a paper piping bag (1) Cut a square from a sheet of baking paper, fold it in half diagonally, cut it in half along the fold to make two triangles.

Shaping the paper piping bag (2) Hold the apex of the triangle towards you, wrap one point of the triangle around to form a cone shape, then wriggle the three points of the triangle until they line up perfectly.

Securing the paper piping bag (3) Staple the piping bag so that the staple holds the three points of the triangle in place. Half-fill the bag with icing, snip a tiny piece from the point of the bag, pipe a little icing to judge if the hole is large enough, if not, snip more paper from the point of the bag.

Colouring coconut Use disposable gloves to stop the colouring staining your skin. Place the coconut into a bowl and rub drops of colouring through the coconut until it's evenly coloured. This method can be used to colour sugar too.

Colouring sugar Place the sugar into a strong resealable plastic bag; add a little food colouring. Massage the colouring through the sugar until it's evenly coloured. This method can also be used for colouring coconut.

Using licorice Use sharp scissors for cutting and trimming licorice into various shapes and sizes.

Making glacé icing Stir the icing over hot water until it's smooth and pourable. The icing must only ever be warm, not hot. Pour the warmed icing over the cake as quickly as possible, preferably without trying to spread it out with a spatula. The icing can be trimmed at the base after it has set.

Melting chocolate Melt chocolate over hot water, it's important that the water in the pan doesn't touch the bottom of the bowl, so that the chocolate doesn't overheat and spoil.

Piping chocolate discs Use either small piping bags fitted with a plain piping tube, or a paper piping bag. Half-fill the bag with melted chocolate; pipe discs of chocolate onto a baking-paper-lined tray. Tap the tray on the bench to make the chocolate spread slightly, then leave the discs to set at room temperature.

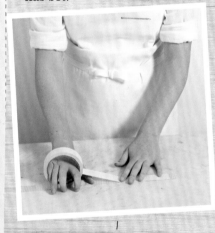

Backing ribbon Sometimes ribbon needs to be backed, so that it doesn't become stained by the icing it's in contact with. Use a strip of adhesive tape the same width as the ribbon, and apply to the back of the ribbon. You might need help to keep the ribbon straight while doing this.

Positioning skewers for tiered cakes The skewers are needed to support the weight of the top cake. Place the top cake on a cake board. Insert the skewers into the bottom cake, through to the cake board. Mark the height of the skewers; remove them, then trim them so they are level with the top of the bottom cake. Position skewers in the cake.

Positioning the top cake tier Carefully sit the top tier on the skewers. There will be a small gap between the two cakes, cover this with icing or decorations. Remove the top tier, using a metal spatula, before cutting the cakes. Remove the skewers before cutting and serving the cake.

Lollies

If you can't find any of the lollies we used in this book, use something similar - the results will be just as good.

1. Chocolate ripple biscuits
2. Furry friends slab
3. Curly wurly 4. Rainbow sour straps 5. Dark eating chocolate 6. Milk eating chocolate 7-9. Dark, milk and white buttons 10. Wagon wheel 11-12. Jelly beans
13. Rainbow nerd rope
14-15. Chocolate-coated peanuts and sultanas
16. Flake bar 17-18. Rainbow and chocolate sprinkles
19. Silver cachous 20. Green sprinkles 21. Fruit roll-ups
22. Wine gums 23-24. Blue and orange sprinkles 25. Tic tacs
26. Milk bottles 27. Mentos mints 28. Hundreds and thousands 29. Fruit & cola wheels 30. Jols forest berries pastilles 31. Liquorice allsorts
32. Metallic cachous 33. Yellow and white sugar pearls

34. Icing flowers
35. Spearmint (mint) leaves
36. Jelly snakes 37. Mini toblerone bar 38-39. Mini chocolate chips 40. M&Ms
41. Candy letters 42. Chocolate-coated honeycomb 43. Sour straps 44. Hershey's kisses
45. Licorice strap 46. Black licorice (smooth) 47. Green apple tang liquorice
48. Strawberry liquorice bites
49. Gumballs 50. Mini musks
51. Sour worms 52. Noodle snack pack 53. Milo Duos
54. Smarties 55. Rainbow choc drops 56. Choc rocks
57. Raspberries 58. Candied sugar heart 59. Icing butterfly
60. Icing flowers 61. Jelly tots
62. Jubes 63. Fruit jelly rings
64. Milo powder 65. Butterfly sprinkles 66. Kool mints
67. Milk arrowroot biscuits

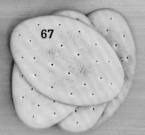

Glossary

almonds

blanched brown skins removed.
flaked paper-thin slices.
ground also called almond meal; nuts are powdered to a coarse flour texture for use in baking or as a thickening agent.

allspice

Also known as pimento or jamaican pepper; so-named because is tastes like a combination of nutmeg, cumin, clove and cinnamon - all spices.

baking paper

Also called parchment, silicon paper or non-stick baking paper; not to be confused with greaseproof or waxed paper. Used to line cake pans; also to make piping bags.

baking powder

A raising agent consisting mainly of two parts cream of tartar to one part bicarbonate of (baking) soda.

bicarbonate of soda

Also called baking soda; used as a leavening (rising) agent in baking.

biscuits

Also known as cookies.

butter

We use salted butter unless stated otherwise. Unsalted or 'sweet' butter has no added salt. 125g (4 ounces) is equal to 1 stick of butter.

buttermilk

Originally the term given to the slightly sour liquid left after butter was churned from cream, today it is made similarly to yogurt. Sold in the refrigerated section in supermarkets.

cereal

Coco Pops chocolate-flavoured puffed rice.
Froot Loops fruit-flavoured puffed rice.
puffed rice gluten-free cereal made from whole brown rice grains.
Rice Bubbles puffed rice product made with malt extract.

chocolate

Choc Bits also called chocolate chips or chocolate morsels; available in milk, white and dark chocolate. Made of cocoa liquor, cocoa butter, sugar and an emulsifier; they hold their shape when baked, so are ideal for decorating.
choc Melts discs of compounded milk, white or dark chocolate ideal for melting and moulding.
dark cooking also called compounded chocolate; made with vegetable oil. Is good for cooking as it sets at room temperature.
dark eating also called semi-sweet or luxury chocolate; made of a high percentage of cocoa liquor and cocoa butter, and little added sugar. Unless stated otherwise, we use dark eating chocolate in this book.
milk eating most popular eating chocolate, mild and very sweet; similar in make-up to dark chocolate, with the difference being the addition of milk solids.

white eating contains no cocoa solids but derives its sweet flavour from cocoa butter. Very sensitive to heat, so watch carelfully.

chocolate hazelnut spread

We use Nutella; made of cocoa powder, hazelnuts, sugar and milk.

cinnamon

Available as sticks (quills) and ground into powder; one of the world's most common spices.

cocoa powder

Also called unsweetened cocoa; cocoa beans (cacao seeds) that have been fermented, roasted, shelled, then ground into a powder.

Coconut

cream obtained commercially from the first pressing of the coconut flesh alone, without the addition of water; the second pressing (less rich) is sold as the milk. Available in cans and cartons at supermarkets.
desiccated concentrated, dried, unsweetened and finely shredded coconut flesh.
essence synthetically made from flavouring, oil and alcohol.
flaked dried flaked coconut flesh.
shredded unsweetened thin strips of dried coconut flesh.

corn syrup

A sweet syrup made by heating cornstarch with water under pressure. It comes in light and dark types and is used in baking and in confectionery making.

cornflour

Also also known as cornstarch; used as a thickening agent in cooking. Wheaten cornflour is made from wheat rather than corn (maize) and gives sponge cakes a lighter texture (due to the fact wheaten cornflour has some gluten).

cream

pouring also called pure cream. It has no additives, and contains a minimum fat content of 35 per cent.
thickened a whipping cream that contains a thickener. Has a minimum fat content of 35 per cent.

cream of tartar

The acid ingredient in baking powder; added to confectionery mixtures to help prevent sugar from crystallising. Keeps frostings creamy and improves volume when beating egg whites.

custard powder

Instant mixture used to make pouring custard; similar to North American instant pudding mixes.

eggs

We use large chicken eggs (60g) in our recipes unless stated otherwise. If a recipe calls for raw or barely cooked eggs, exercise caution if there is a salmonella problem in your area.

flour

besan also called chickpea flour or gram; made from ground chickpeas so is gluten-free and high in protein.

plain an all-purpose white flour made from wheat.
rice very fine, almost powdery, gluten-free flour; made from ground white rice.
self-raising plain or wholemeal all-purpose flour combined with baking powder in the proportion of 1 cup flour to 2 teaspoons baking powder. Also called self-rising flour.

food colouring

Vegetable-based substance available in liquid, paste or gel form. Used to change the colour of various foods

gelatine

A thickening agent. Available in sheet form (leaf gelatine) or as a powder – 3 teaspoons powdered gelatine (8g or one sachet) is roughly equivalent to four gelatine leaves.

ginger

fresh also called green or root ginger; the thick gnarled root of a tropical plant.
glacé fresh ginger root preserved in a sugar syrup; crystallised ginger can be substituted if rinsed with warm water and dried before using.
ground also known as powdered ginger; used as a flavouring in cakes, pies and puddings but cannot be substituted for fresh ginger.

glucose syrup

Also known as liquid glucose; a clear, thick liquid often made from wheat or corn starch.

golden syrup

A by-product of refined sugarcane; pure maple syrup or honey can be substituted.

honey

Honey sold in a squeezable container is not suitable for the recipes in this book, as it is too runny.

ice-cream

Use good-quality ice-cream; ice-cream varieties differ from manufacturer to manufacturer depending on the quantities of air and fat incorporated into the mixture.

jam

Also called conserve or preserve.

lollies

Also called sweets or candy.

milk

We use full-cream homogenised milk unless stated otherwise.

mixing the cakes

We recommend mixing no more than 3 cakes mixes in the large bowl of your stand mixer at any one time. If you need to use more than 3 cake mixes, make them up in batches. If the recipe states only half a mix is needed, make up the whole cake and use half to make the cake, and the other half to make cupcakes for the party (or more of the same cakes, if the recipe is for cupcakes).

milo

A chocolate malted sweetened milk drink base.

mixed fruit

Consists of a mixture of sultanas, raisins, currants, mixed peel and sometimes glacé cherries.

Glossary

mixed peel
Candied citrus peel.

mixed spice
A classic mixture generally containing caraway, allspice, coriander, cumin, nutmeg and ginger, although cinnamon and other spices can be added.

modelling paste
Also known a BAS relief paste, gum paste, flower modelling paste and pastillage. Sets very hard, and is used to make all types of decorations for cakes. Work with small amounts at a time and keep the remaining paste airtight, wrapped in plastic wrap, to stop it drying out. Models made from the paste will need anywhere from 1 hour to 2 days to dry completely before using. Colour modelling paste in the same way as ready-made icing.

nutmeg
A strong and very pungent spice ground from the dried nut of an evergreen tree native to Indonesia. Usually found ground, but the flavour is more intense from a whole nut, available from spice shops, so it's best to grate your own.

oil
cooking spray we use cholesterol-free spray made from canola oil.
vegetable oils sourced from plants rather than animal fats.

pistachios
Pale green, delicately flavoured nut inside hard off-white shells. To peel, soak shelled nuts in boiling water for about 5 minutes; drain, then pat dry with absorbent paper. Rub skins with cloth to peel.

popcorn
A variety of corn that is sold as kernels for popping, or can be bought ready popped.

poppy seeds
Small, dried, bluish-grey seeds of the poppy plant, with a crunchy texture and a nutty flavour. Purchase whole or ground in most supermarkets.

raisins
Dried sweet grapes (traditionally muscatel grapes).

ready-made white icing
Also called soft icing, ready-to-roll icing (RTR), fondant sugar, sugar paste, plastic icing and soft icing. Is sweet tasting, and has a dough-like consistency when kneaded. Available from the baking section in most supermarkets.

roasting/toasting
Roast nuts and dry coconut in the oven to restore their fresh flavour and release their aromatic essential oils. Spread evenly onto an oven tray and roast in a moderate oven (180°C/350°F) for about 5 minutes. Desiccated coconut, pine nuts and sesame seeds roast more evenly if stirred over low heat in a heavy-based frying pan; their natural oils will help turn them golden brown. Remove immediately from the pan or tray, to stop them from burning.

sour cream
Thick, commercially-cultured sour cream with a minimum fat content of 35 per cent.

star anise
A dried star-shaped pod with an astringent aniseed flavour.

sugar
brown a soft, finely granulated sugar retaining molasses for its characteristic colour and flavour.
caster also known as superfine or finely granulated table sugar. The fine crystals dissolve easily making it perfect for cakes and meringues.
demerara small-grained golden-coloured crystal sugar.
icing also called confectioners' or powdered sugar; granulated sugar is crushed together with a small amount of added cornflour.
pure icing also called confectioners' or powdered sugar; does not contain any cornflour (is gluten free).
raw natural brown granulated sugar.
vanilla granulated or caster sugar flavoured with a vanilla bean; can be stored indefinitely.
white a coarsely granulated table sugar; also called crystal sugar, unless stated otherwise.

sultanas
Also called golden raisins; dried seedless white grapes.

vanilla
bean dried, long, thin pod from a tropical golden orchid grown; the minuscule black seeds inside are used to impart a luscious vanilla flavour in baking and desserts.
extract beans soaked in alcohol. Essence is not a suitable substitute.

yogurt
We use plain full-cream yogurt in our recipes unless stated otherwise.

Conversion chart

Measures

One Australian metric measuring cup holds approximately 250ml; one Australian metric tablespoon holds 20ml; one Australian metric teaspoon holds 5ml.

The difference between one country's measuring cups and another's is within a two- or three-teaspoon variance, and will not affect your cooking results. North America, New Zealand and the United Kingdom all use a 15ml tablespoon.

All cup and spoon measurements are level. The most accurate way of measuring dry ingredients is to weigh them. When measuring liquids, use a clear glass or plastic jug with metric markings.

We use large eggs with an average weight of 60g.

Dry measures

METRIC	IMPERIAL
15g	½oz
30g	1oz
60g	2oz
90g	3oz
125g	4oz (¼lb)
155g	5oz
185g	6oz
220g	7oz
250g	8oz (½lb)
280g	9oz
315g	10oz
345g	11oz
375g	12oz (¾lb)
410g	13oz
440g	14oz
470g	15oz
500g	16oz (1lb)
750g	24oz (1½lb)
1kg	32oz (2lb)

Liquid measures

METRIC	IMPERIAL
30ml	1 fluid oz
60ml	2 fluid oz
100ml	3 fluid oz
125ml	4 fluid oz
150ml	5 fluid oz (¼ pint)
190ml	6 fluid oz
250ml	8 fluid oz
300ml	10 fluid oz (½ pint)
500ml	16 fluid oz
600ml	20 fluid oz (1 pint)
1000ml (1 litre)	1¾ pints

Length measures

METRIC	IMPERIAL
3mm	⅛in
6mm	¼in
1cm	½in
2cm	¾in
2.5cm	1in
5cm	2in
6cm	2½in
8cm	3in
10cm	4in
13cm	5¼in
15cm	6in
18cm	7¼in
20cm	8in
23cm	9¼in
25cm	10in
28cm	11¼in
30cm	12in (1ft)

Oven temperatures

The oven temperatures in this book are for conventional ovens; if you have a fan-forced oven, decrease the temperature by 10-20 degrees.

	°C (CELSIUS)	°F (FAHRENHEIT)
Very slow	120	250
Slow	150	300
Moderately slow	160	325
Moderate	180	350
Moderately hot	200	400
Hot	220	425
Very hot	240	475

Index

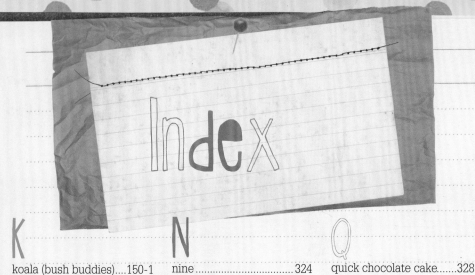

Index